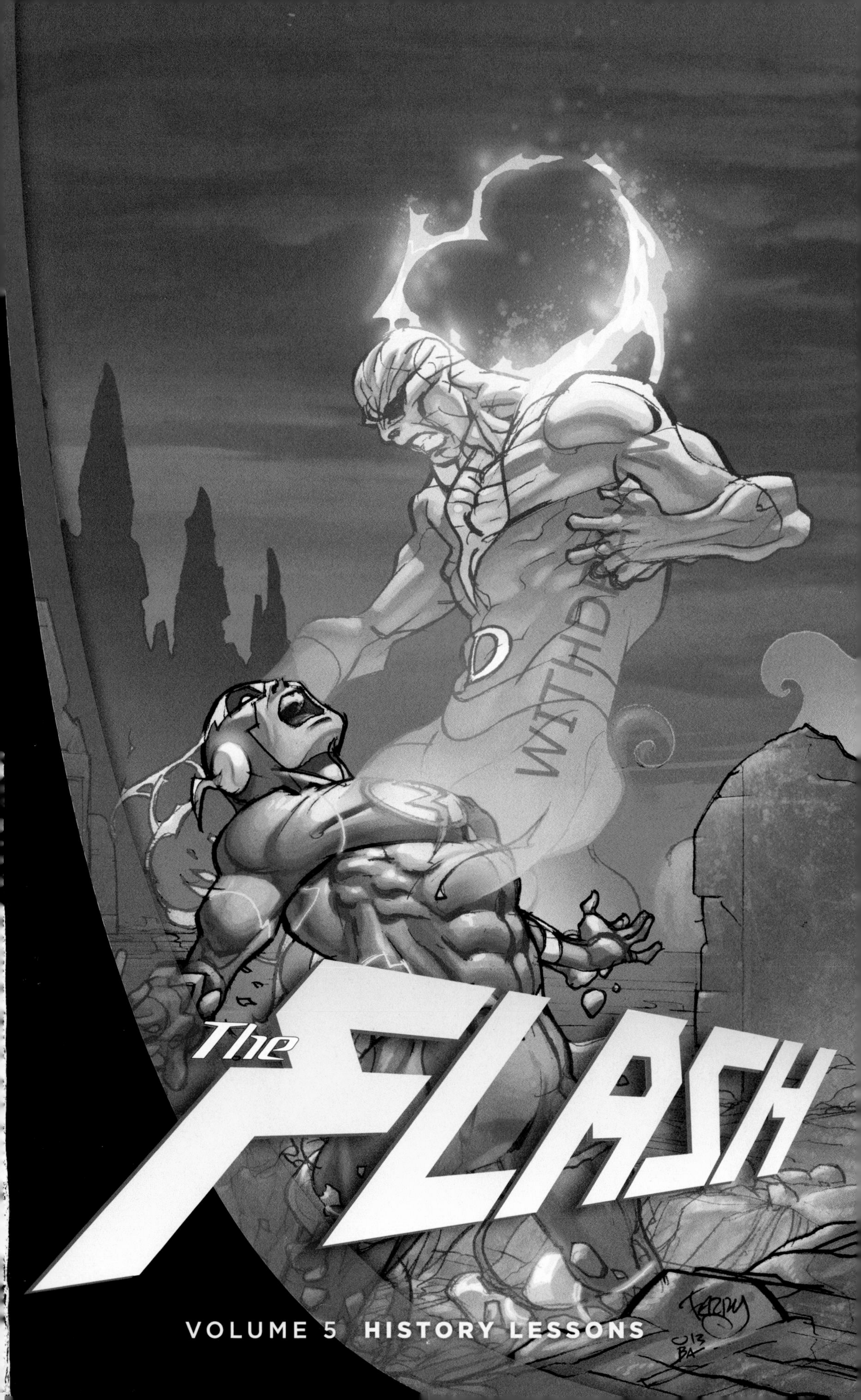
The
FLASH

VOLUME 5 HISTORY LESSONS

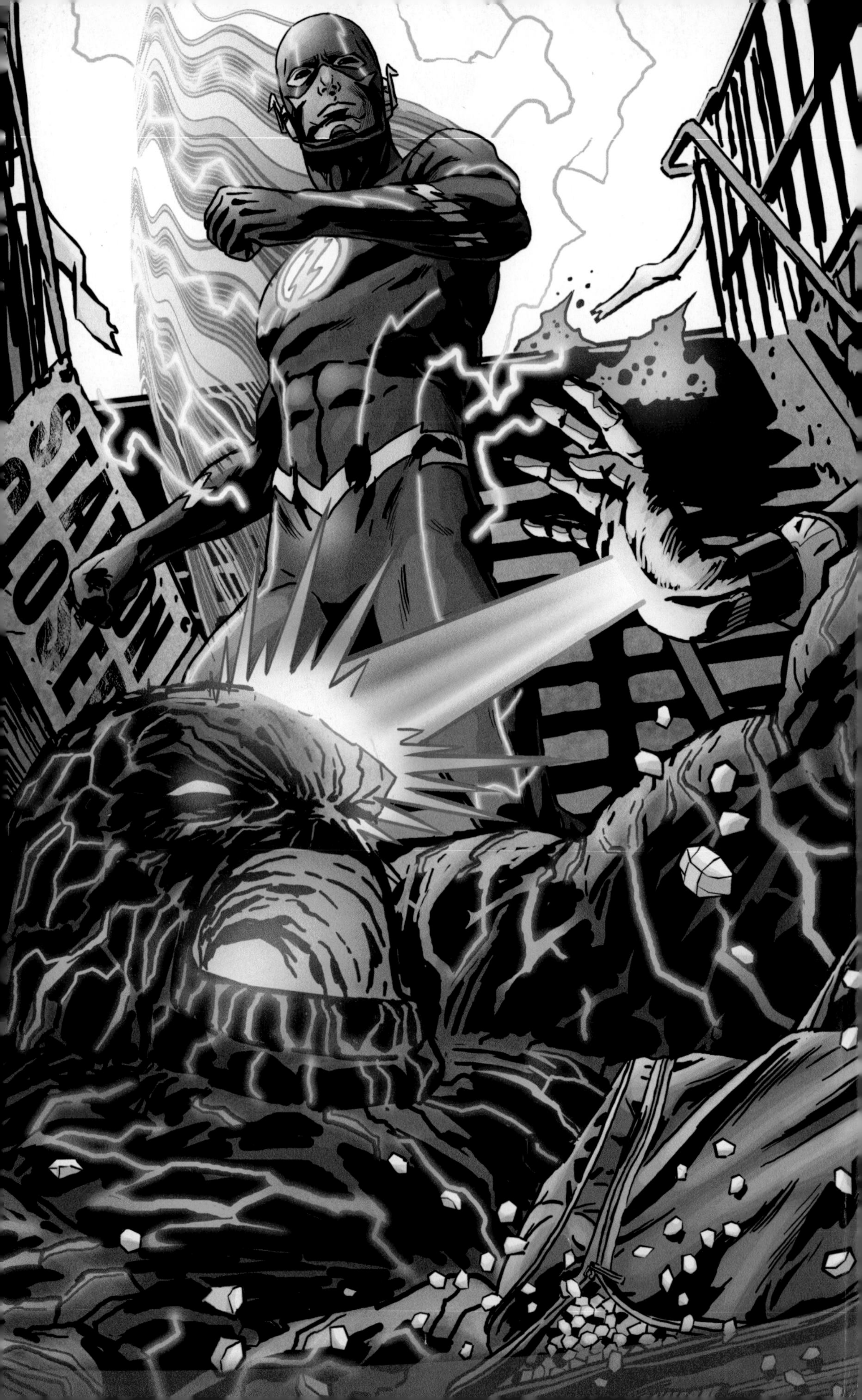

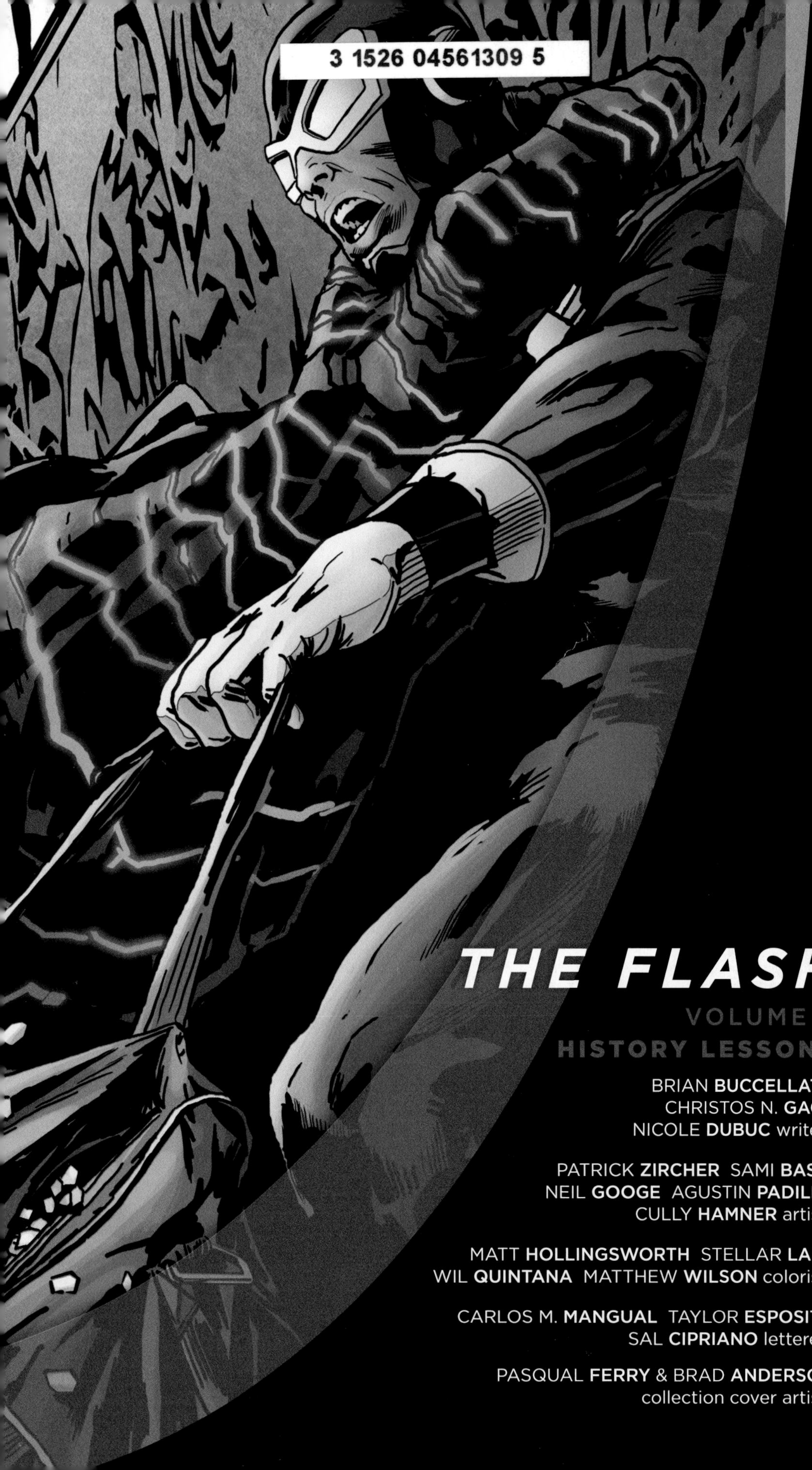

THE FLASH

VOLUME 5

HISTORY LESSONS

BRIAN **BUCCELLATO**
CHRISTOS N. **GAGE**
NICOLE **DUBUC** writers

PATRICK **ZIRCHER** SAMI **BASRI**
NEIL **GOOGE** AGUSTIN **PADILLA**
CULLY **HAMNER** artists

MATT **HOLLINGSWORTH** STELLAR **LABS**
WIL **QUINTANA** MATTHEW **WILSON** colorists

CARLOS M. **MANGUAL** TAYLOR **ESPOSITO**
SAL **CIPRIANO** letterers

PASQUAL **FERRY** & BRAD **ANDERSON**
collection cover artists

BRIAN CUNNINGHAM WIL MOSS Editors – Original Series HARVEY RICHARDS Associate Editor – Original Series
KATE DURRÉ Assistant Editor – Original Series LIZ ERICKSON Editor
ROBBIN BROSTERMAN Design Director – Books ROBBIE BIEDERMAN Publication Design

BOB HARRAS Senior VP – Editor-in-Chief, DC Comics

DIANE NELSON President DAN DIDIO and JIM LEE Co-Publishers GEOFF JOHNS Chief Creative Officer
AMIT DESAI Senior VP – Marketing and Franchise Management
AMY GENKINS Senior VP – Business and Legal Affairs NAIRI GARDINER Senior VP – Finance
JEFF BOISON VP – Publishing Planning MARK CHIARELLO VP – Art Direction and Design
JOHN CUNNINGHAM VP – Marketing TERRI CUNNINGHAM VP – Editorial Administration
LARRY GANEM VP – Talent Relations and Services ALISON GILL Senior VP – Manufacturing and Operations
HANK KANALZ Senior VP – Vertigo and Integrated Publishing JAY KOGAN VP – Business and Legal Affairs, Publishing
JACK MAHAN VP – Business Affairs, Talent NICK NAPOLITANO VP – Manufacturing Administration SUE POHJA VP – Book Sales
FRED RUIZ VP – Manufacturing Operations COURTNEY SIMMONS Senior VP – Publicity BOB WAYNE Senior VP – Sales

THE FLASH VOLUME 5: HISTORY LESSONS

DC Comics, 1700 Broadway, New York, NY 10019
A Warner Bros. Entertainment Company.
Printed by RR Donnelley, Salem, VA, USA. 12/19/14. First Printing

ISBN: 978-1-4012-4950-2

SUSTAINABLE FORESTRY INITIATIVE Certified Chain of Custody
20% Certified Forest Content,
80% Certified Sourcing
www.sfiprogram.org
SFI-01042
APPLIES TO TEXT STOCK ONLY

Library of Congress Cataloging-in-Publication Data

Buccellato, Brian.
The Flash. Volume 5, History lessons / Brian Buccellato, Patrick Zircher.
pages cm. — (The New 52!)
ISBN 978-1-4012-4950-2 (hardback)
1. Graphic novels. I. Zircher, Patrick, illustrator. II. Title. III. Title: History lessons.

PN6728.F53B84 2015
741.5'973—dc23

2014033188

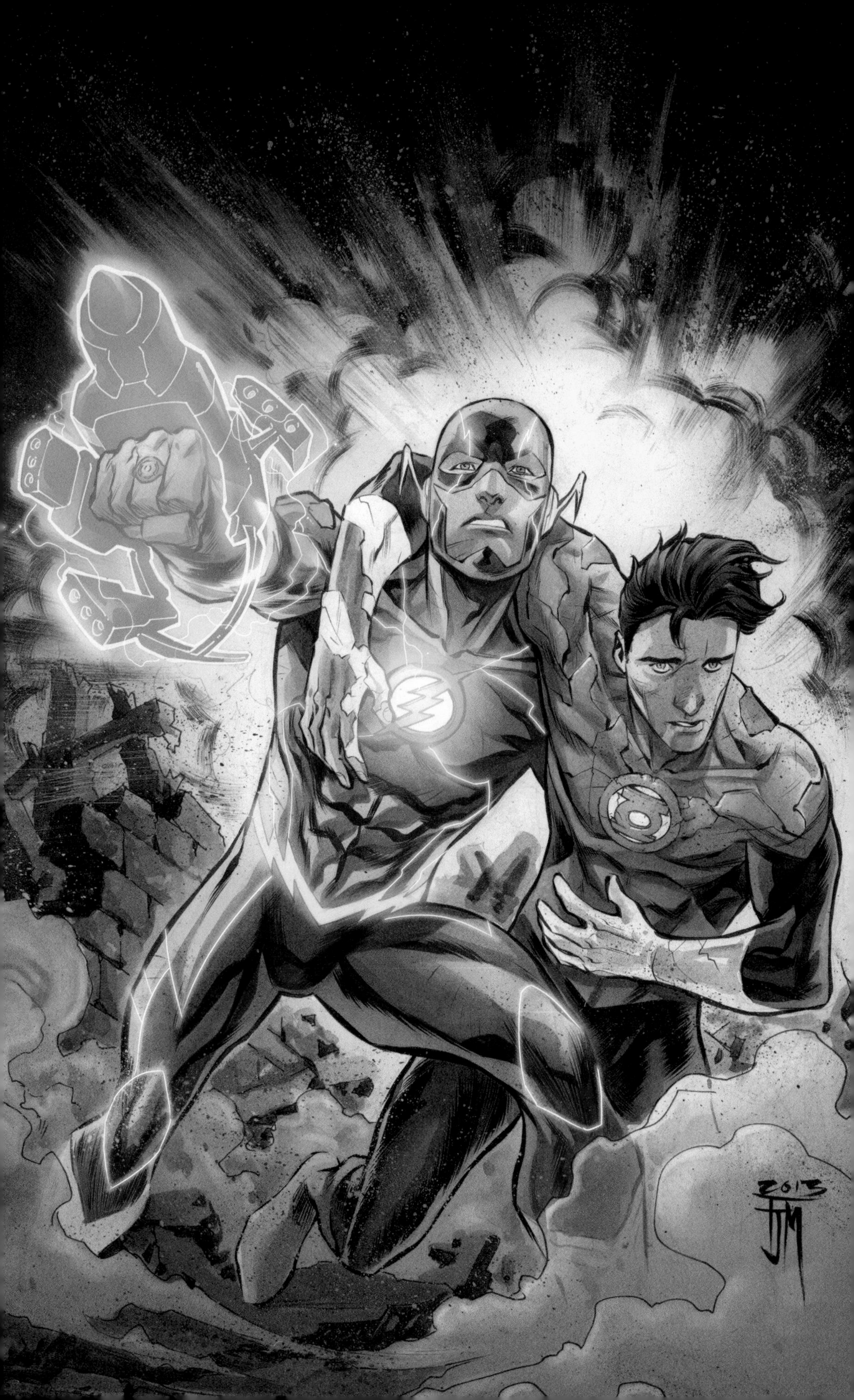

THE QUICK AND THE GREEN
BRIAN BUCCELLATO writer SAMI BASRI artist
DETAILS
NICOLE DUBUC writer CULLY HAMNER artist cover art by FRANCIS MANAPUL & BRIAN BUCCELLATO

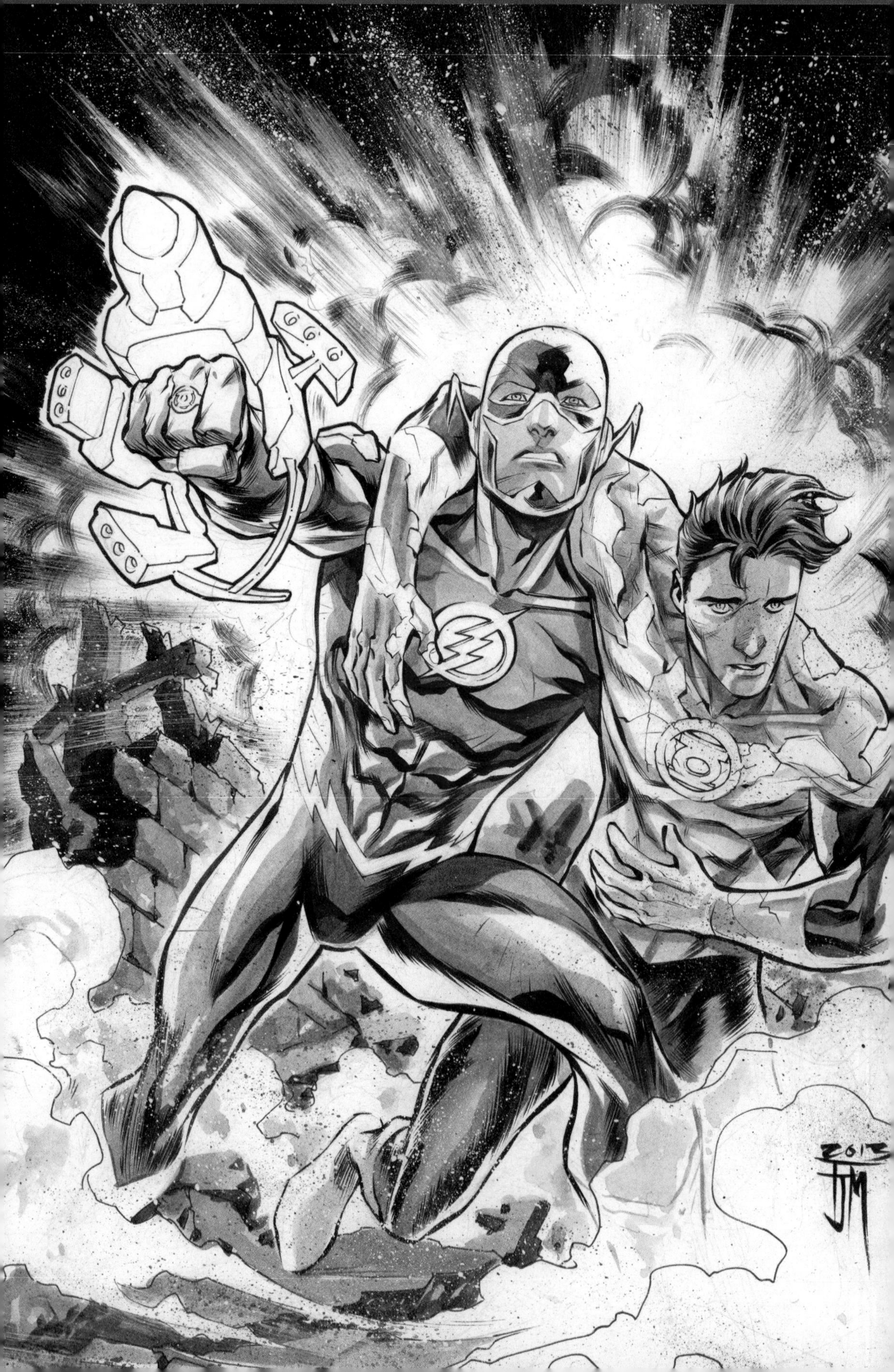
2013

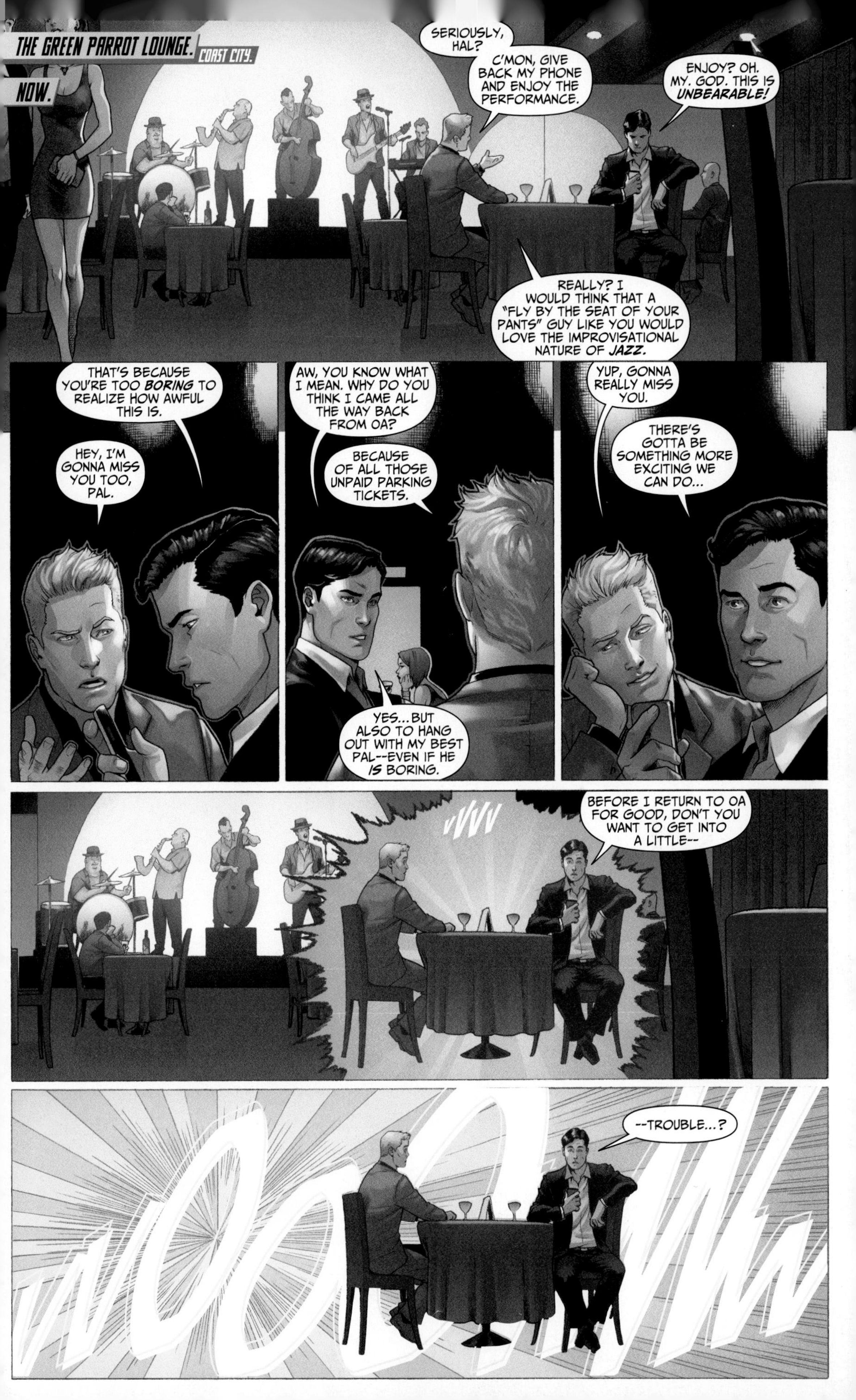
THE GREEN PARROT LOUNGE.
COAST CITY.
NOW.
SERIOUSLY, HAL?
C'MON, GIVE BACK MY PHONE AND ENJOY THE PERFORMANCE.
ENJOY? OH. MY. GOD. THIS IS UNBEARABLE!
REALLY? I WOULD THINK THAT A "FLY BY THE SEAT OF YOUR PANTS" GUY LIKE YOU WOULD LOVE THE IMPROVISATIONAL NATURE OF JAZZ.
THAT'S BECAUSE YOU'RE TOO BORING TO REALIZE HOW AWFUL THIS IS.
HEY, I'M GONNA MISS YOU TOO, PAL.
AW, YOU KNOW WHAT I MEAN. WHY DO YOU THINK I CAME ALL THE WAY BACK FROM OA?
BECAUSE OF ALL THOSE UNPAID PARKING TICKETS.
YES...BUT ALSO TO HANG OUT WITH MY BEST PAL--EVEN IF HE IS BORING.
YUP, GONNA REALLY MISS YOU.
THERE'S GOTTA BE SOMETHING MORE EXCITING WE CAN DO...
vVVV
BEFORE I RETURN TO OA FOR GOOD, DON'T YOU WANT TO GET INTO A LITTLE--
--TROUBLE...?

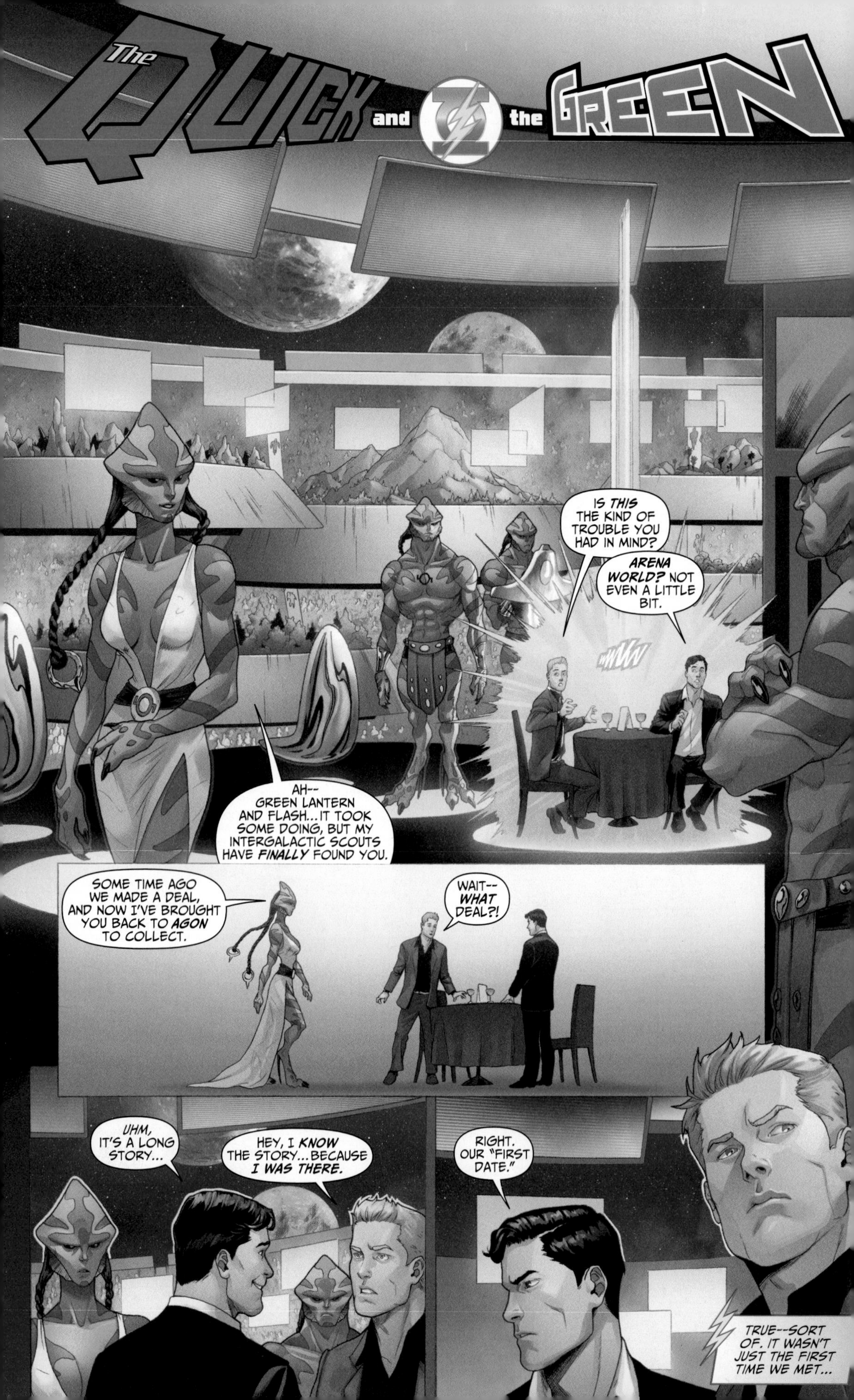
The QUICK and the GREEN
IS THIS THE KIND OF TROUBLE YOU HAD IN MIND?
ARENA WORLD? NOT EVEN A LITTLE BIT.
WWW
AH-- GREEN LANTERN AND FLASH...IT TOOK SOME DOING, BUT MY INTERGALACTIC SCOUTS HAVE FINALLY FOUND YOU.
SOME TIME AGO WE MADE A DEAL, AND NOW I'VE BROUGHT YOU BACK TO AGON TO COLLECT.
WAIT-- WHAT DEAL?!
UHM, IT'S A LONG STORY...
HEY, I KNOW THE STORY...BECAUSE I WAS THERE.
RIGHT. OUR "FIRST DATE."
TRUE--SORT OF. IT WASN'T JUST THE FIRST TIME WE MET...

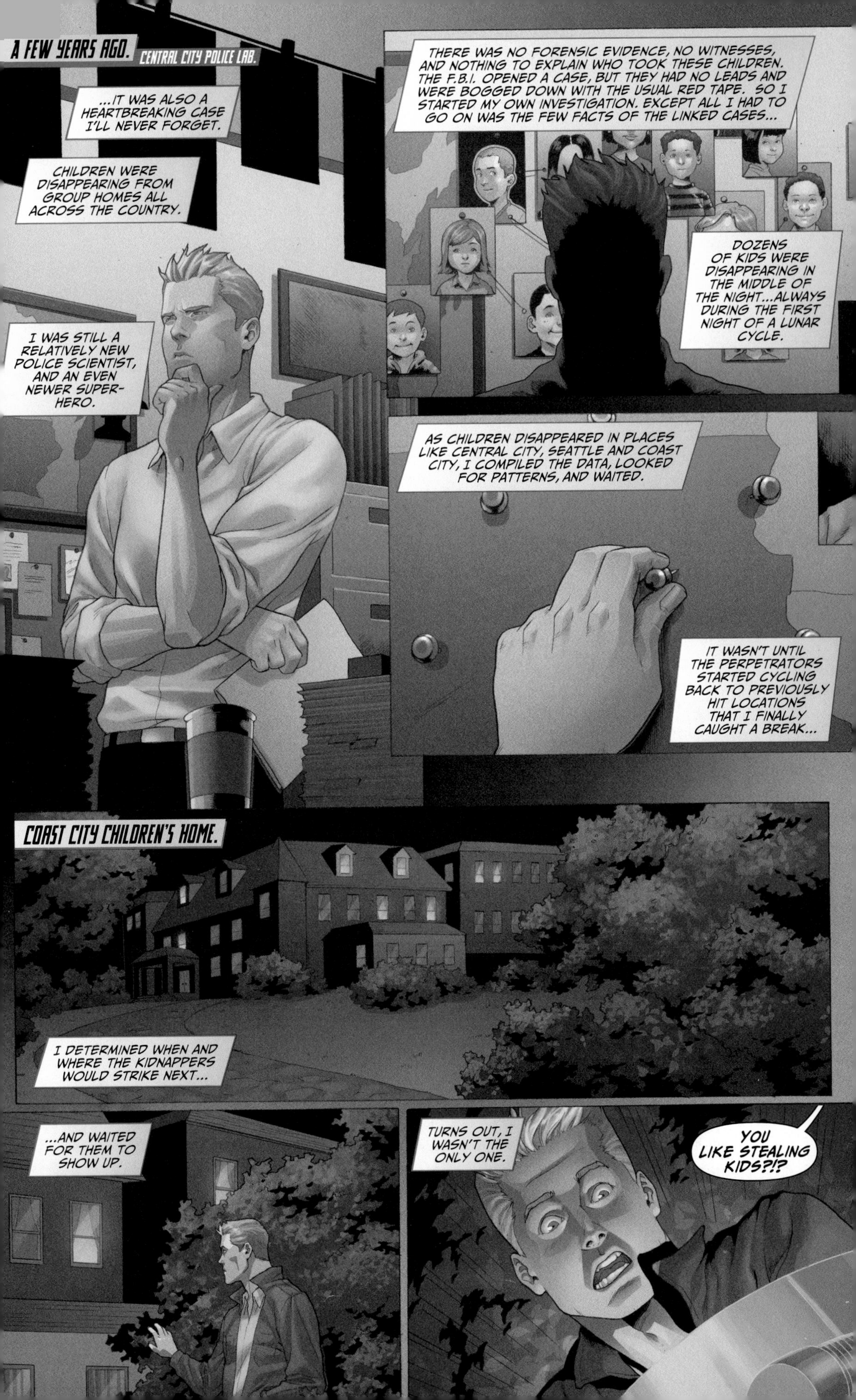
A FEW YEARS AGO.
CENTRAL CITY POLICE LAB.
...IT WAS ALSO A HEARTBREAKING CASE I'LL NEVER FORGET.
CHILDREN WERE DISAPPEARING FROM GROUP HOMES ALL ACROSS THE COUNTRY.
I WAS STILL A RELATIVELY NEW POLICE SCIENTIST, AND AN EVEN NEWER SUPER-HERO.
THERE WAS NO FORENSIC EVIDENCE, NO WITNESSES, AND NOTHING TO EXPLAIN WHO TOOK THESE CHILDREN. THE F.B.I. OPENED A CASE, BUT THEY HAD NO LEADS AND WERE BOGGED DOWN WITH THE USUAL RED TAPE. SO I STARTED MY OWN INVESTIGATION. EXCEPT ALL I HAD TO GO ON WAS THE FEW FACTS OF THE LINKED CASES...
DOZENS OF KIDS WERE DISAPPEARING IN THE MIDDLE OF THE NIGHT...ALWAYS DURING THE FIRST NIGHT OF A LUNAR CYCLE.
AS CHILDREN DISAPPEARED IN PLACES LIKE CENTRAL CITY, SEATTLE AND COAST CITY, I COMPILED THE DATA, LOOKED FOR PATTERNS, AND WAITED.
IT WASN'T UNTIL THE PERPETRATORS STARTED CYCLING BACK TO PREVIOUSLY HIT LOCATIONS THAT I FINALLY CAUGHT A BREAK...
COAST CITY CHILDREN'S HOME.
I DETERMINED WHEN AND WHERE THE KIDNAPPERS WOULD STRIKE NEXT...
...AND WAITED FOR THEM TO SHOW UP.
TURNS OUT, I WASN'T THE ONLY ONE.
YOU LIKE STEALING KIDS?!?

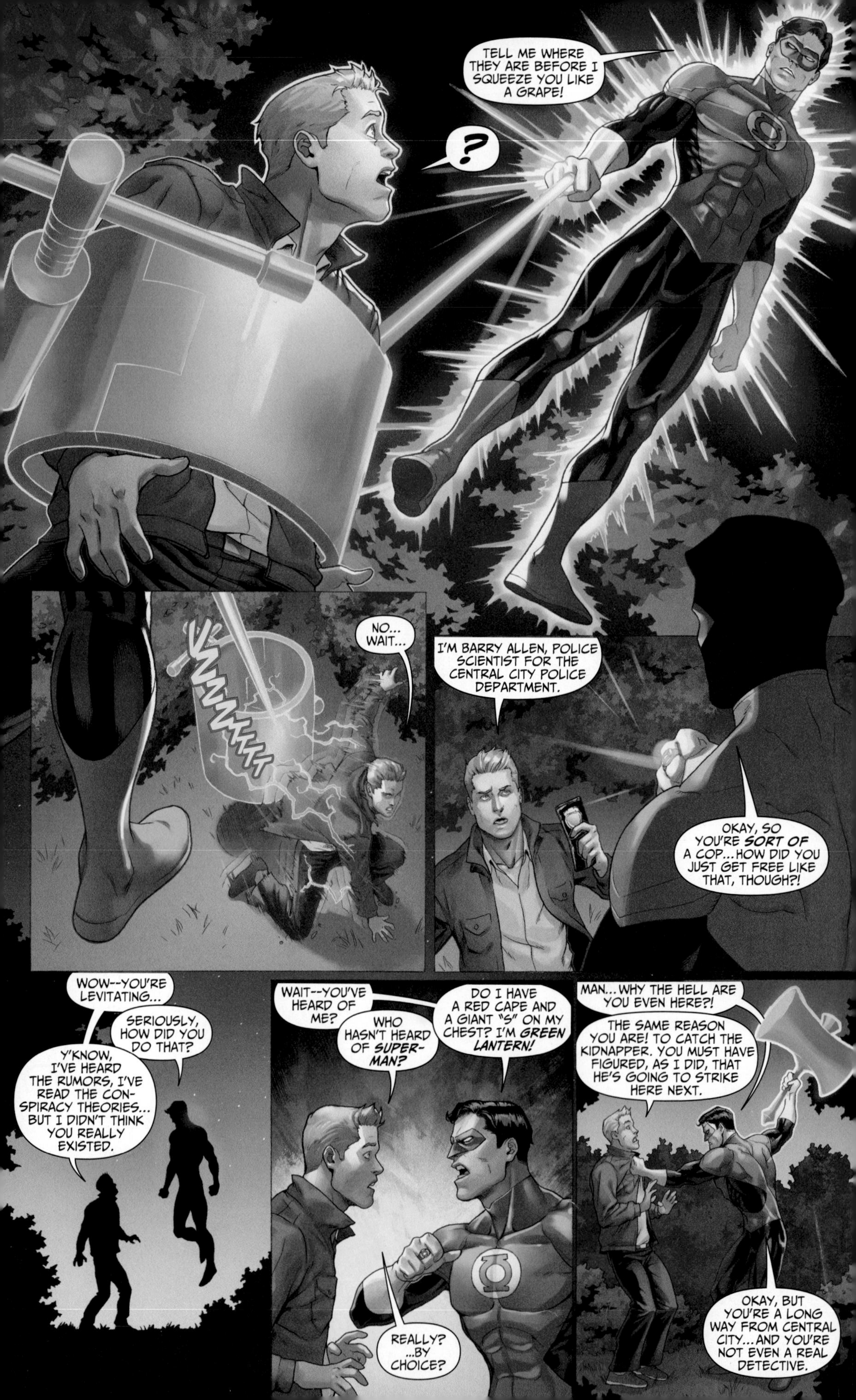
TELL ME WHERE THEY ARE BEFORE I SQUEEZE YOU LIKE A GRAPE!
?
NO... WAIT...
VWWWKKK
I'M BARRY ALLEN, POLICE SCIENTIST FOR THE CENTRAL CITY POLICE DEPARTMENT.
OKAY, SO YOU'RE SORT OF A COP...HOW DID YOU JUST GET FREE LIKE THAT, THOUGH?!
WOW--YOU'RE LEVITATING...
SERIOUSLY, HOW DID YOU DO THAT?
Y'KNOW, I'VE HEARD THE RUMORS, I'VE READ THE CONSPIRACY THEORIES... BUT I DIDN'T THINK YOU REALLY EXISTED.
WAIT--YOU'VE HEARD OF ME?
WHO HASN'T HEARD OF SUPERMAN?
DO I HAVE A RED CAPE AND A GIANT "S" ON MY CHEST? I'M GREEN LANTERN!
REALLY? ...BY CHOICE?
MAN...WHY THE HELL ARE YOU EVEN HERE?!
THE SAME REASON YOU ARE! TO CATCH THE KIDNAPPER. YOU MUST HAVE FIGURED, AS I DID, THAT HE'S GOING TO STRIKE HERE NEXT.
OKAY, BUT YOU'RE A LONG WAY FROM CENTRAL CITY...AND YOU'RE NOT EVEN A REAL DETECTIVE.

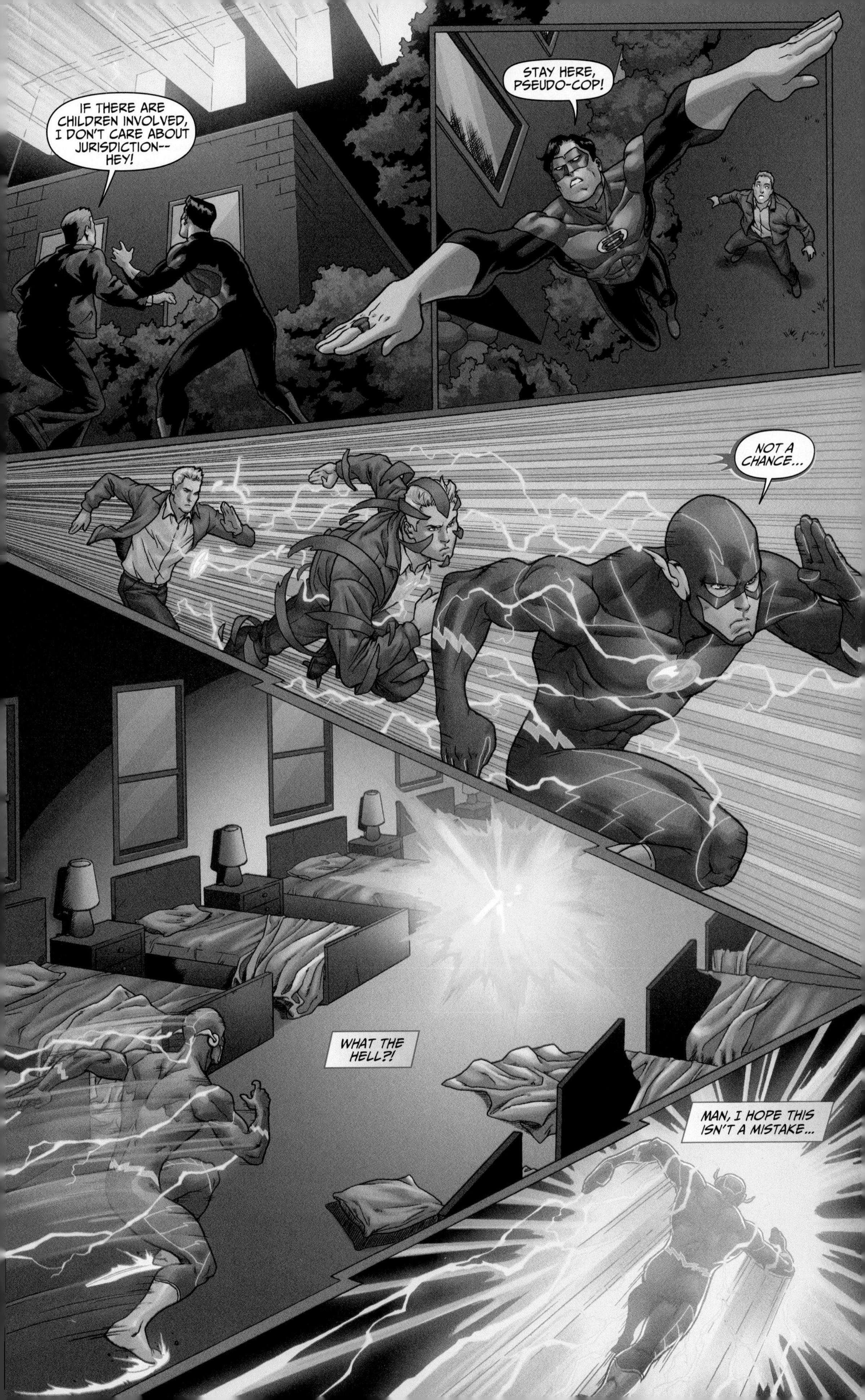
IF THERE ARE CHILDREN INVOLVED, I DON'T CARE ABOUT JURISDICTION-- HEY!
STAY HERE, PSEUDO-COP!
NOT A CHANCE...
WHAT THE HELL?!
MAN, I HOPE THIS ISN'T A MISTAKE...

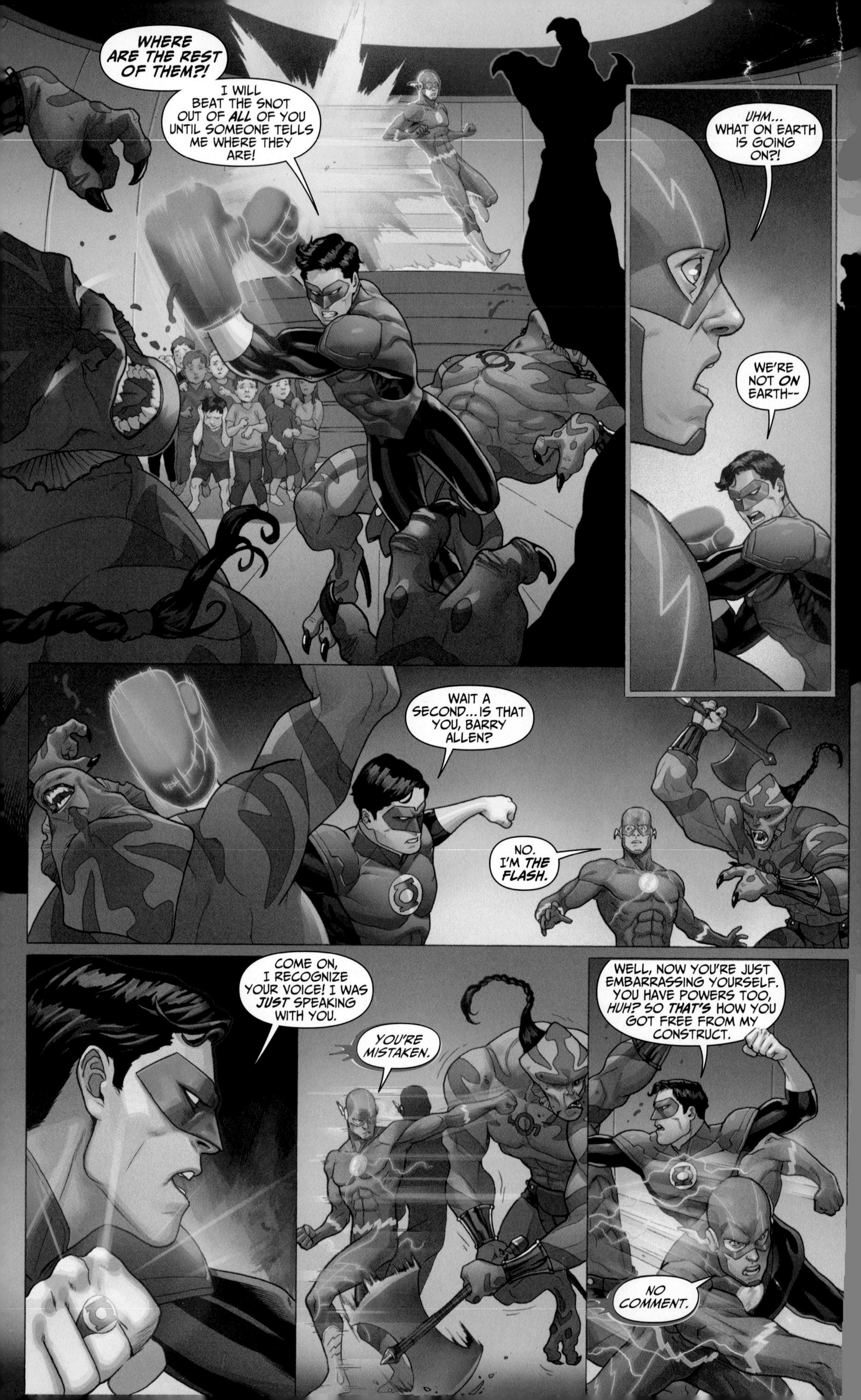
WHERE ARE THE REST OF THEM?!
I WILL BEAT THE SNOT OUT OF ALL OF YOU UNTIL SOMEONE TELLS ME WHERE THEY ARE!
UHM... WHAT ON EARTH IS GOING ON?!
WE'RE NOT ON EARTH--
WAIT A SECOND...IS THAT YOU, BARRY ALLEN?
NO. I'M THE FLASH.
COME ON, I RECOGNIZE YOUR VOICE! I WAS JUST SPEAKING WITH YOU.
YOU'RE MISTAKEN.
WELL, NOW YOU'RE JUST EMBARRASSING YOURSELF. YOU HAVE POWERS TOO, HUH? SO THAT'S HOW YOU GOT FREE FROM MY CONSTRUCT.
NO COMMENT.

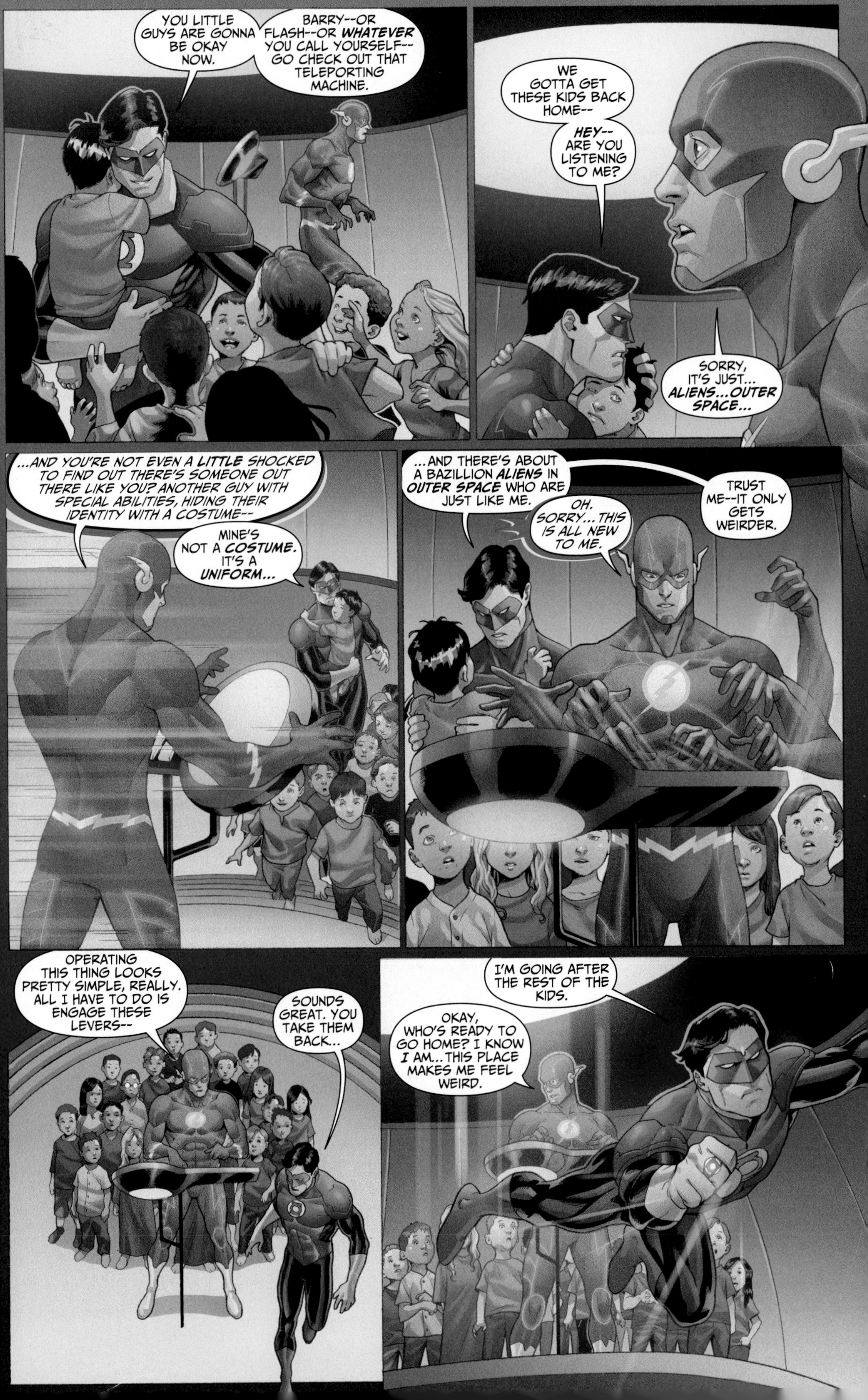
YOU LITTLE GUYS ARE GONNA BE OKAY NOW.
BARRY--OR FLASH--OR WHATEVER YOU CALL YOURSELF--GO CHECK OUT THAT TELEPORTING MACHINE.
WE GOTTA GET THESE KIDS BACK HOME--
HEY-- ARE YOU LISTENING TO ME?
SORRY, IT'S JUST... ALIENS...OUTER SPACE...
...AND YOU'RE NOT EVEN A LITTLE SHOCKED TO FIND OUT THERE'S SOMEONE OUT THERE LIKE YOU? ANOTHER GUY WITH SPECIAL ABILITIES, HIDING THEIR IDENTITY WITH A COSTUME--
MINE'S NOT A COSTUME. IT'S A UNIFORM...
...AND THERE'S ABOUT A BAZILLION ALIENS IN OUTER SPACE WHO ARE JUST LIKE ME.
OH. SORRY... THIS IS ALL NEW TO ME.
TRUST ME--IT ONLY GETS WEIRDER.
OPERATING THIS THING LOOKS PRETTY SIMPLE, REALLY. ALL I HAVE TO DO IS ENGAGE THESE LEVERS--
SOUNDS GREAT. YOU TAKE THEM BACK...
I'M GOING AFTER THE REST OF THE KIDS.
OKAY, WHO'S READY TO GO HOME? I KNOW I AM...THIS PLACE MAKES ME FEEL WEIRD.

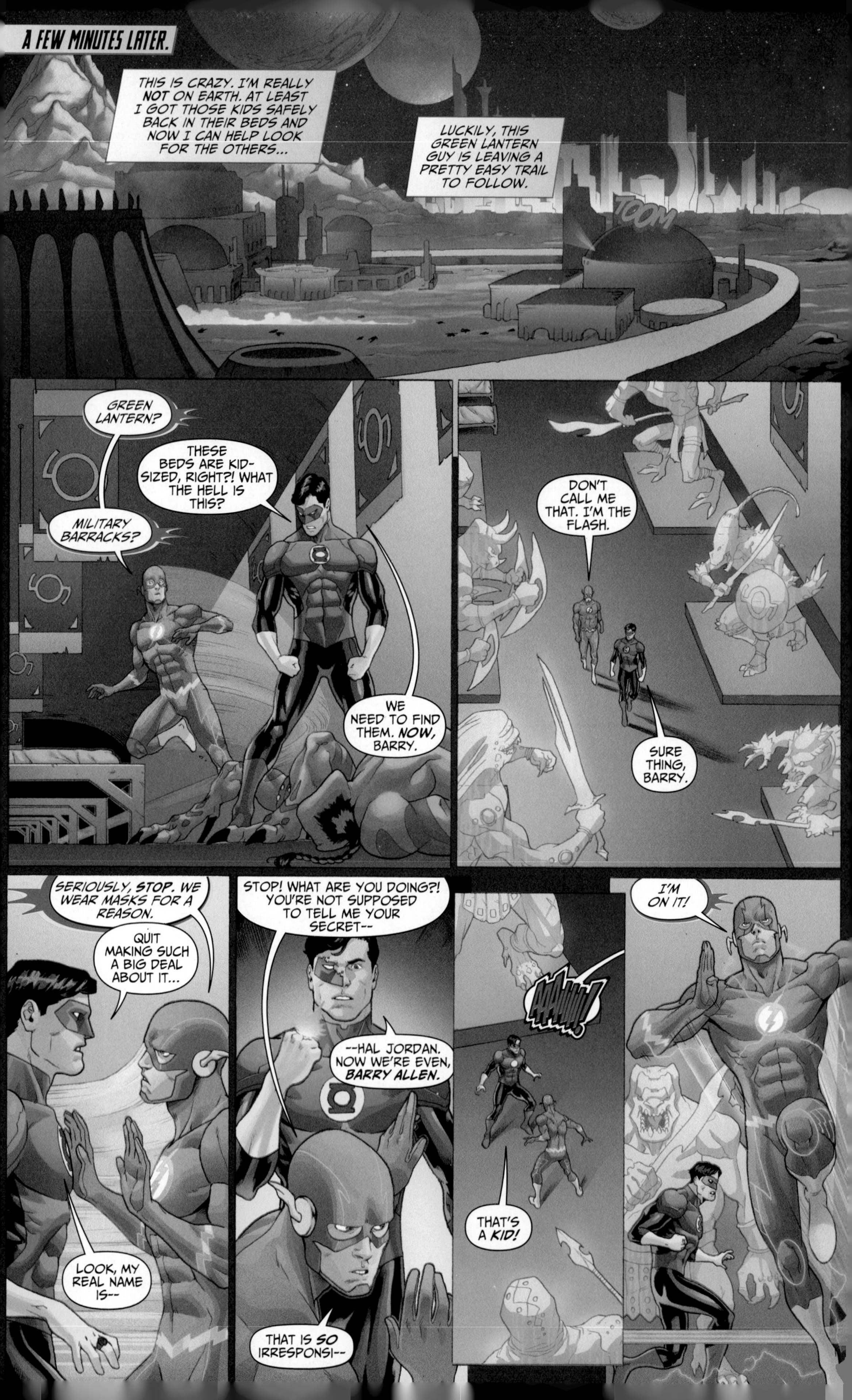
A FEW MINUTES LATER.
THIS IS CRAZY. I'M REALLY NOT ON EARTH. AT LEAST I GOT THOSE KIDS SAFELY BACK IN THEIR BEDS AND NOW I CAN HELP LOOK FOR THE OTHERS...
LUCKILY, THIS GREEN LANTERN GUY IS LEAVING A PRETTY EASY TRAIL TO FOLLOW.
TOOM
GREEN LANTERN?
THESE BEDS ARE KID-SIZED, RIGHT?! WHAT THE HELL IS THIS?
MILITARY BARRACKS?
WE NEED TO FIND THEM. NOW, BARRY.
DON'T CALL ME THAT. I'M THE FLASH.
SURE THING, BARRY.
SERIOUSLY, STOP. WE WEAR MASKS FOR A REASON.
QUIT MAKING SUCH A BIG DEAL ABOUT IT...
LOOK, MY REAL NAME IS--
STOP! WHAT ARE YOU DOING?! YOU'RE NOT SUPPOSED TO TELL ME YOUR SECRET--
--HAL JORDAN. NOW WE'RE EVEN, BARRY ALLEN.
THAT IS SO IRRESPONSI--
AAAHHH!
THAT'S A KID!
I'M ON IT!

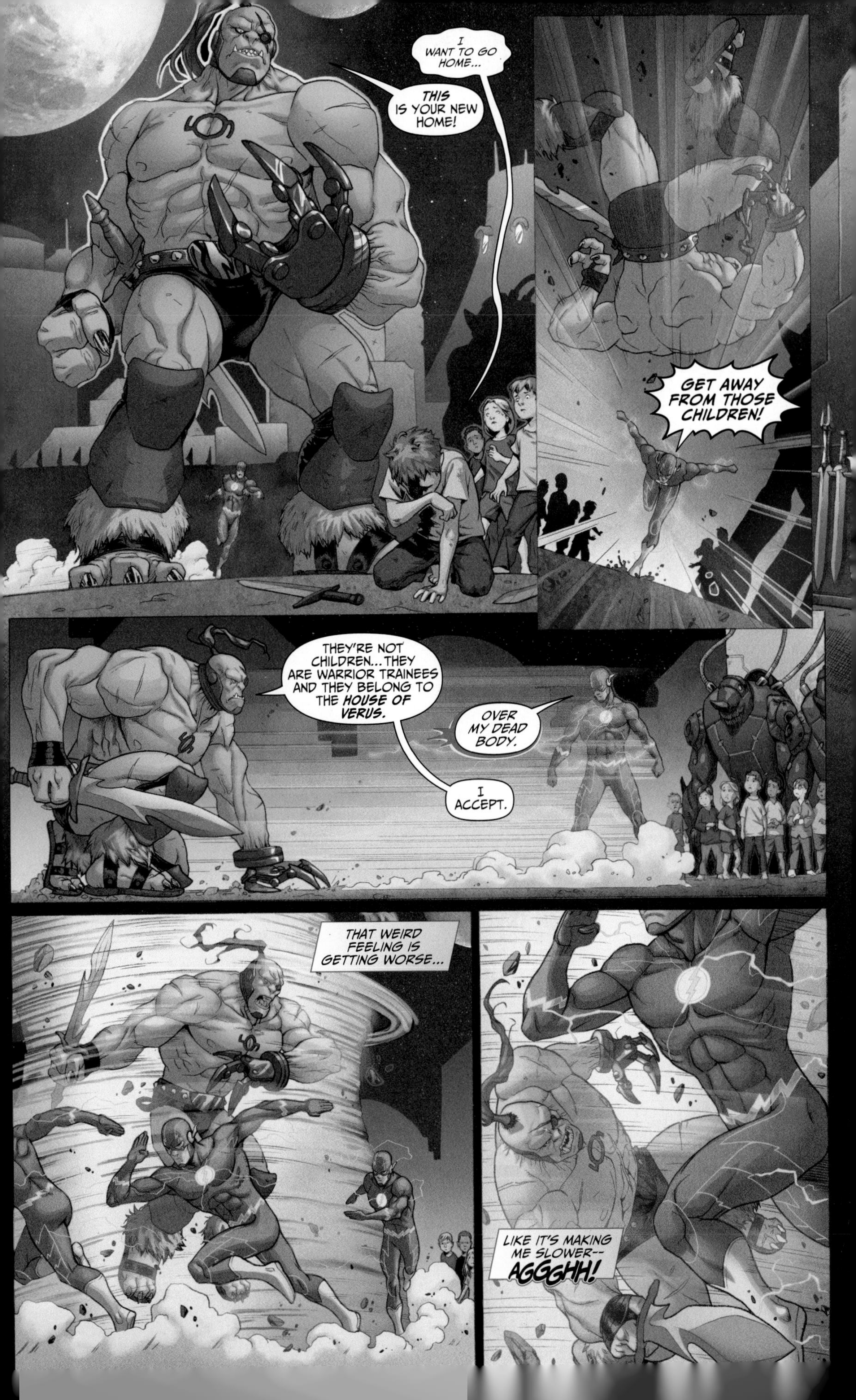

I WANT TO GO HOME...
THIS IS YOUR NEW HOME!
GET AWAY FROM THOSE CHILDREN!
THEY'RE NOT CHILDREN...THEY ARE WARRIOR TRAINEES AND THEY BELONG TO THE HOUSE OF VERUS.
OVER MY DEAD BODY.
I ACCEPT.
THAT WEIRD FEELING IS GETTING WORSE...
LIKE IT'S MAKING ME SLOWER--
AGGGHH!

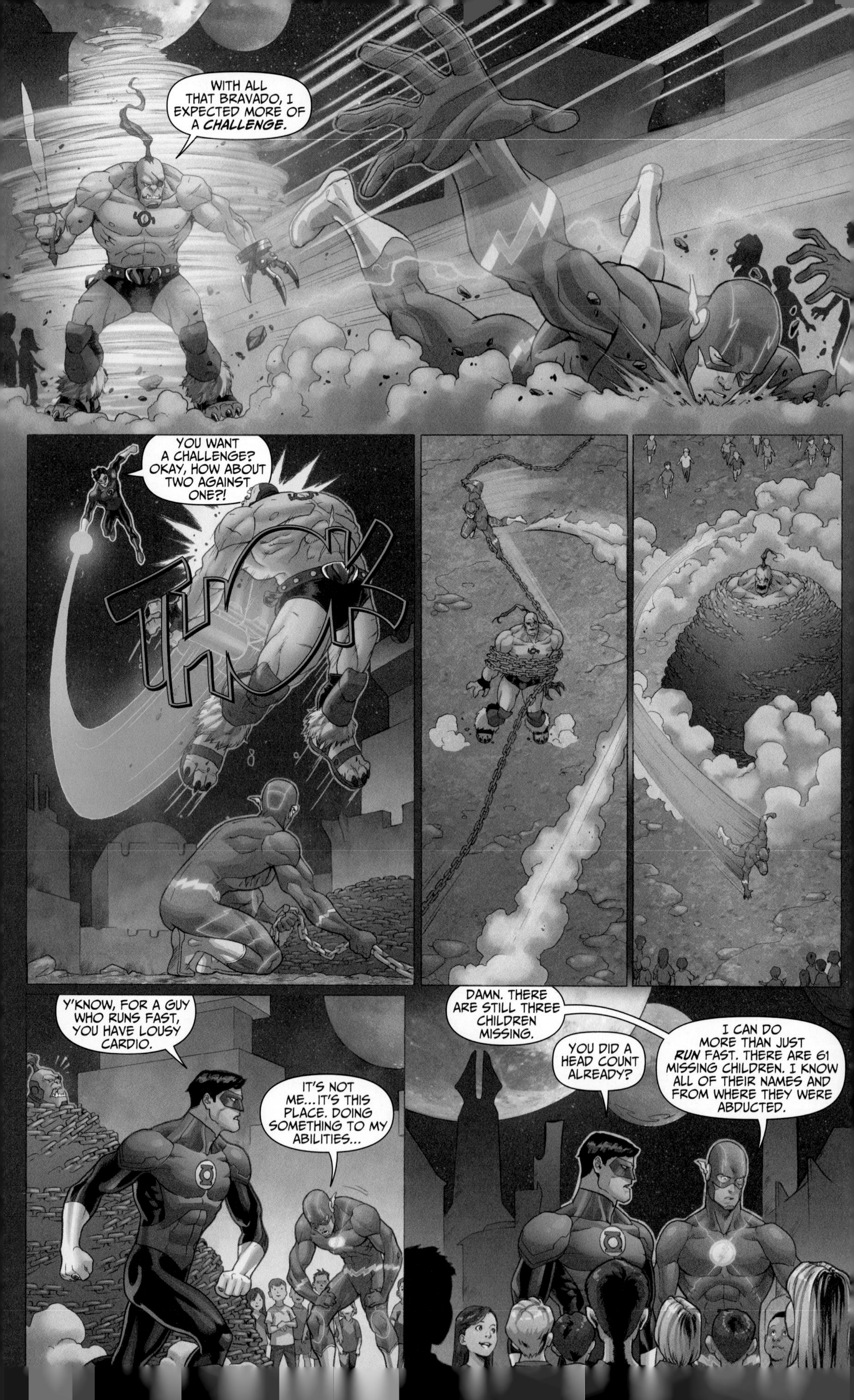

WITH ALL THAT BRAVADO, I EXPECTED MORE OF A *CHALLENGE.*
YOU WANT A CHALLENGE? OKAY, HOW ABOUT TWO AGAINST ONE?!
THOK
Y'KNOW, FOR A GUY WHO RUNS FAST, YOU HAVE LOUSY CARDIO.
IT'S NOT ME...IT'S THIS PLACE. DOING SOMETHING TO MY ABILITIES...
DAMN. THERE ARE STILL THREE CHILDREN MISSING.
YOU DID A HEAD COUNT ALREADY?
I CAN DO MORE THAN JUST *RUN* FAST. THERE ARE 61 MISSING CHILDREN. I KNOW ALL OF THEIR NAMES AND FROM WHERE THEY WERE ABDUCTED.

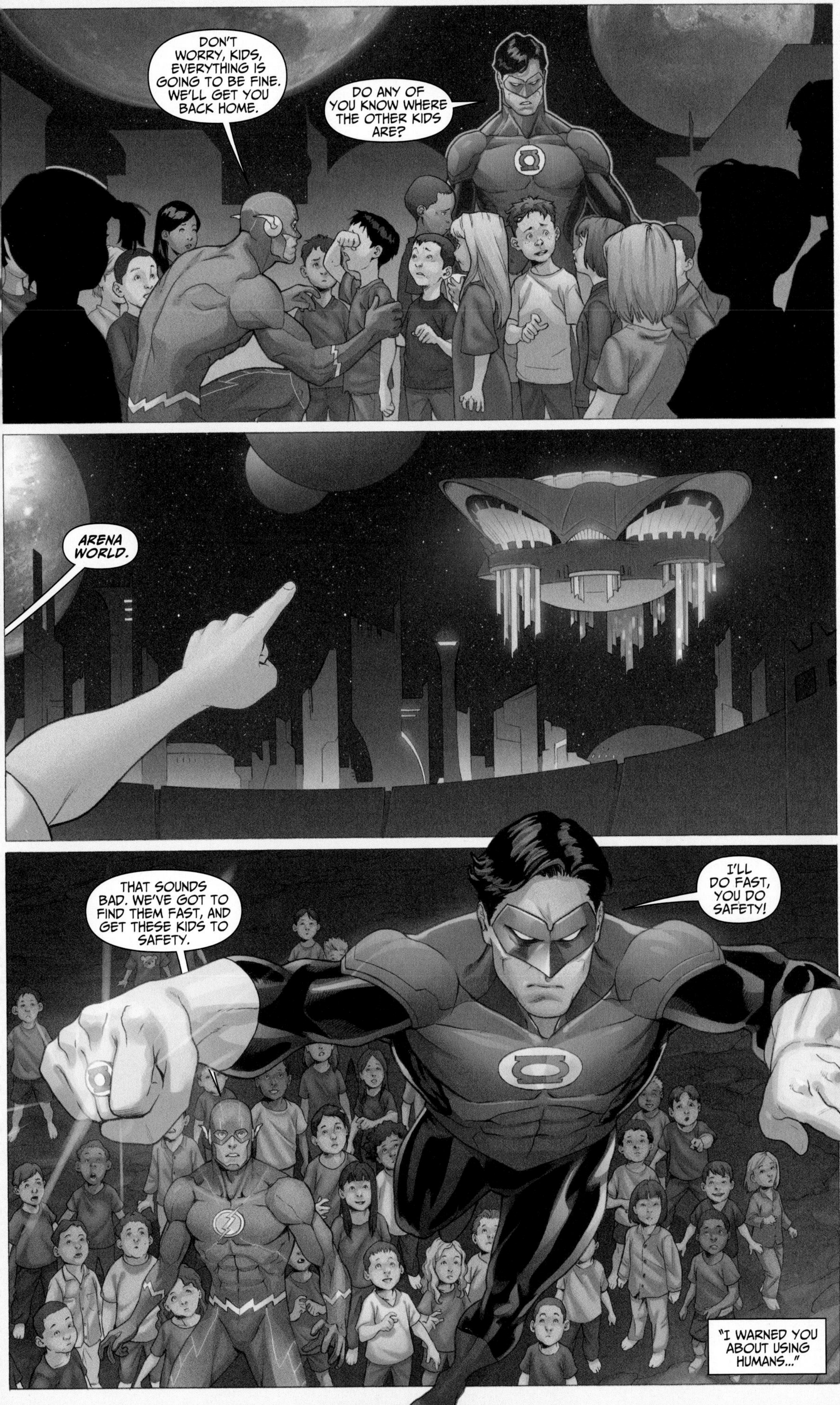
DON'T WORRY, KIDS, EVERYTHING IS GOING TO BE FINE. WE'LL GET YOU BACK HOME.
DO ANY OF YOU KNOW WHERE THE OTHER KIDS ARE?
ARENA WORLD.
THAT SOUNDS BAD. WE'VE GOT TO FIND THEM FAST, AND GET THESE KIDS TO SAFETY.
I'LL DO FAST, YOU DO SAFETY!
"I WARNED YOU ABOUT USING HUMANS..."

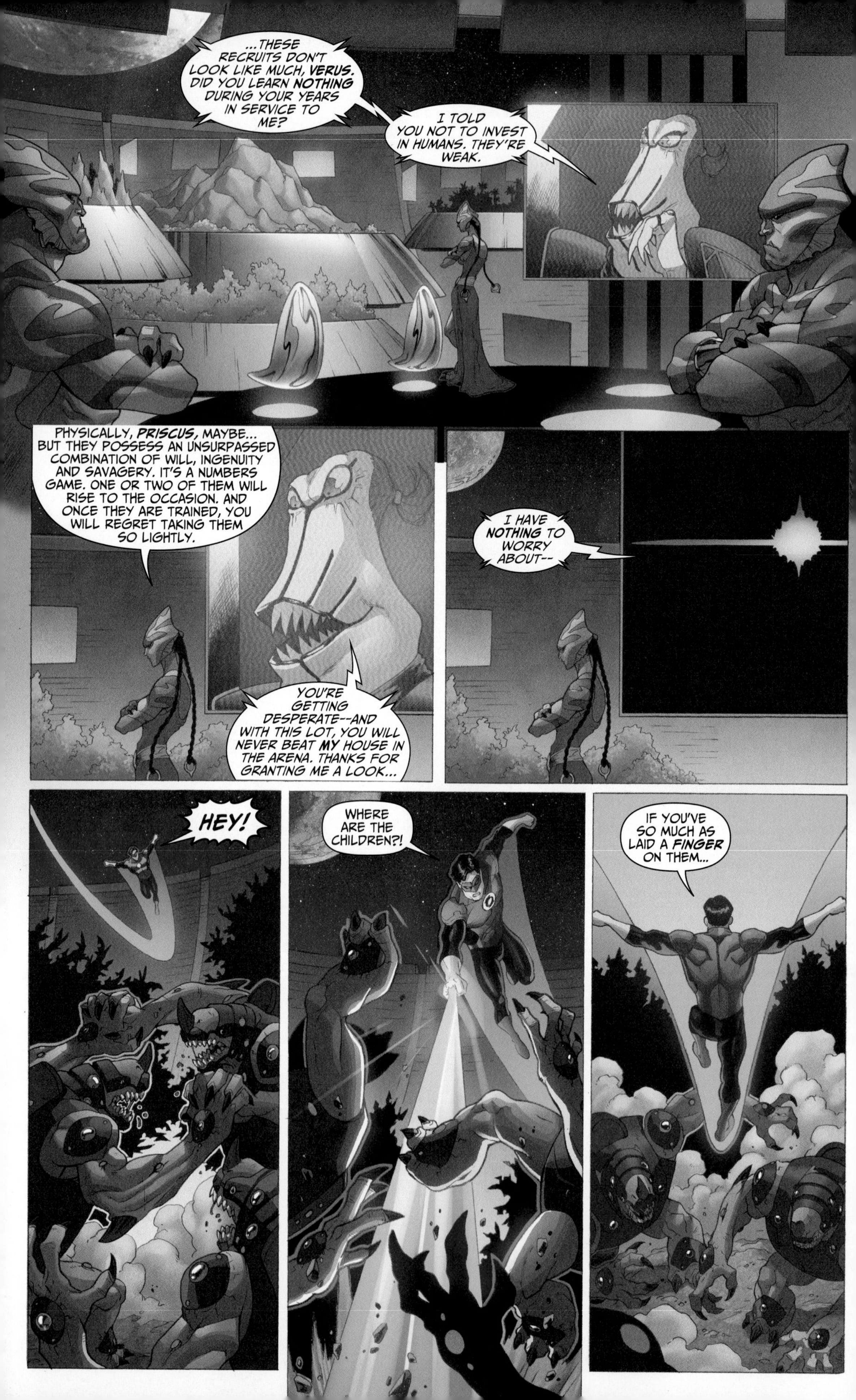
...THESE RECRUITS DON'T LOOK LIKE MUCH, VERUS. DID YOU LEARN NOTHING DURING YOUR YEARS IN SERVICE TO ME?
I TOLD YOU NOT TO INVEST IN HUMANS. THEY'RE WEAK.
PHYSICALLY, PRISCUS, MAYBE... BUT THEY POSSESS AN UNSURPASSED COMBINATION OF WILL, INGENUITY AND SAVAGERY. IT'S A NUMBERS GAME. ONE OR TWO OF THEM WILL RISE TO THE OCCASION. AND ONCE THEY ARE TRAINED, YOU WILL REGRET TAKING THEM SO LIGHTLY.
YOU'RE GETTING DESPERATE--AND WITH THIS LOT, YOU WILL NEVER BEAT MY HOUSE IN THE ARENA. THANKS FOR GRANTING ME A LOOK...
I HAVE NOTHING TO WORRY ABOUT--
HEY!
WHERE ARE THE CHILDREN?!
IF YOU'VE SO MUCH AS LAID A FINGER ON THEM...

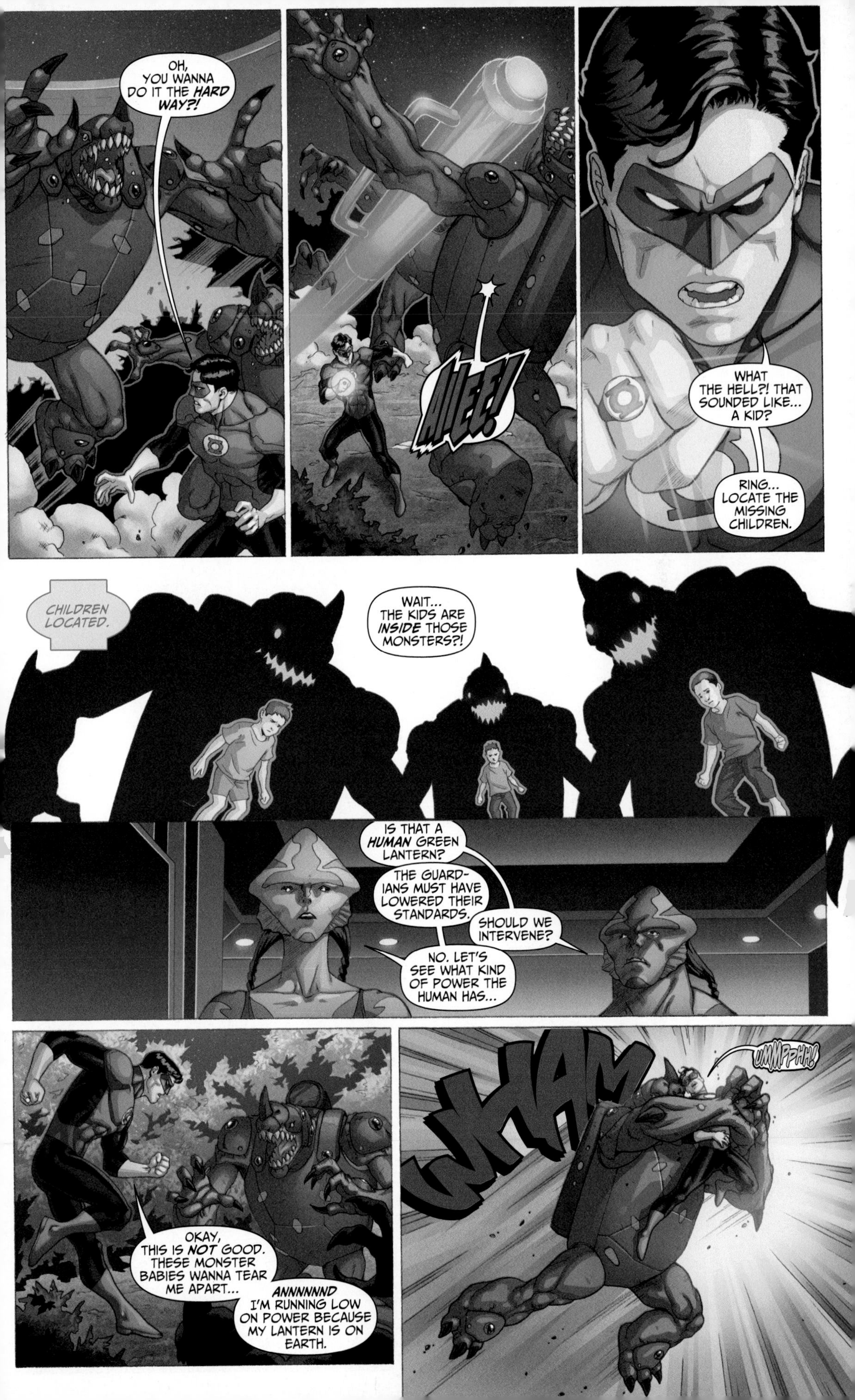
OH, YOU WANNA DO IT THE *HARD WAY?!*
AIIEEE!
WHAT THE HELL?! THAT SOUNDED LIKE... A KID?
RING... LOCATE THE MISSING CHILDREN.
CHILDREN LOCATED.
WAIT... THE KIDS ARE *INSIDE* THOSE MONSTERS?!
IS THAT A *HUMAN* GREEN LANTERN?
THE GUARDIANS MUST HAVE LOWERED THEIR STANDARDS.
SHOULD WE INTERVENE?
NO. LET'S SEE WHAT KIND OF POWER THE HUMAN HAS...
OKAY, THIS IS *NOT* GOOD. THESE MONSTER BABIES WANNA TEAR ME APART...
ANNNNNND I'M RUNNING LOW ON POWER BECAUSE MY LANTERN IS ON EARTH.
WHAM
UMMPPHH!

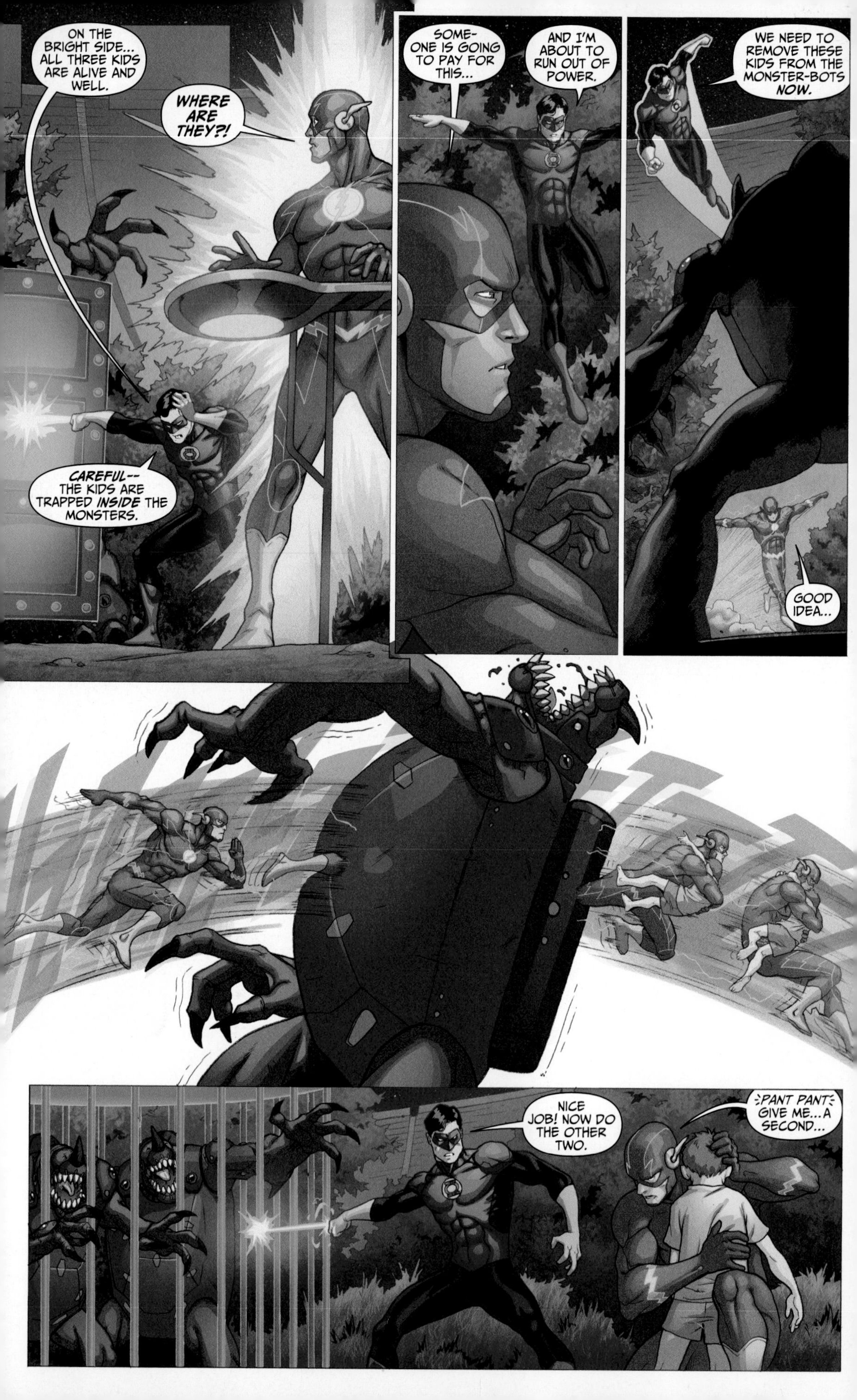
ON THE BRIGHT SIDE... ALL THREE KIDS ARE ALIVE AND WELL.
WHERE ARE THEY?!
CAREFUL-- THE KIDS ARE TRAPPED *INSIDE* THE MONSTERS.
SOME-ONE IS GOING TO PAY FOR THIS...
AND I'M ABOUT TO RUN OUT OF POWER.
WE NEED TO REMOVE THESE KIDS FROM THE MONSTER-BOTS *NOW.*
GOOD IDEA...
NICE JOB! NOW DO THE OTHER TWO.
PANT PANT GIVE ME...A SECOND...

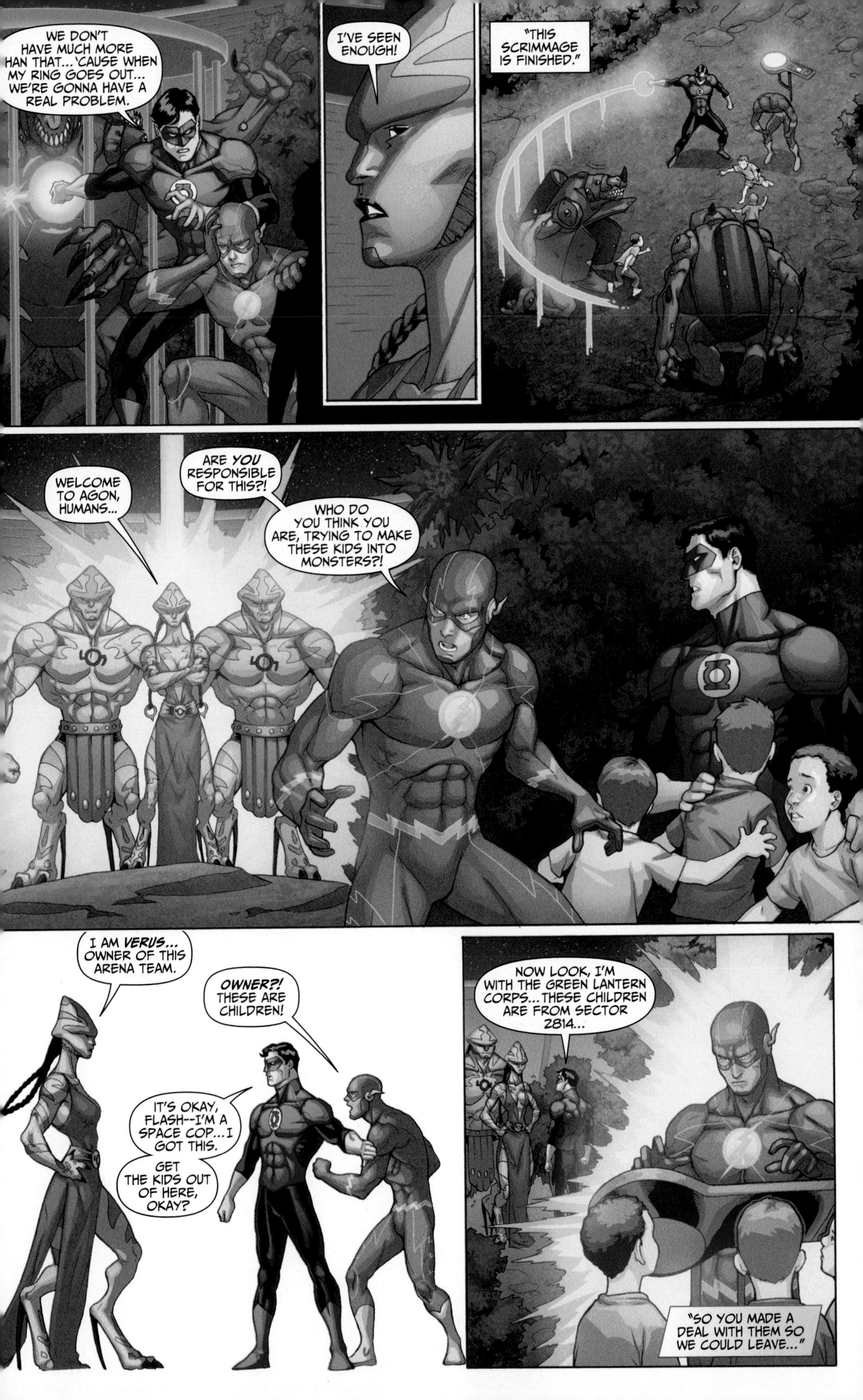
WE DON'T HAVE MUCH MORE HAN THAT... 'CAUSE WHEN MY RING GOES OUT... WE'RE GONNA HAVE A REAL PROBLEM.
I'VE SEEN ENOUGH!
"THIS SCRIMMAGE IS FINISHED."
WELCOME TO AGON, HUMANS...
ARE YOU RESPONSIBLE FOR THIS?!
WHO DO YOU THINK YOU ARE, TRYING TO MAKE THESE KIDS INTO MONSTERS?!
I AM VERUS... OWNER OF THIS ARENA TEAM.
OWNER?! THESE ARE CHILDREN!
IT'S OKAY, FLASH--I'M A SPACE COP...I GOT THIS.
GET THE KIDS OUT OF HERE, OKAY?
NOW LOOK, I'M WITH THE GREEN LANTERN CORPS...THESE CHILDREN ARE FROM SECTOR 2814...
"SO YOU MADE A DEAL WITH THEM SO WE COULD LEAVE..."

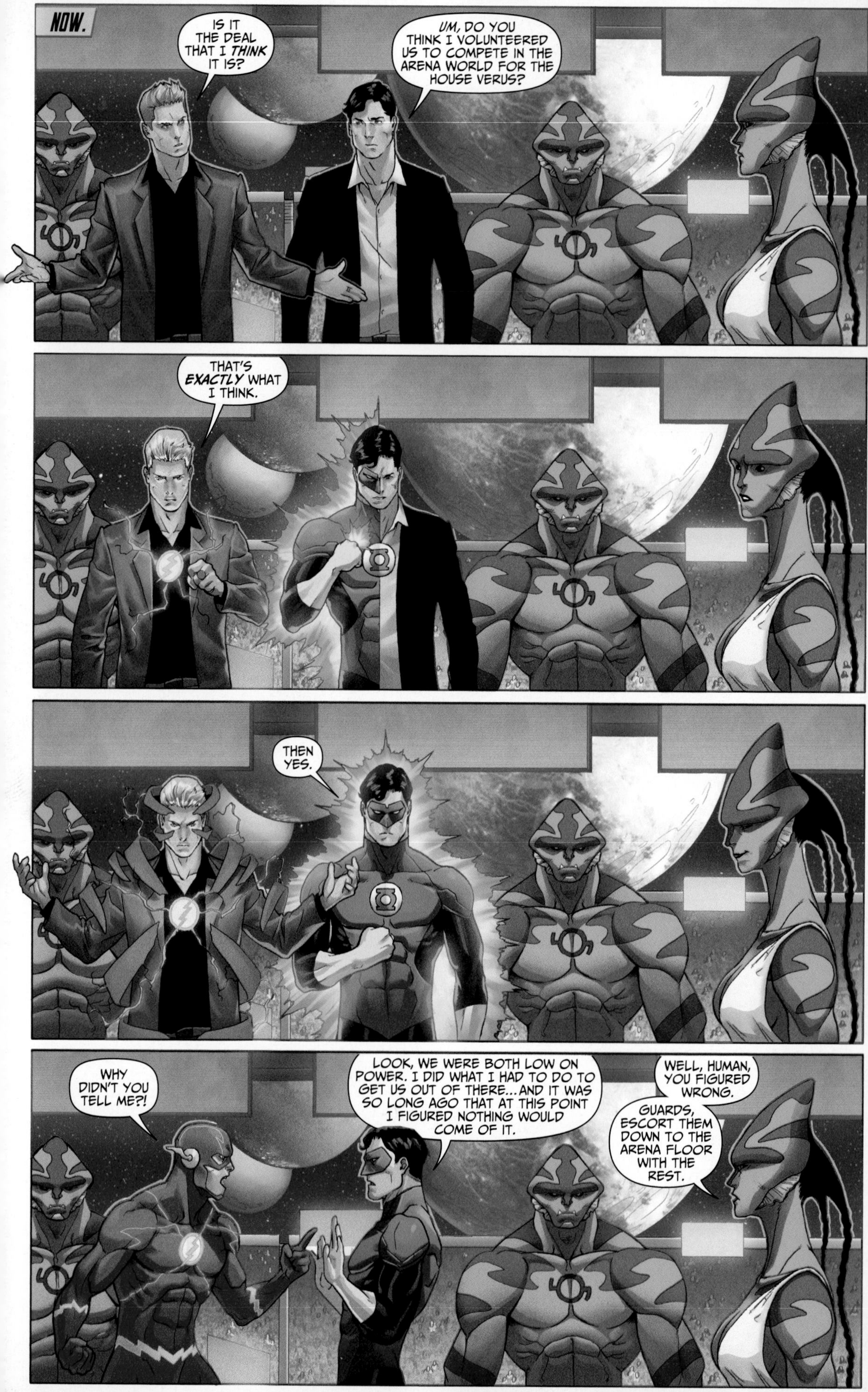
NOW.
IS IT THE DEAL THAT I *THINK* IT IS?
UM, DO YOU THINK I VOLUNTEERED US TO COMPETE IN THE ARENA WORLD FOR THE HOUSE VERUS?
THAT'S *EXACTLY* WHAT I THINK.
THEN YES.
WHY DIDN'T YOU TELL ME?!
LOOK, WE WERE BOTH LOW ON POWER. I DID WHAT I HAD TO DO TO GET US OUT OF THERE...AND IT WAS SO LONG AGO THAT AT THIS POINT I FIGURED NOTHING WOULD COME OF IT.
WELL, HUMAN, YOU FIGURED WRONG.
GUARDS, ESCORT THEM DOWN TO THE ARENA FLOOR WITH THE REST.

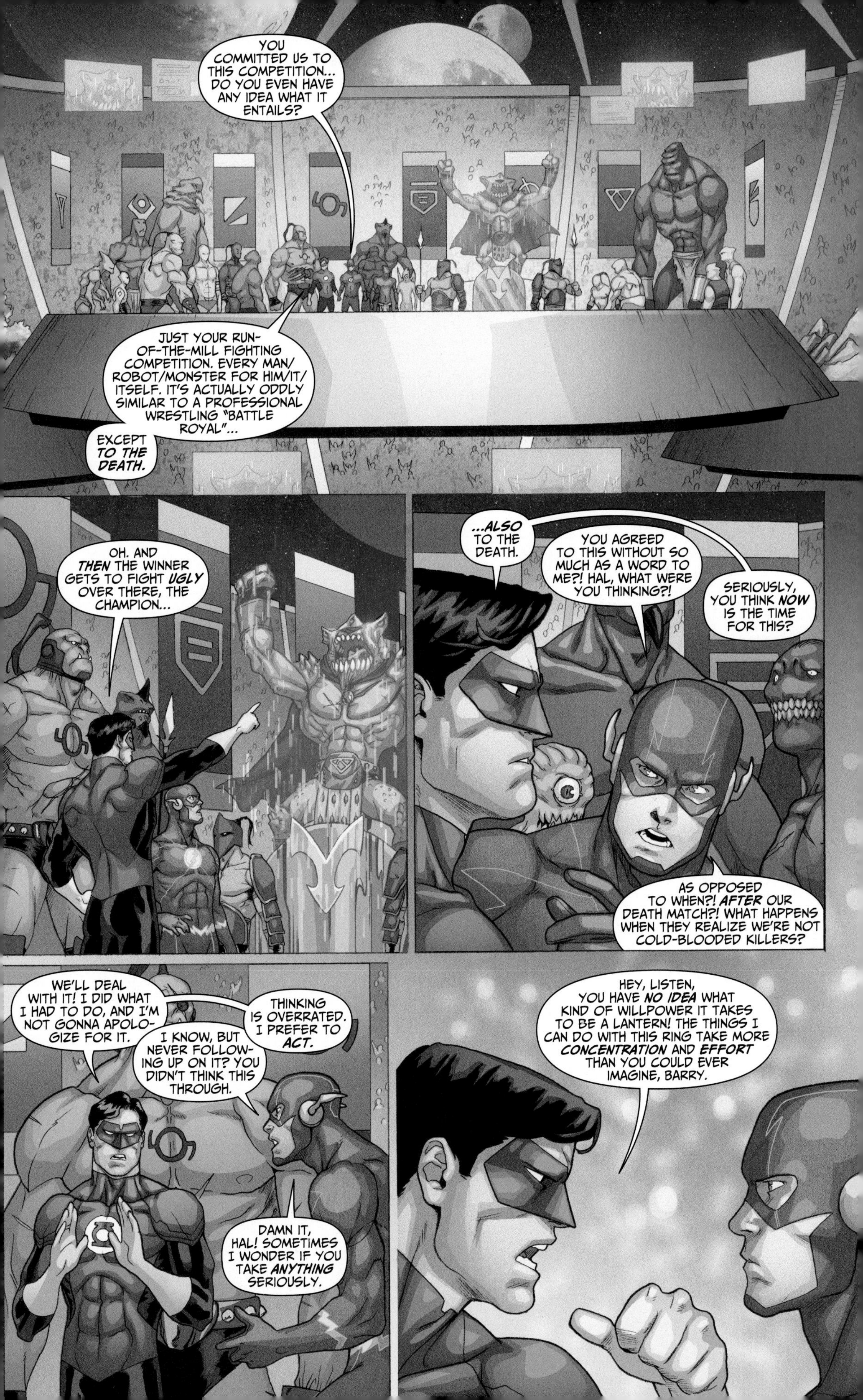

YOU COMMITTED US TO THIS COMPETITION... DO YOU EVEN HAVE ANY IDEA WHAT IT ENTAILS?
JUST YOUR RUN-OF-THE-MILL FIGHTING COMPETITION. EVERY MAN/ROBOT/MONSTER FOR HIM/IT/ITSELF. IT'S ACTUALLY ODDLY SIMILAR TO A PROFESSIONAL WRESTLING "BATTLE ROYAL"...
EXCEPT TO THE DEATH.
OH. AND THEN THE WINNER GETS TO FIGHT UGLY OVER THERE, THE CHAMPION...
...ALSO TO THE DEATH.
YOU AGREED TO THIS WITHOUT SO MUCH AS A WORD TO ME?! HAL, WHAT WERE YOU THINKING?!
SERIOUSLY, YOU THINK NOW IS THE TIME FOR THIS?
AS OPPOSED TO WHEN?! AFTER OUR DEATH MATCH?! WHAT HAPPENS WHEN THEY REALIZE WE'RE NOT COLD-BLOODED KILLERS?
WE'LL DEAL WITH IT! I DID WHAT I HAD TO DO, AND I'M NOT GONNA APOLOGIZE FOR IT.
THINKING IS OVERRATED. I PREFER TO ACT.
I KNOW, BUT NEVER FOLLOWING UP ON IT? YOU DIDN'T THINK THIS THROUGH.
DAMN IT, HAL! SOMETIMES I WONDER IF YOU TAKE ANYTHING SERIOUSLY.
HEY, LISTEN, YOU HAVE NO IDEA WHAT KIND OF WILLPOWER IT TAKES TO BE A LANTERN! THE THINGS I CAN DO WITH THIS RING TAKE MORE CONCENTRATION AND EFFORT THAN YOU COULD EVER IMAGINE, BARRY.

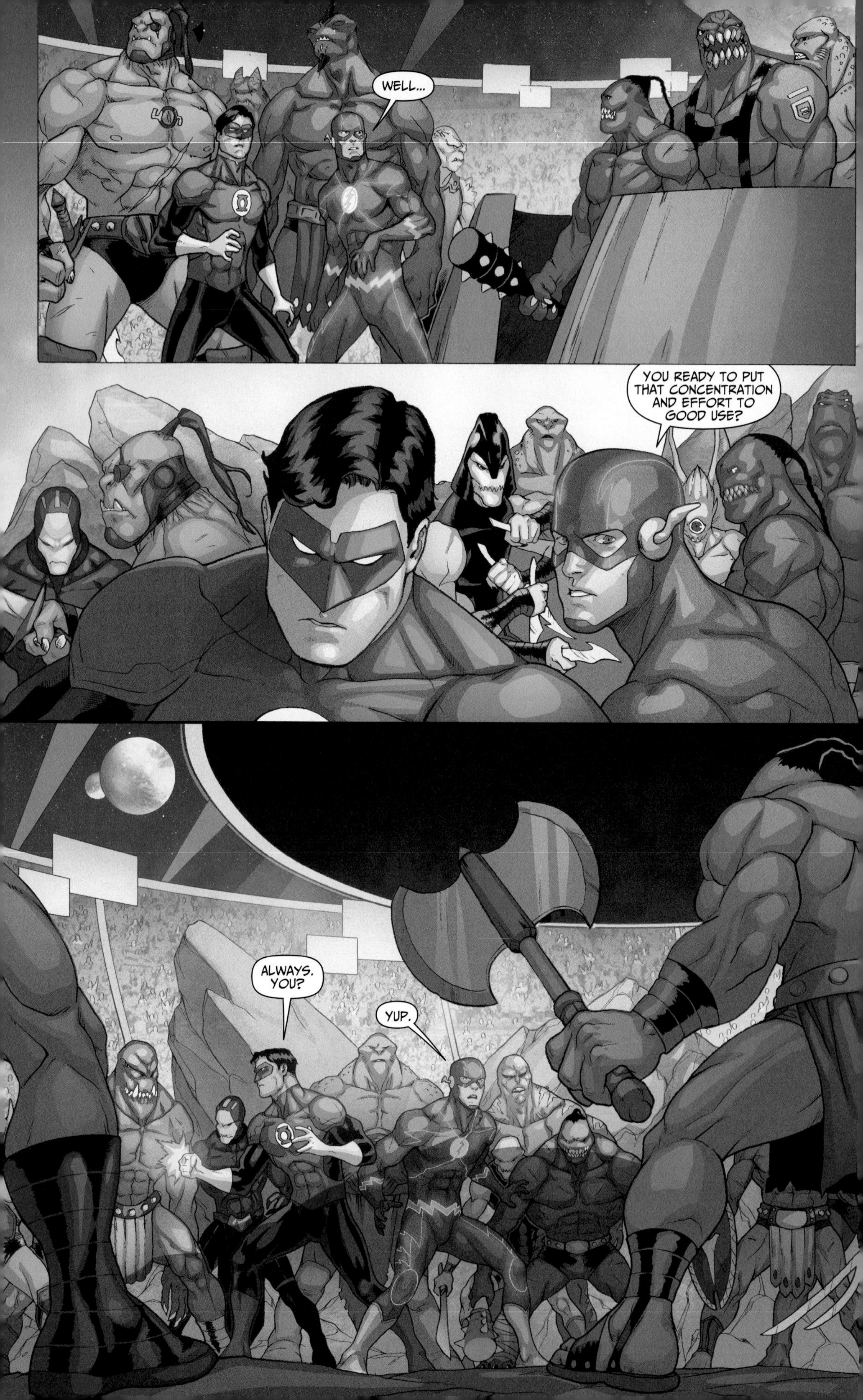
WELL...
YOU READY TO PUT THAT CONCENTRATION AND EFFORT TO GOOD USE?
ALWAYS. YOU?
YUP.

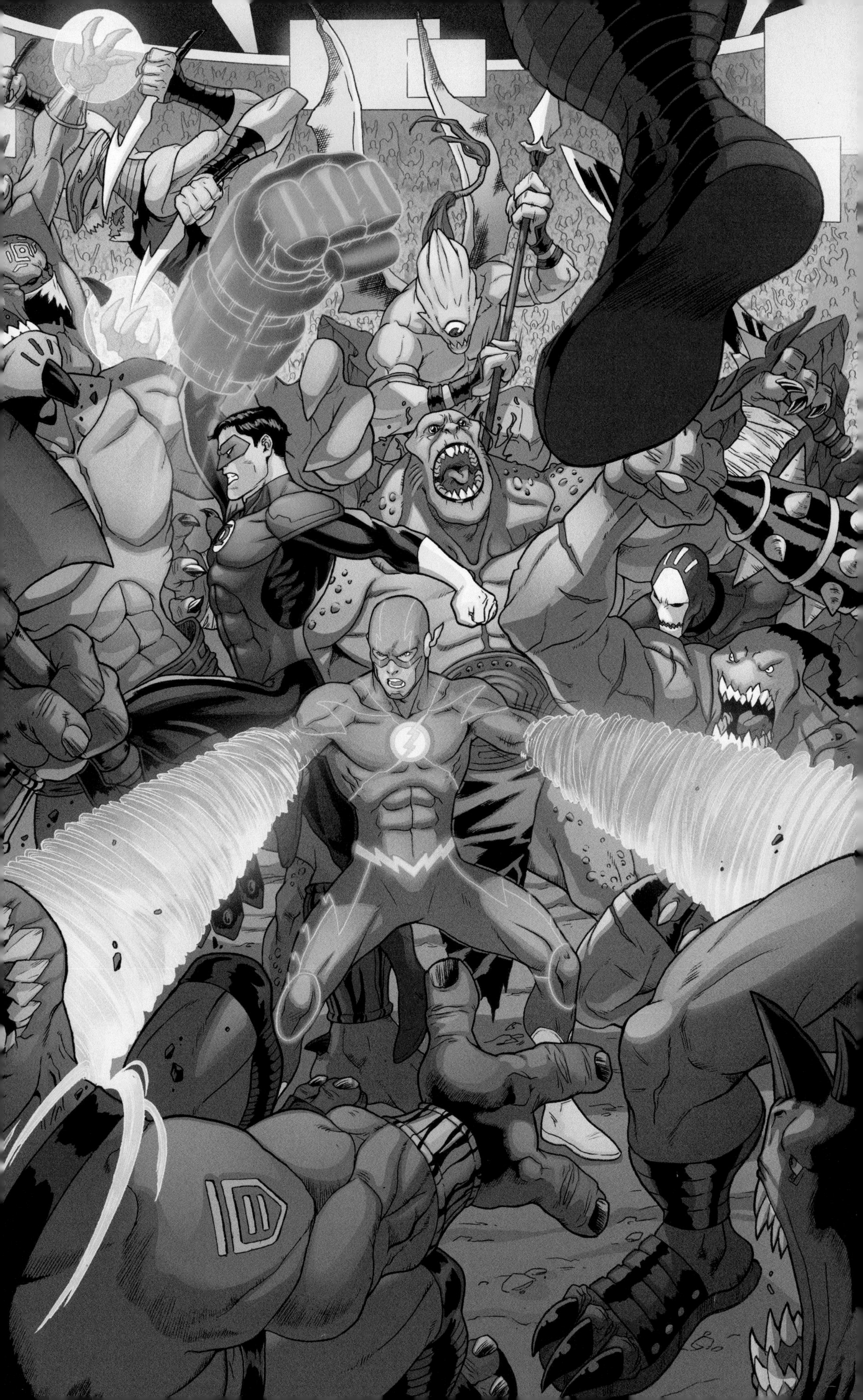

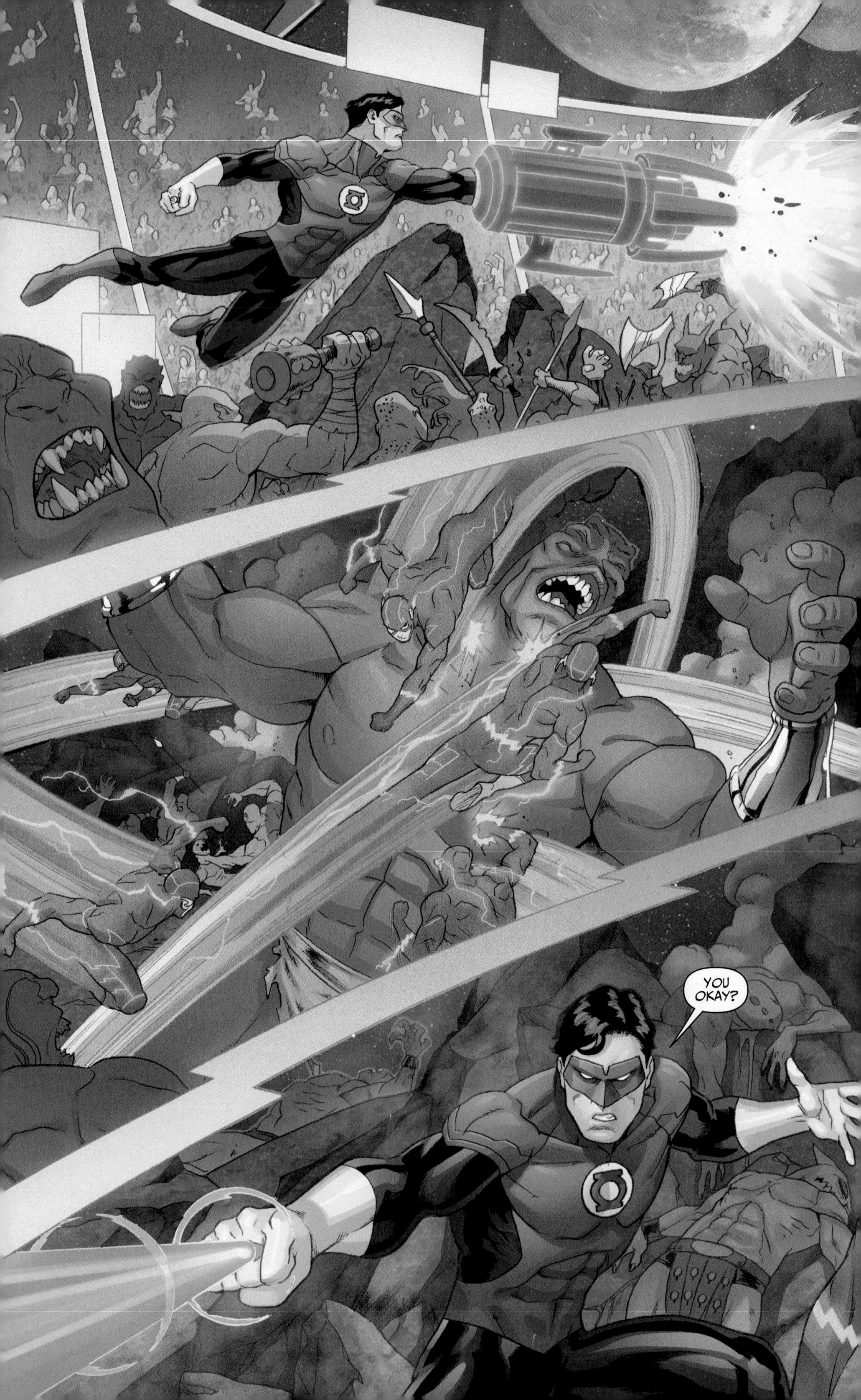
YOU OKAY?

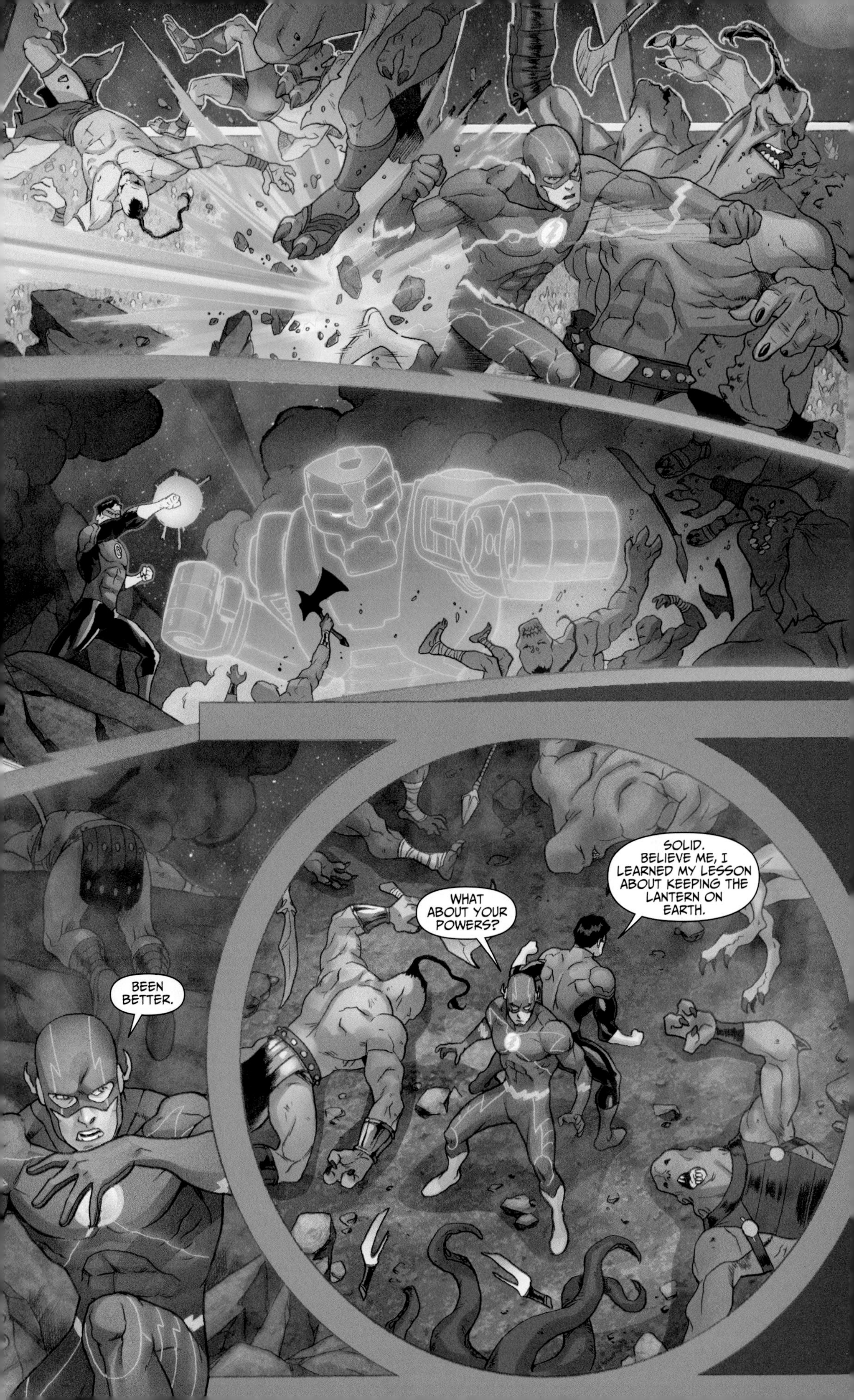
BEEN BETTER.
WHAT ABOUT YOUR POWERS?
SOLID. BELIEVE ME, I LEARNED MY LESSON ABOUT KEEPING THE LANTERN ON EARTH.

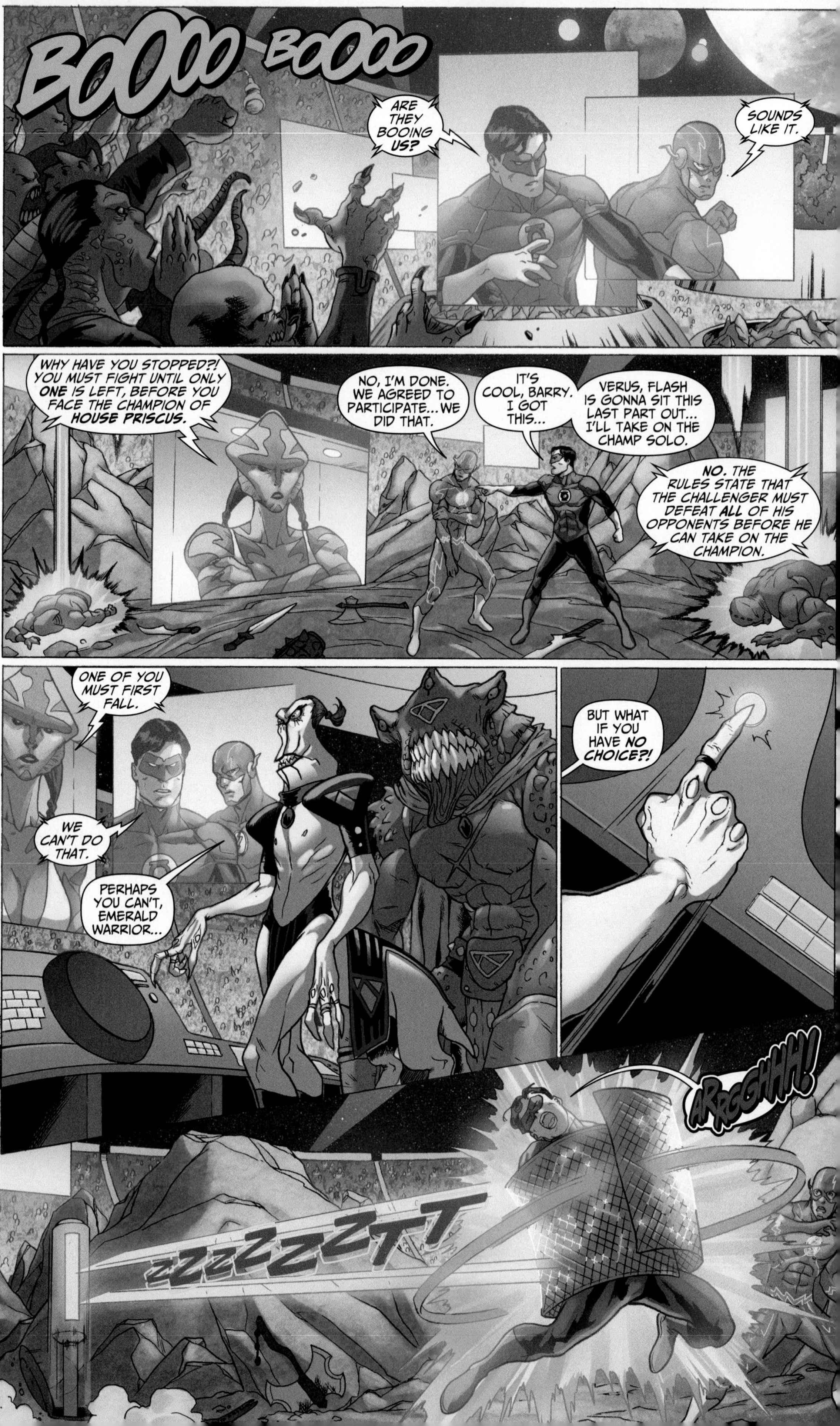
BOOOO BOOOO
ARE THEY BOOING US?
SOUNDS LIKE IT.
WHY HAVE YOU STOPPED?! YOU MUST FIGHT UNTIL ONLY ONE IS LEFT, BEFORE YOU FACE THE CHAMPION OF HOUSE PRISCUS.
NO, I'M DONE. WE AGREED TO PARTICIPATE... WE DID THAT.
IT'S COOL, BARRY. I GOT THIS...
VERUS, FLASH IS GONNA SIT THIS LAST PART OUT... I'LL TAKE ON THE CHAMP SOLO.
NO. THE RULES STATE THAT THE CHALLENGER MUST DEFEAT ALL OF HIS OPPONENTS BEFORE HE CAN TAKE ON THE CHAMPION.
ONE OF YOU MUST FIRST FALL.
WE CAN'T DO THAT.
PERHAPS YOU CAN'T, EMERALD WARRIOR...
BUT WHAT IF YOU HAVE NO CHOICE?!
ARRGGHHH!
ZZZZZZZT!

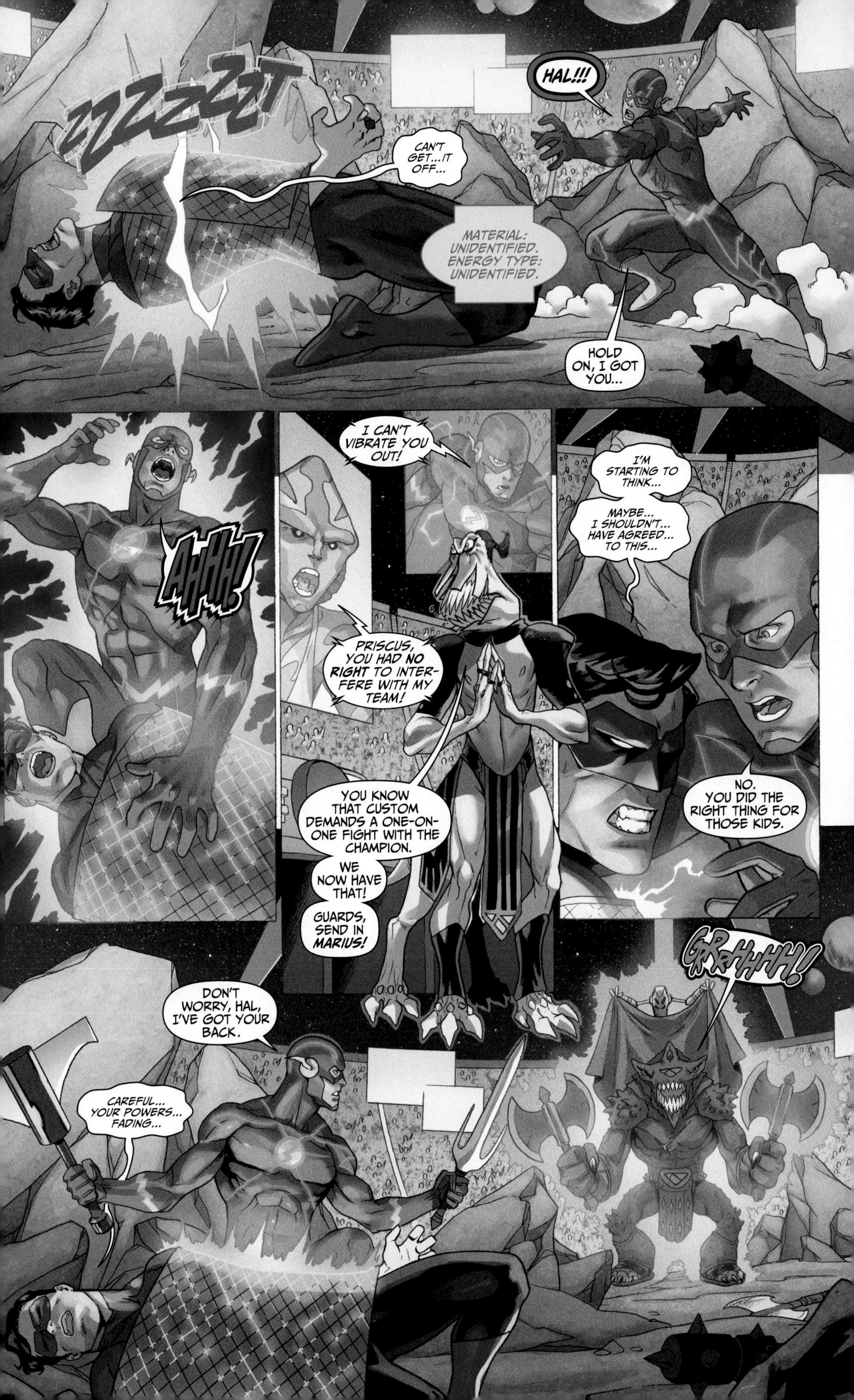

ZZZZZZZT
HAL!!!
CAN'T GET...IT OFF...
MATERIAL: UNIDENTIFIED. ENERGY TYPE: UNIDENTIFIED.
HOLD ON, I GOT YOU...
AHHH!
I CAN'T VIBRATE YOU OUT!
PRISCUS, YOU HAD NO RIGHT TO INTERFERE WITH MY TEAM!
YOU KNOW THAT CUSTOM DEMANDS A ONE-ON-ONE FIGHT WITH THE CHAMPION.
WE NOW HAVE THAT!
GUARDS, SEND IN MARIUS!
I'M STARTING TO THINK...
MAYBE... I SHOULDN'T... HAVE AGREED... TO THIS...
NO. YOU DID THE RIGHT THING FOR THOSE KIDS.
GRRHHHH!
DON'T WORRY, HAL, I'VE GOT YOUR BACK.
CAREFUL... YOUR POWERS... FADING...

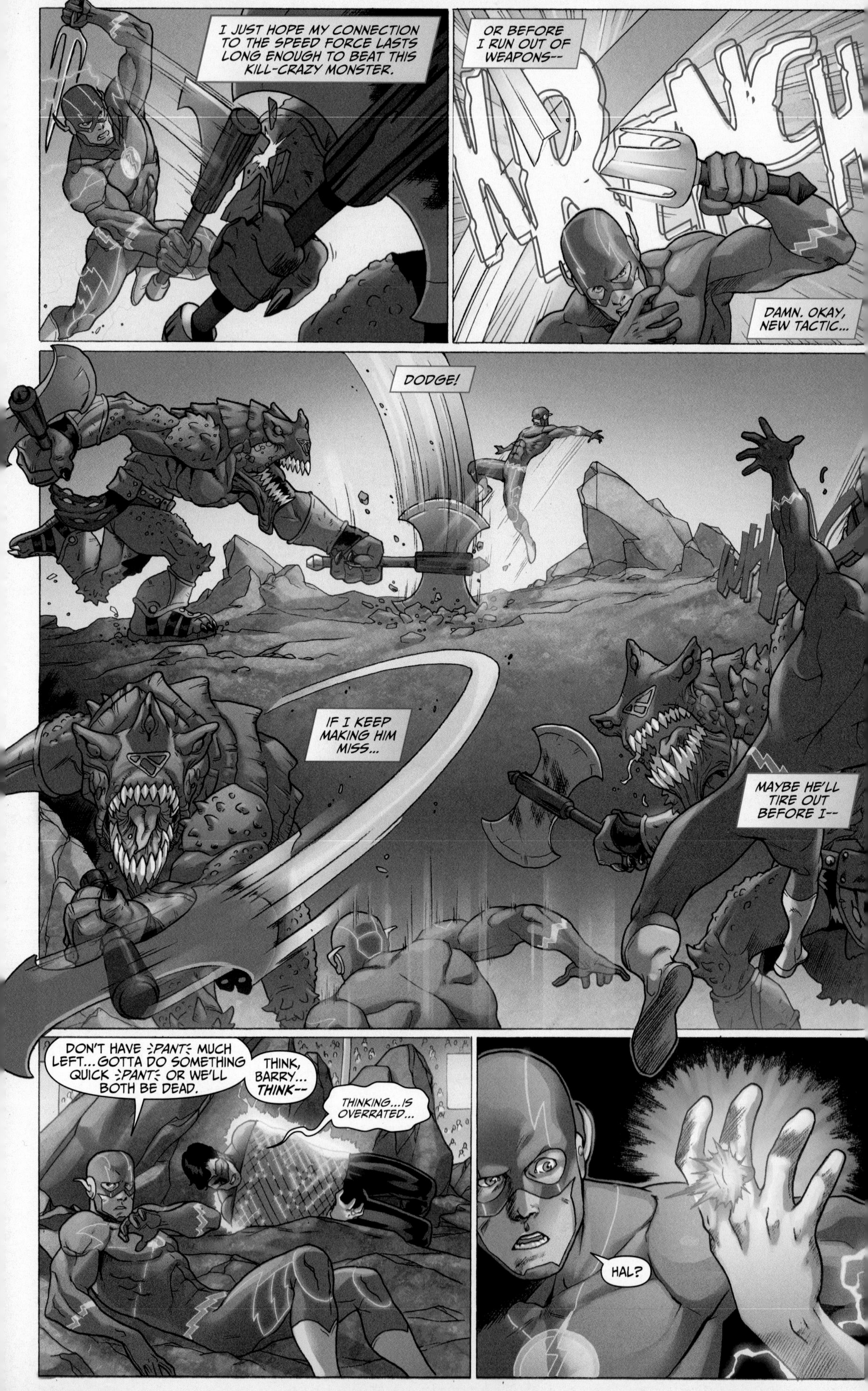
I JUST HOPE MY CONNECTION TO THE SPEED FORCE LASTS LONG ENOUGH TO BEAT THIS KILL-CRAZY MONSTER.
OR BEFORE I RUN OUT OF WEAPONS--
DAMN. OKAY, NEW TACTIC...
DODGE!
IF I KEEP MAKING HIM MISS...
MAYBE HE'LL TIRE OUT BEFORE I--
DON'T HAVE ⁃PANT⁃ MUCH LEFT...GOTTA DO SOMETHING QUICK ⁃PANT⁃ OR WE'LL BOTH BE DEAD.
THINK, BARRY... THINK--
THINKING...IS OVERRATED...
HAL?

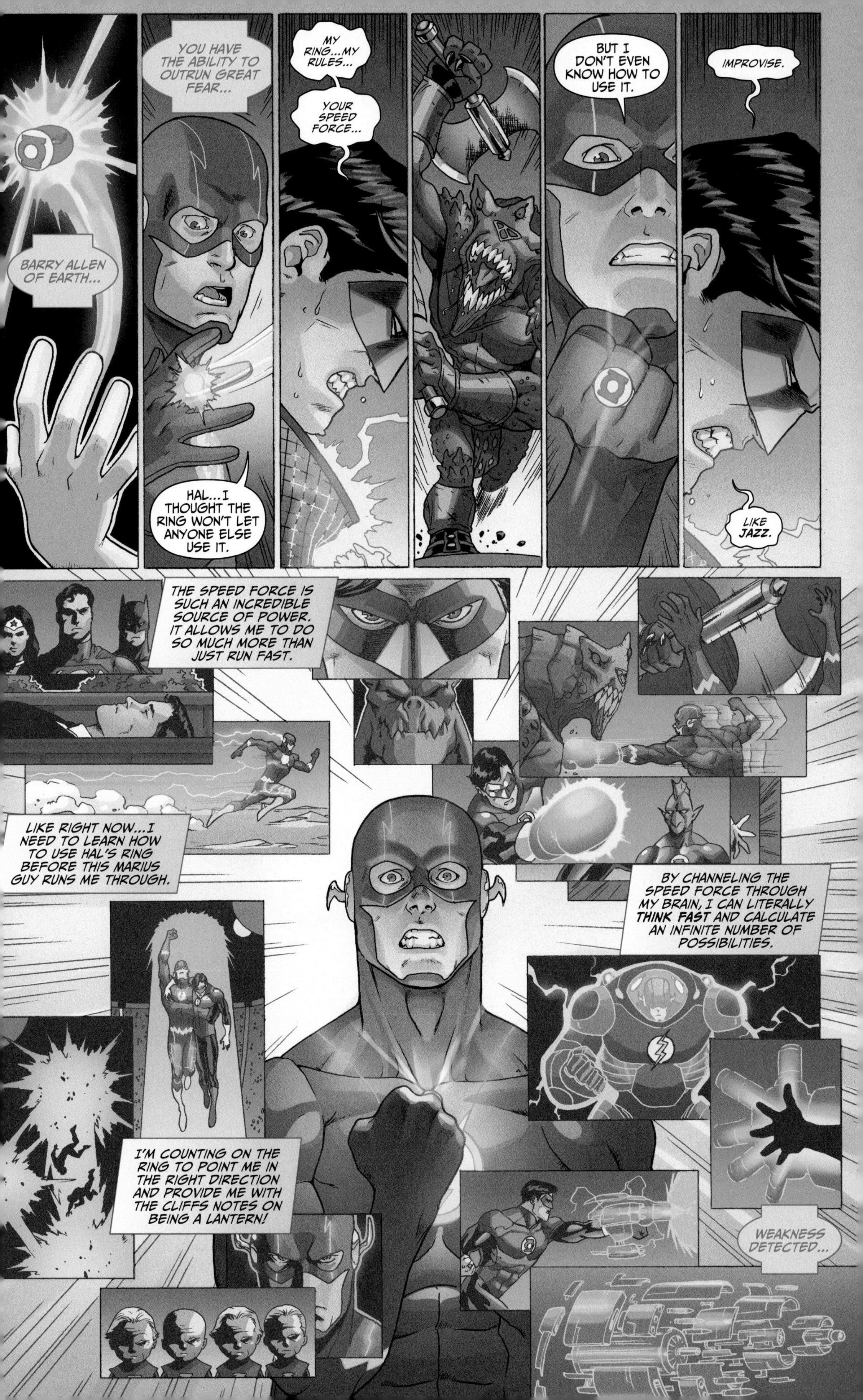
BARRY ALLEN OF EARTH...
YOU HAVE THE ABILITY TO OUTRUN GREAT FEAR...
HAL...I THOUGHT THE RING WON'T LET ANYONE ELSE USE IT.
MY RING...MY RULES...
YOUR SPEED FORCE...
BUT I DON'T EVEN KNOW HOW TO USE IT.
IMPROVISE.
LIKE JAZZ.
THE SPEED FORCE IS SUCH AN INCREDIBLE SOURCE OF POWER. IT ALLOWS ME TO DO SO MUCH MORE THAN JUST RUN FAST.
LIKE RIGHT NOW...I NEED TO LEARN HOW TO USE HAL'S RING BEFORE THIS MARIUS GUY RUNS ME THROUGH.
BY CHANNELING THE SPEED FORCE THROUGH MY BRAIN, I CAN LITERALLY THINK FAST AND CALCULATE AN INFINITE NUMBER OF POSSIBILITIES.
I'M COUNTING ON THE RING TO POINT ME IN THE RIGHT DIRECTION AND PROVIDE ME WITH THE CLIFFS NOTES ON BEING A LANTERN!
WEAKNESS DETECTED...

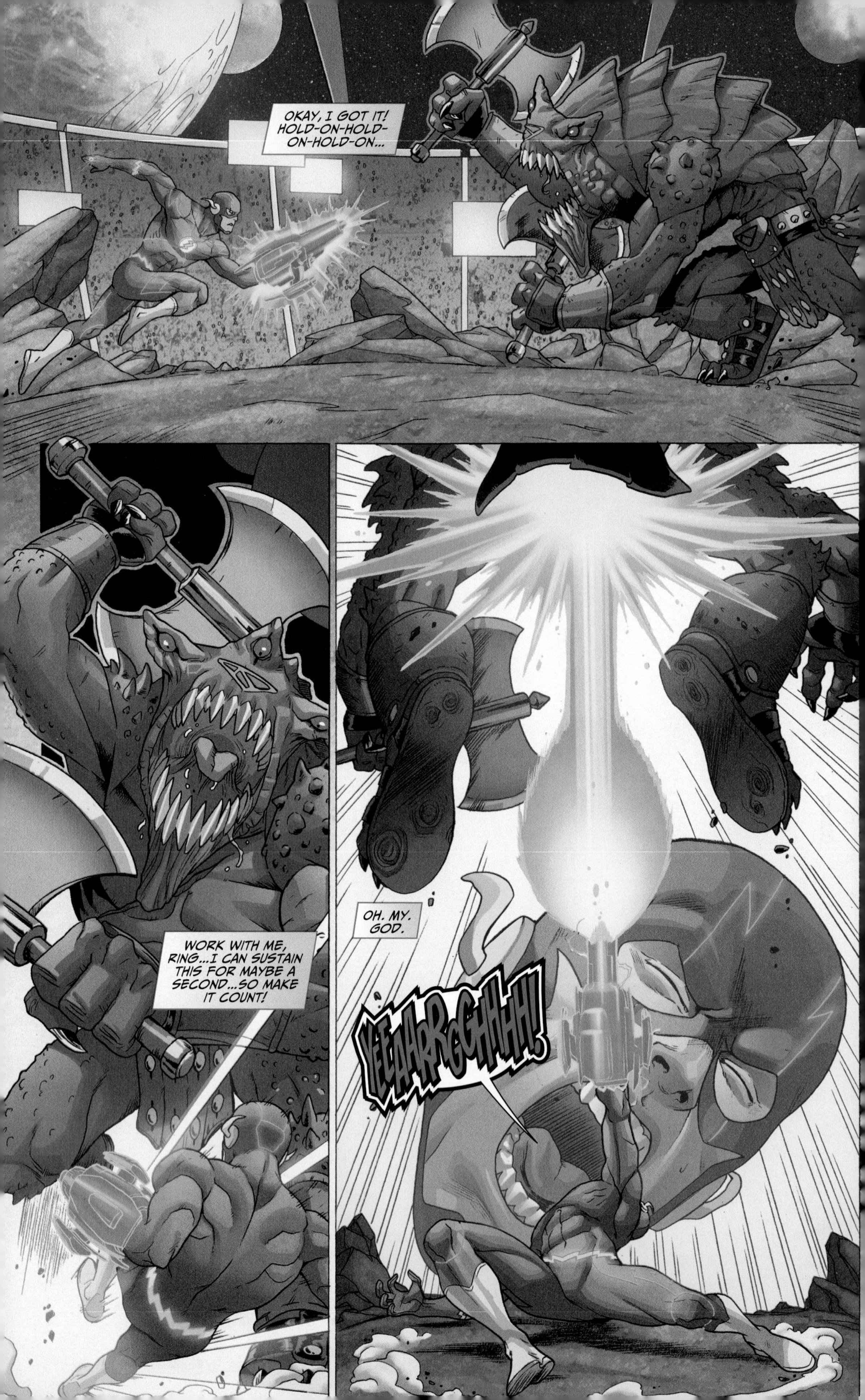
OKAY, I GOT IT! HOLD-ON-HOLD-ON-HOLD-ON...
WORK WITH ME, RING...I CAN SUSTAIN THIS FOR MAYBE A SECOND...SO MAKE IT COUNT!
OH. MY. GOD.
YEEAARRGHHH!

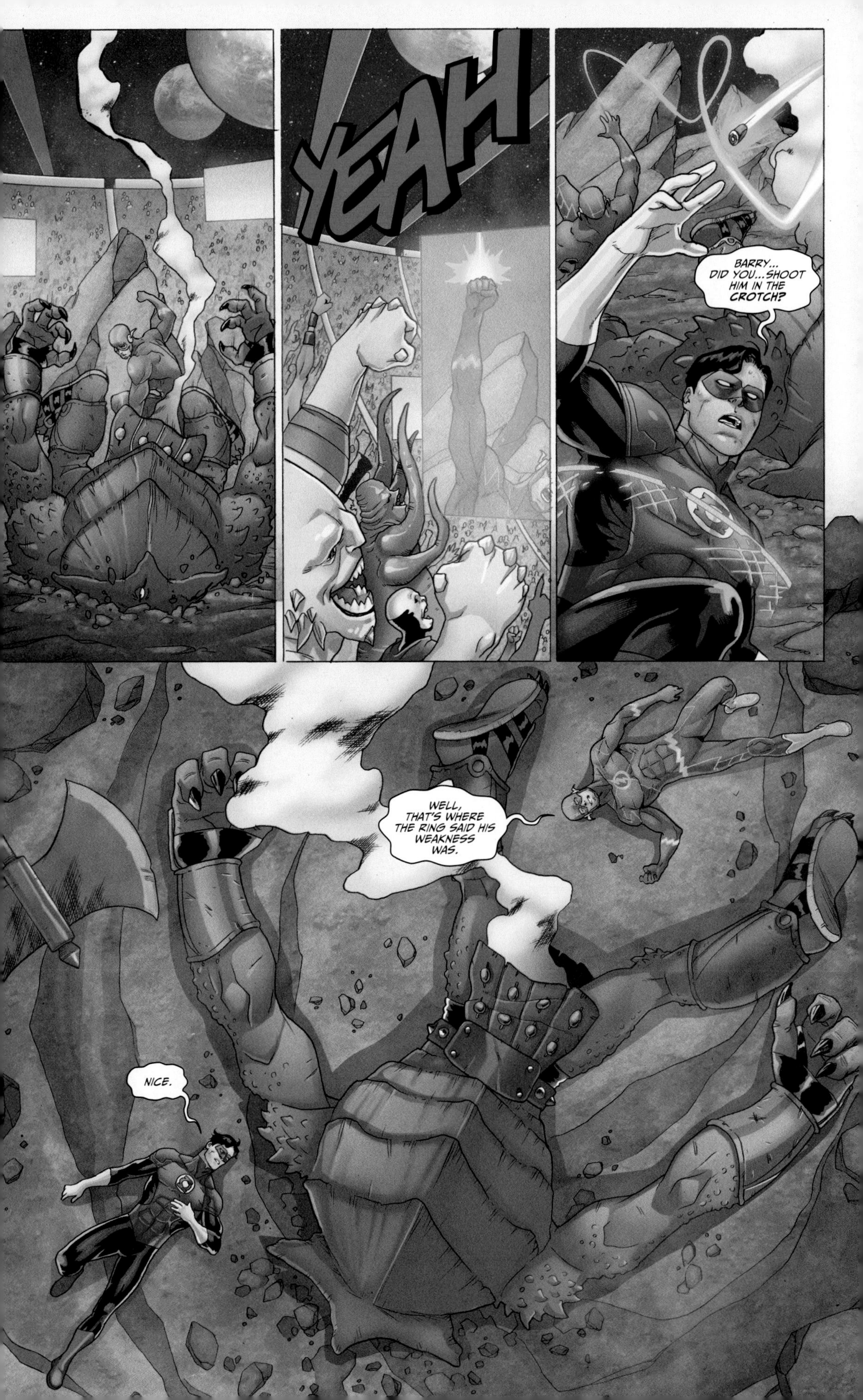
YEAH
BARRY... DID YOU...SHOOT HIM IN THE CROTCH?
WELL, THAT'S WHERE THE RING SAID HIS WEAKNESS WAS.
NICE.

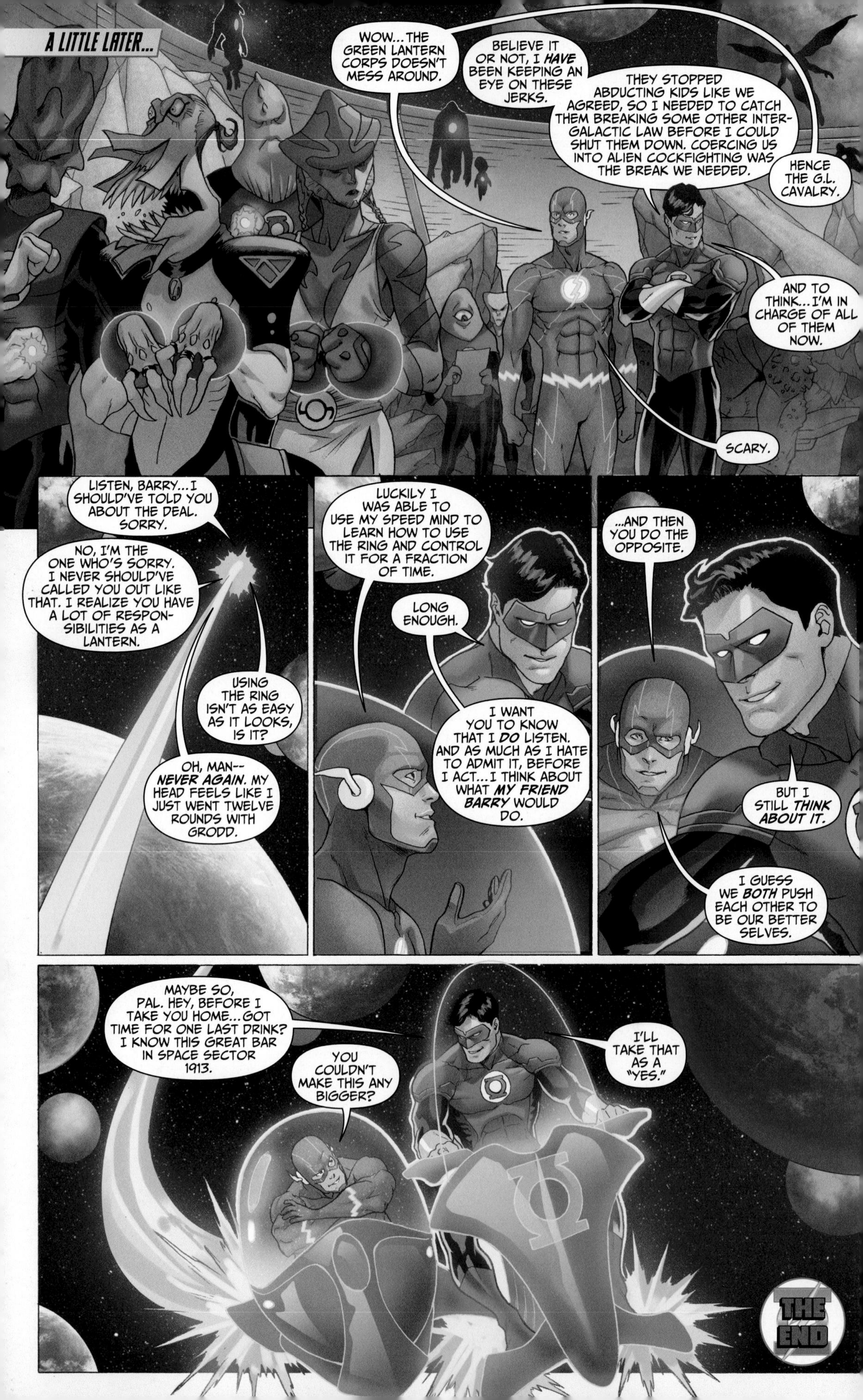
A LITTLE LATER...
WOW...THE GREEN LANTERN CORPS DOESN'T MESS AROUND.
BELIEVE IT OR NOT, I HAVE BEEN KEEPING AN EYE ON THESE JERKS.
THEY STOPPED ABDUCTING KIDS LIKE WE AGREED, SO I NEEDED TO CATCH THEM BREAKING SOME OTHER INTER-GALACTIC LAW BEFORE I COULD SHUT THEM DOWN. COERCING US INTO ALIEN COCKFIGHTING WAS THE BREAK WE NEEDED.
HENCE THE G.L. CAVALRY.
AND TO THINK...I'M IN CHARGE OF ALL OF THEM NOW.
SCARY.
LISTEN, BARRY...I SHOULD'VE TOLD YOU ABOUT THE DEAL. SORRY.
NO, I'M THE ONE WHO'S SORRY. I NEVER SHOULD'VE CALLED YOU OUT LIKE THAT. I REALIZE YOU HAVE A LOT OF RESPON-SIBILITIES AS A LANTERN.
USING THE RING ISN'T AS EASY AS IT LOOKS, IS IT?
OH, MAN-- NEVER AGAIN. MY HEAD FEELS LIKE I JUST WENT TWELVE ROUNDS WITH GRODD.
LUCKILY I WAS ABLE TO USE MY SPEED MIND TO LEARN HOW TO USE THE RING AND CONTROL IT FOR A FRACTION OF TIME.
LONG ENOUGH.
I WANT YOU TO KNOW THAT I DO LISTEN. AND AS MUCH AS I HATE TO ADMIT IT, BEFORE I ACT...I THINK ABOUT WHAT MY FRIEND BARRY WOULD DO.
...AND THEN YOU DO THE OPPOSITE.
BUT I STILL THINK ABOUT IT.
I GUESS WE BOTH PUSH EACH OTHER TO BE OUR BETTER SELVES.
MAYBE SO, PAL. HEY, BEFORE I TAKE YOU HOME...GOT TIME FOR ONE LAST DRINK? I KNOW THIS GREAT BAR IN SPACE SECTOR 1913.
YOU COULDN'T MAKE THIS ANY BIGGER?
I'LL TAKE THAT AS A "YES."
THE END

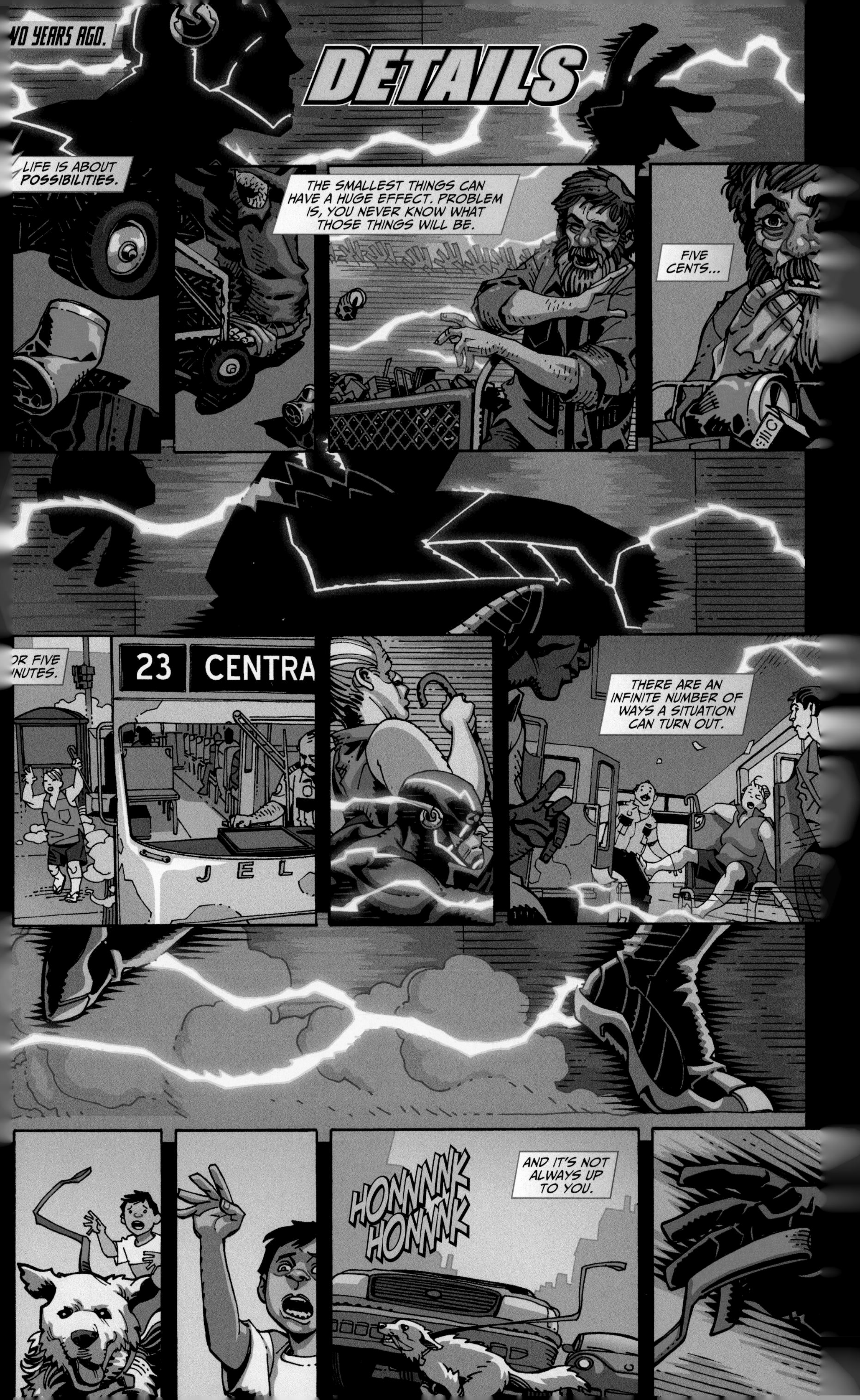
WO YEARS AGO.
DETAILS
LIFE IS ABOUT POSSIBILITIES.
THE SMALLEST THINGS CAN HAVE A HUGE EFFECT. PROBLEM IS, YOU NEVER KNOW WHAT THOSE THINGS WILL BE.
FIVE CENTS...
OR FIVE MINUTES.
23 CENTRA
THERE ARE AN INFINITE NUMBER OF WAYS A SITUATION CAN TURN OUT.
HONNNNK HONNNK
AND IT'S NOT ALWAYS UP TO YOU.

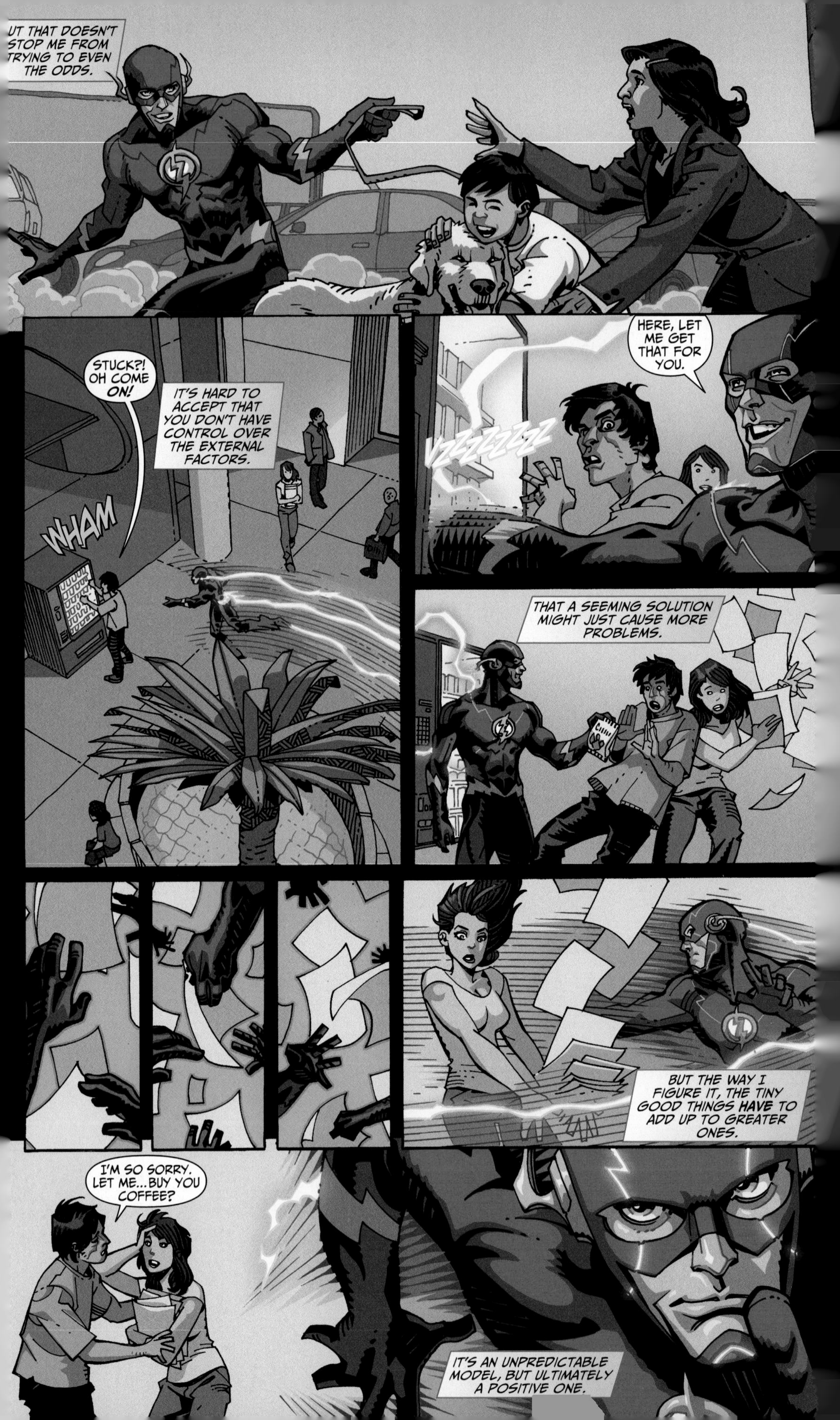
UT THAT DOESN'T STOP ME FROM TRYING TO EVEN THE ODDS.
STUCK?! OH COME ON!
IT'S HARD TO ACCEPT THAT YOU DON'T HAVE CONTROL OVER THE EXTERNAL FACTORS.
WHAM
HERE, LET ME GET THAT FOR YOU.
VZZZZZZZ
THAT A SEEMING SOLUTION MIGHT JUST CAUSE MORE PROBLEMS.
BUT THE WAY I FIGURE IT, THE TINY GOOD THINGS HAVE TO ADD UP TO GREATER ONES.
I'M SO SORRY. LET ME...BUY YOU COFFEE?
IT'S AN UNPREDICTABLE MODEL, BUT ULTIMATELY A POSITIVE ONE.

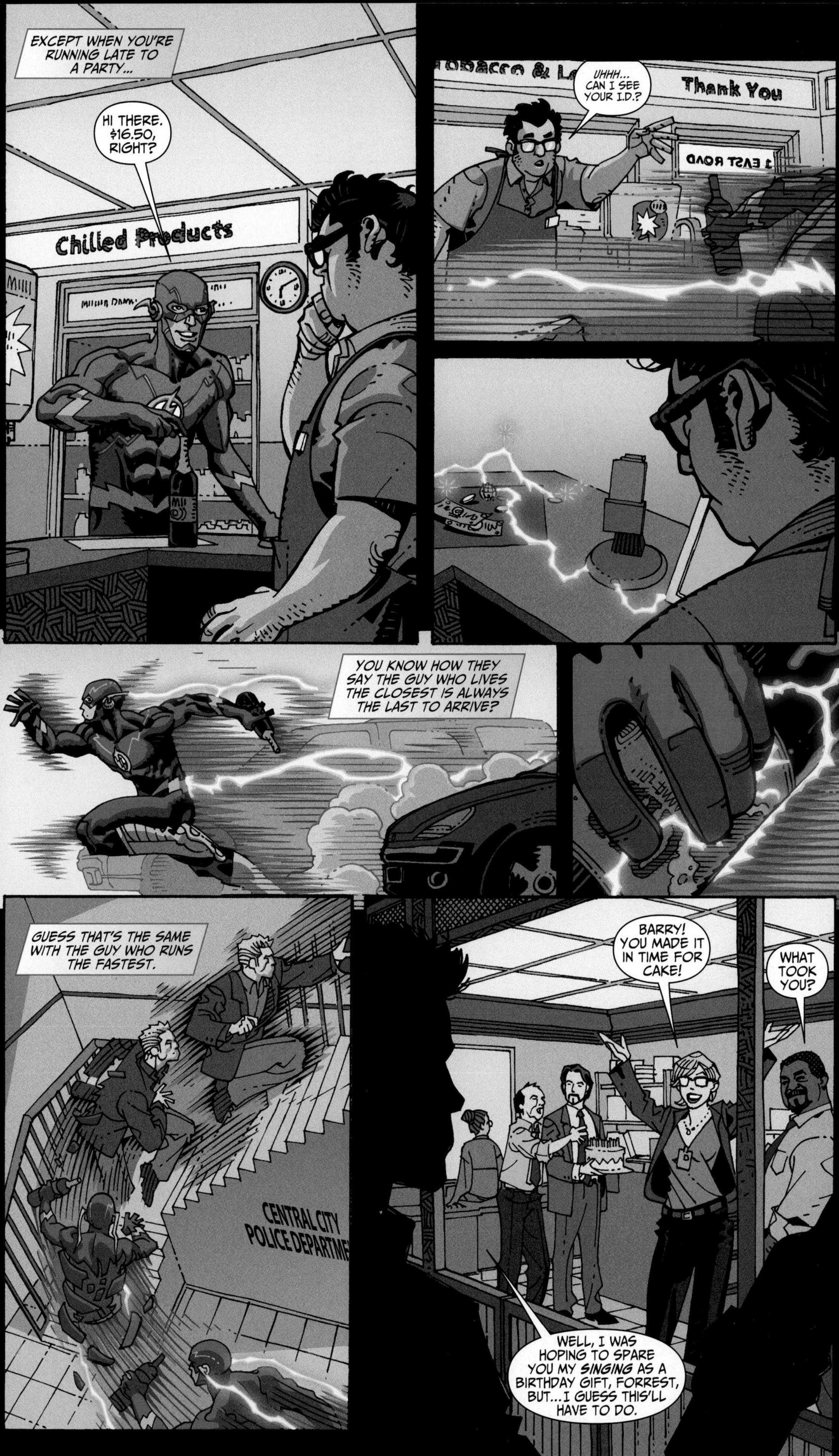
EXCEPT WHEN YOU'RE RUNNING LATE TO A PARTY...
HI THERE. $16.50, RIGHT?
Chilled Products
Tobacco & L
Thank You
UHHH... CAN I SEE YOUR I.D.?
YOU KNOW HOW THEY SAY THE GUY WHO LIVES THE CLOSEST IS ALWAYS THE LAST TO ARRIVE?
GUESS THAT'S THE SAME WITH THE GUY WHO RUNS THE FASTEST.
CENTRAL CITY POLICE DEPARTME
BARRY! YOU MADE IT IN TIME FOR CAKE!
WHAT TOOK YOU?
WELL, I WAS HOPING TO SPARE YOU MY SINGING AS A BIRTHDAY GIFT, FORREST, BUT...I GUESS THIS'LL HAVE TO DO.

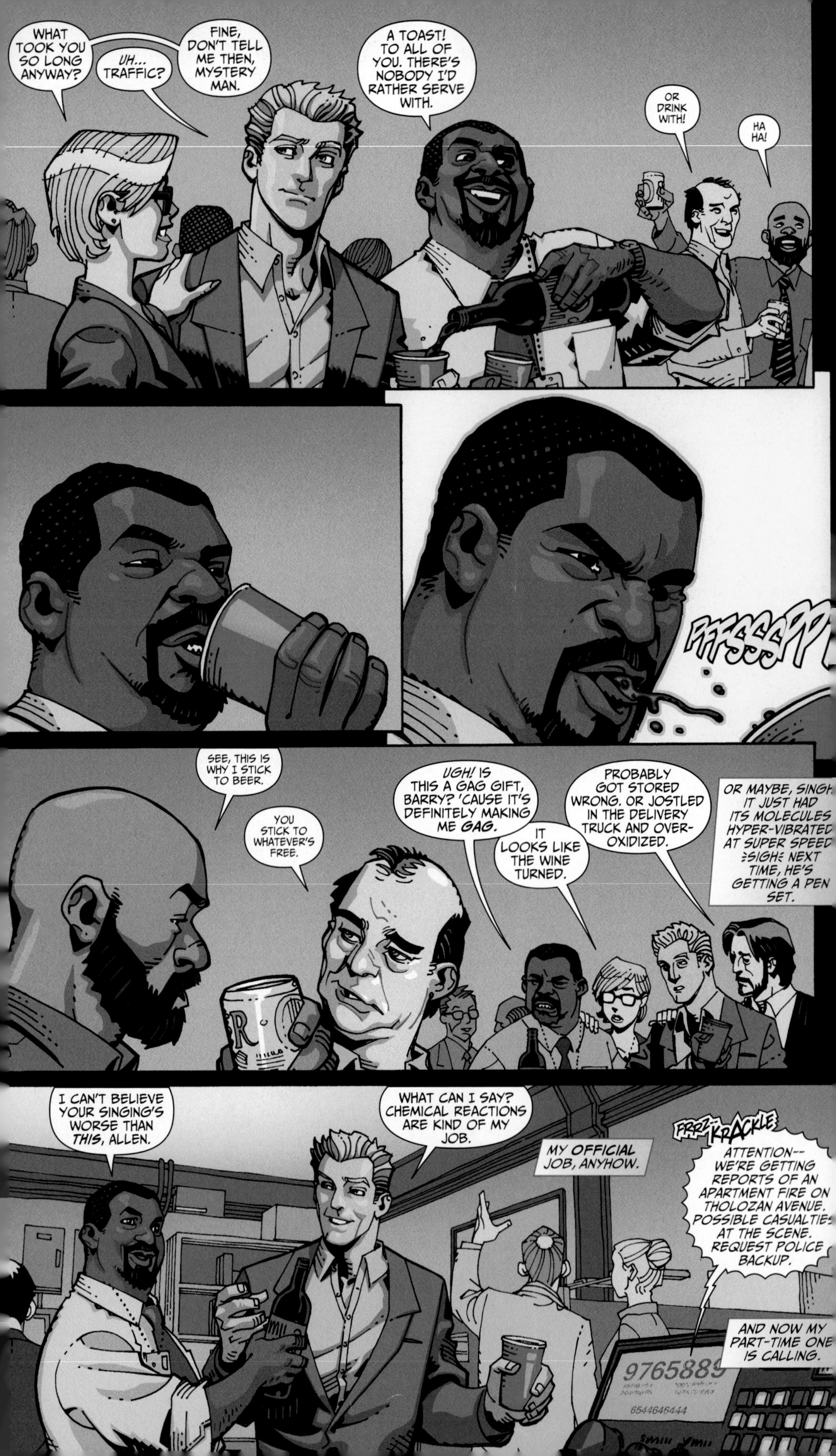
WHAT TOOK YOU SO LONG ANYWAY?
UH... TRAFFIC?
FINE, DON'T TELL ME THEN, MYSTERY MAN.
A TOAST! TO ALL OF YOU. THERE'S NOBODY I'D RATHER SERVE WITH.
OR DRINK WITH!
HA HA!
PFFSSPP
SEE, THIS IS WHY I STICK TO BEER.
YOU STICK TO WHATEVER'S FREE.
UGH! IS THIS A GAG GIFT, BARRY? 'CAUSE IT'S DEFINITELY MAKING ME GAG.
IT LOOKS LIKE THE WINE TURNED.
PROBABLY GOT STORED WRONG. OR JOSTLED IN THE DELIVERY TRUCK AND OVER-OXIDIZED.
OR MAYBE, SINGH, IT JUST HAD ITS MOLECULES HYPER-VIBRATED AT SUPER SPEED. *SIGH* NEXT TIME, HE'S GETTING A PEN SET.
I CAN'T BELIEVE YOUR SINGING'S WORSE THAN THIS, ALLEN.
WHAT CAN I SAY? CHEMICAL REACTIONS ARE KIND OF MY JOB.
MY OFFICIAL JOB, ANYHOW.
FRRZ KRACKLE
ATTENTION-- WE'RE GETTING REPORTS OF AN APARTMENT FIRE ON THOLOZAN AVENUE. POSSIBLE CASUALTIES AT THE SCENE. REQUEST POLICE BACKUP.
AND NOW MY PART-TIME ONE IS CALLING.
9765889
6544646444

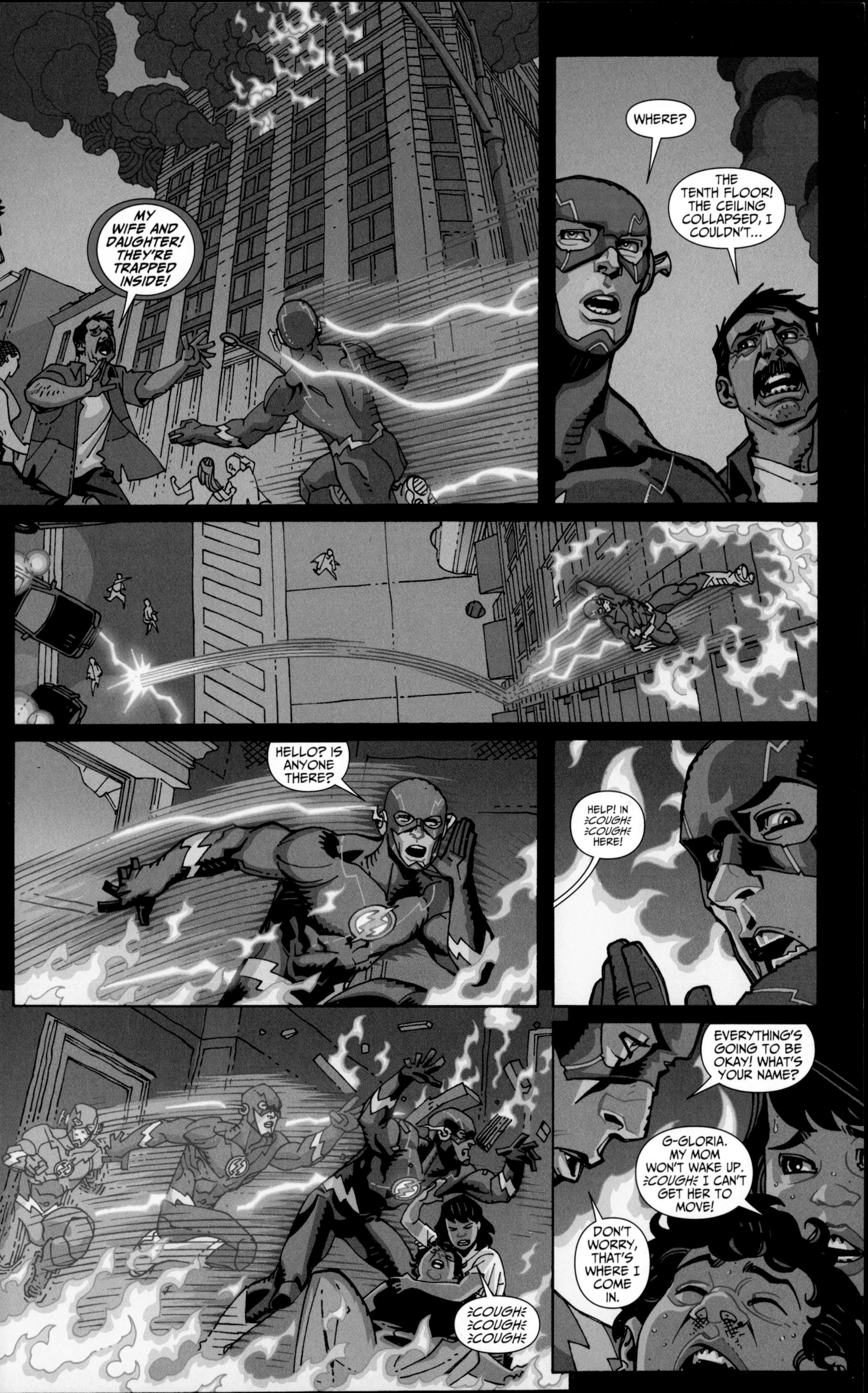
MY WIFE AND DAUGHTER! THEY'RE TRAPPED INSIDE!
WHERE?
THE TENTH FLOOR! THE CEILING COLLAPSED, I COULDN'T...
HELLO? IS ANYONE THERE?
HELP! IN *COUGH* *COUGH* HERE!
EVERYTHING'S GOING TO BE OKAY! WHAT'S YOUR NAME?
G-GLORIA. MY MOM WON'T WAKE UP. *COUGH* I CAN'T GET HER TO MOVE!
DON'T WORRY, THAT'S WHERE I COME IN.
COUGH *COUGH* *COUGH*

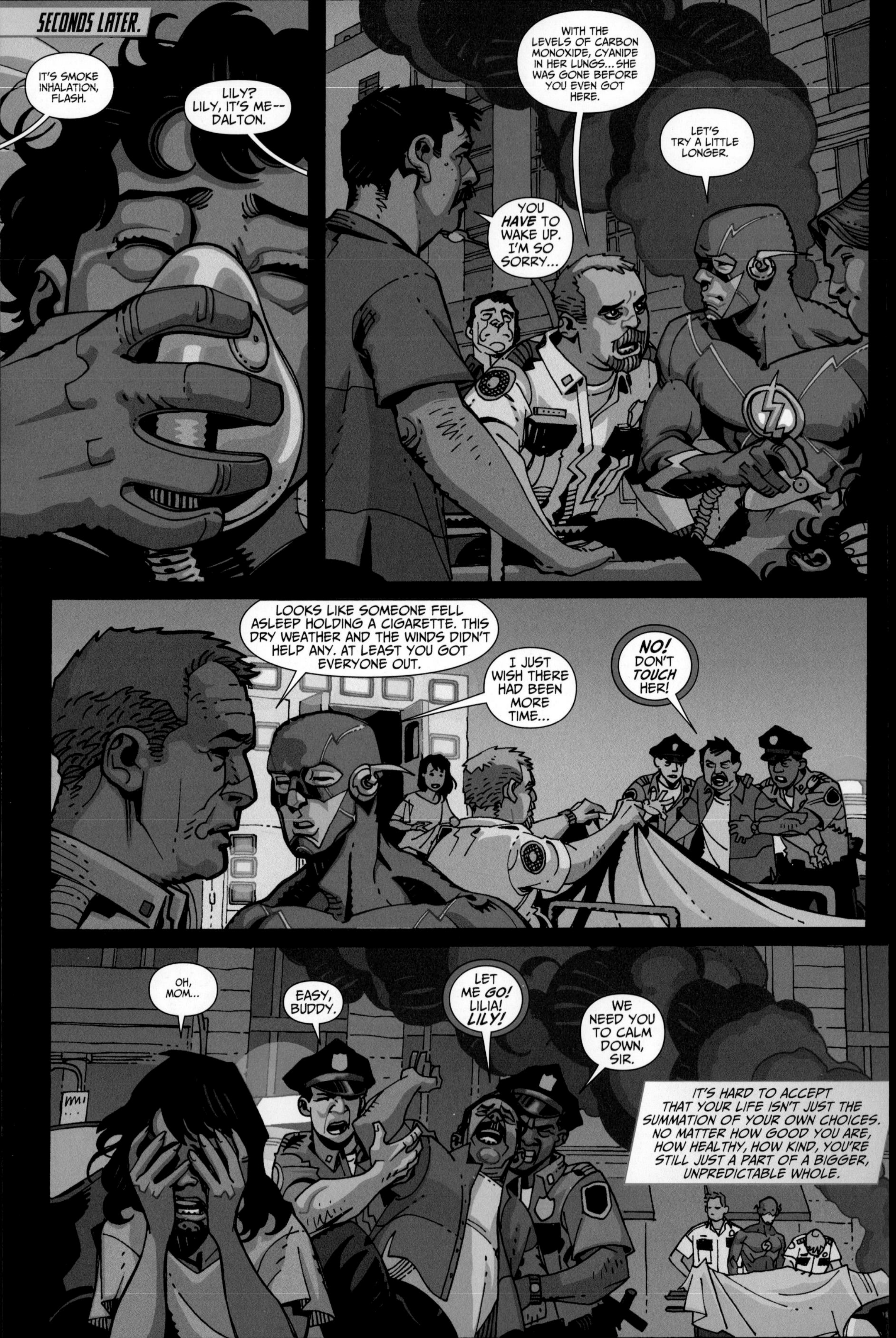

SECONDS LATER.
IT'S SMOKE INHALATION, FLASH.
LILY? LILY, IT'S ME-- DALTON.
WITH THE LEVELS OF CARBON MONOXIDE, CYANIDE IN HER LUNGS... SHE WAS GONE BEFORE YOU EVEN GOT HERE.
LET'S TRY A LITTLE LONGER.
YOU HAVE TO WAKE UP. I'M SO SORRY...
LOOKS LIKE SOMEONE FELL ASLEEP HOLDING A CIGARETTE. THIS DRY WEATHER AND THE WINDS DIDN'T HELP ANY. AT LEAST YOU GOT EVERYONE OUT.
I JUST WISH THERE HAD BEEN MORE TIME...
NO! DON'T TOUCH HER!
OH, MOM...
EASY, BUDDY.
LET ME GO! LILIA! LILY!
WE NEED YOU TO CALM DOWN, SIR.
IT'S HARD TO ACCEPT THAT YOUR LIFE ISN'T JUST THE SUMMATION OF YOUR OWN CHOICES. NO MATTER HOW GOOD YOU ARE, HOW HEALTHY, HOW KIND, YOU'RE STILL JUST A PART OF A BIGGER, UNPREDICTABLE WHOLE.

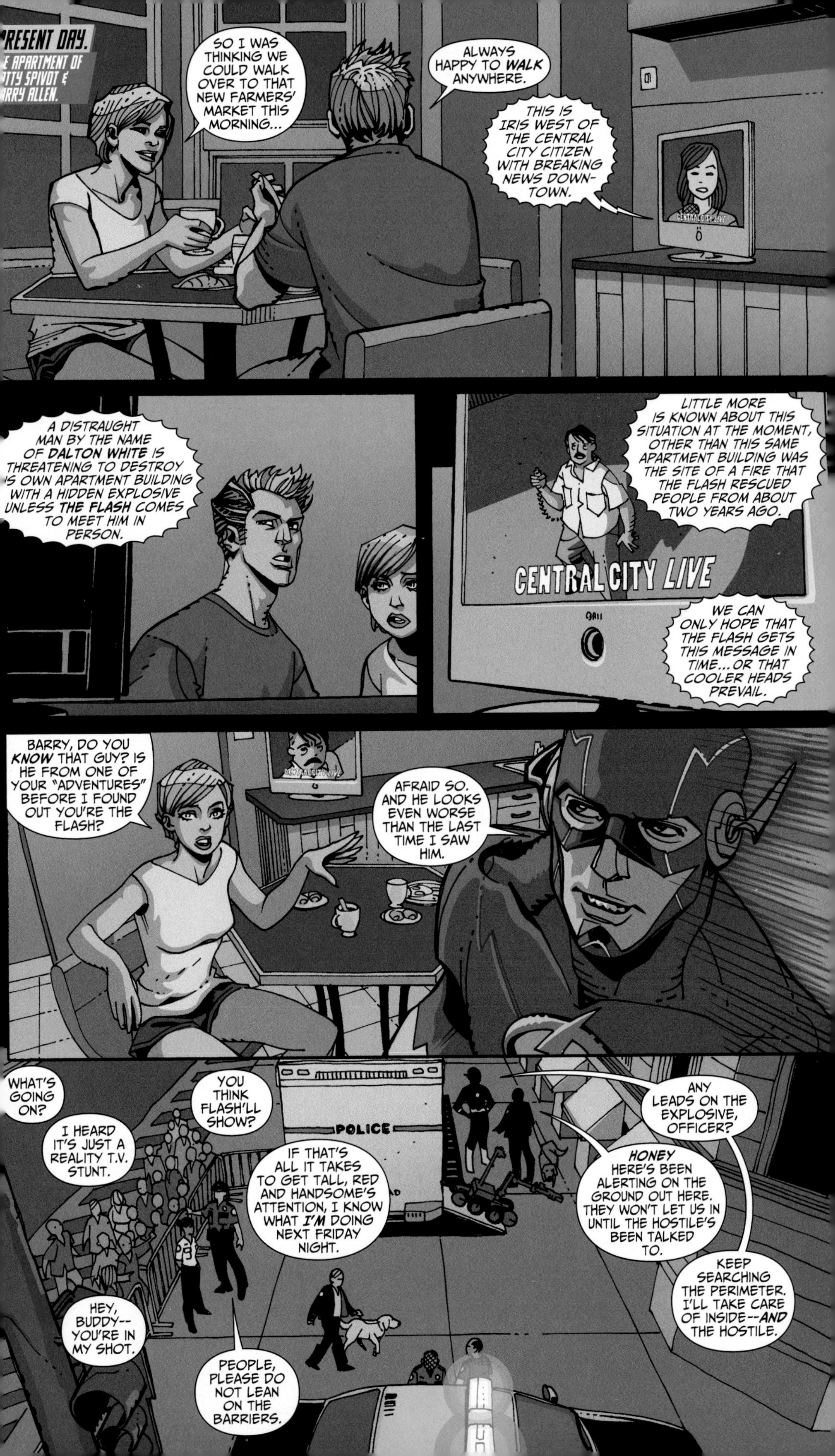
RESENT DAY.
E APARTMENT OF
TTY SPIVOT &
RRY ALLEN.
SO I WAS THINKING WE COULD WALK OVER TO THAT NEW FARMERS' MARKET THIS MORNING...
ALWAYS HAPPY TO WALK ANYWHERE.
THIS IS IRIS WEST OF THE CENTRAL CITY CITIZEN WITH BREAKING NEWS DOWN-TOWN.
CENTRAL CITY LIVE
A DISTRAUGHT MAN BY THE NAME OF DALTON WHITE IS THREATENING TO DESTROY S OWN APARTMENT BUILDING WITH A HIDDEN EXPLOSIVE UNLESS THE FLASH COMES TO MEET HIM IN PERSON.
LITTLE MORE IS KNOWN ABOUT THIS SITUATION AT THE MOMENT, OTHER THAN THIS SAME APARTMENT BUILDING WAS THE SITE OF A FIRE THAT THE FLASH RESCUED PEOPLE FROM ABOUT TWO YEARS AGO.
CENTRAL CITY LIVE
WE CAN ONLY HOPE THAT THE FLASH GETS THIS MESSAGE IN TIME... OR THAT COOLER HEADS PREVAIL.
BARRY, DO YOU KNOW THAT GUY? IS HE FROM ONE OF YOUR "ADVENTURES" BEFORE I FOUND OUT YOU'RE THE FLASH?
AFRAID SO. AND HE LOOKS EVEN WORSE THAN THE LAST TIME I SAW HIM.
WHAT'S GOING ON?
I HEARD IT'S JUST A REALITY T.V. STUNT.
YOU THINK FLASH'LL SHOW?
POLICE
IF THAT'S ALL IT TAKES TO GET TALL, RED AND HANDSOME'S ATTENTION, I KNOW WHAT I'M DOING NEXT FRIDAY NIGHT.
ANY LEADS ON THE EXPLOSIVE, OFFICER?
HONEY HERE'S BEEN ALERTING ON THE GROUND OUT HERE. THEY WON'T LET US IN UNTIL THE HOSTILE'S BEEN TALKED TO.
KEEP SEARCHING THE PERIMETER. I'LL TAKE CARE OF INSIDE--AND THE HOSTILE.
HEY, BUDDY-- YOU'RE IN MY SHOT.
PEOPLE, PLEASE DO NOT LEAN ON THE BARRIERS.

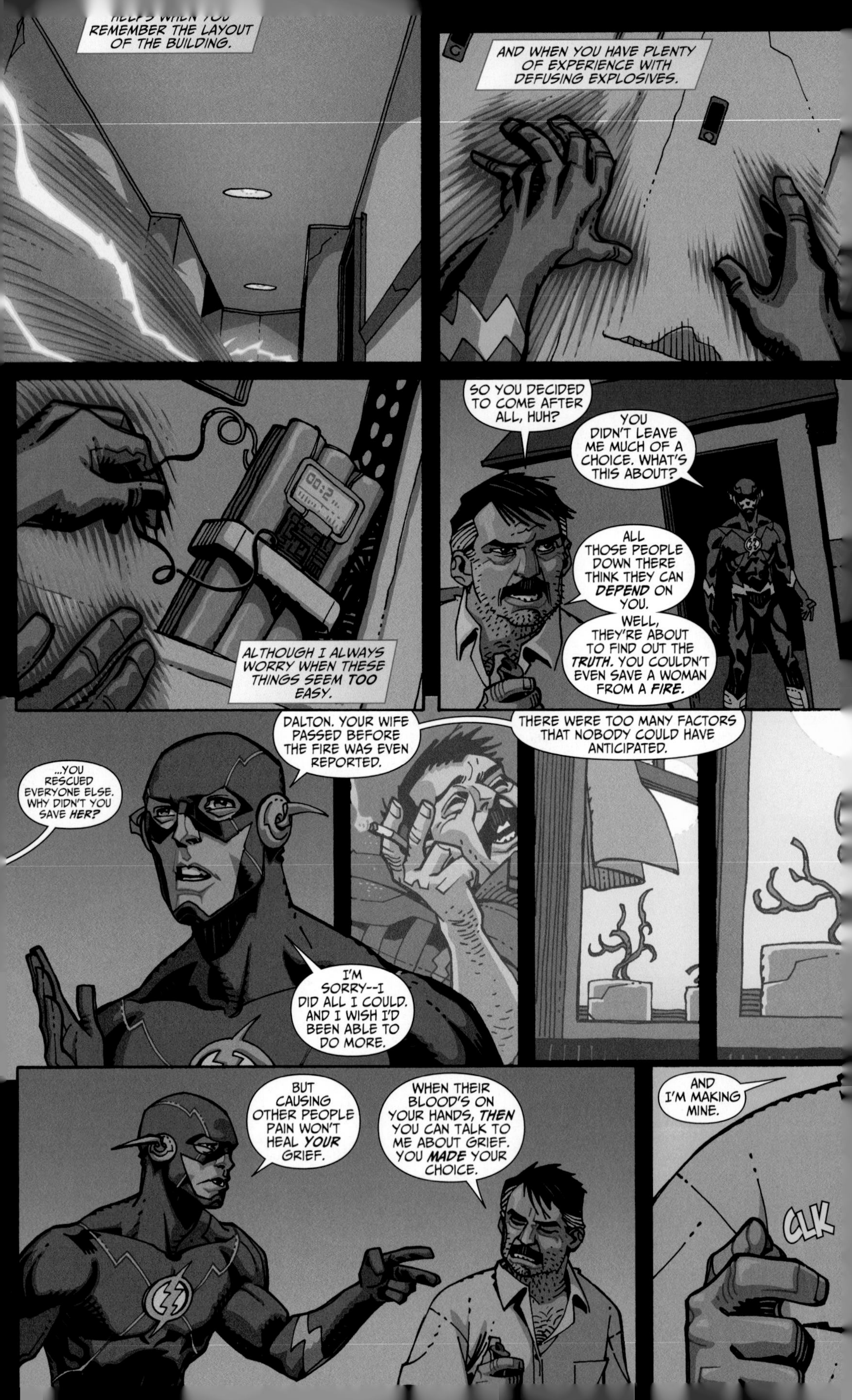
REMEMBER THE LAYOUT OF THE BUILDING.
AND WHEN YOU HAVE PLENTY OF EXPERIENCE WITH DEFUSING EXPLOSIVES.
ALTHOUGH I ALWAYS WORRY WHEN THESE THINGS SEEM TOO EASY.
SO YOU DECIDED TO COME AFTER ALL, HUH?
YOU DIDN'T LEAVE ME MUCH OF A CHOICE. WHAT'S THIS ABOUT?
ALL THOSE PEOPLE DOWN THERE THINK THEY CAN DEPEND ON YOU.
WELL, THEY'RE ABOUT TO FIND OUT THE TRUTH. YOU COULDN'T EVEN SAVE A WOMAN FROM A FIRE.
...YOU RESCUED EVERYONE ELSE. WHY DIDN'T YOU SAVE HER?
DALTON. YOUR WIFE PASSED BEFORE THE FIRE WAS EVEN REPORTED.
THERE WERE TOO MANY FACTORS THAT NOBODY COULD HAVE ANTICIPATED.
I'M SORRY--I DID ALL I COULD. AND I WISH I'D BEEN ABLE TO DO MORE.
BUT CAUSING OTHER PEOPLE PAIN WON'T HEAL YOUR GRIEF.
WHEN THEIR BLOOD'S ON YOUR HANDS, THEN YOU CAN TALK TO ME ABOUT GRIEF. YOU MADE YOUR CHOICE.
AND I'M MAKING MINE.
CLK

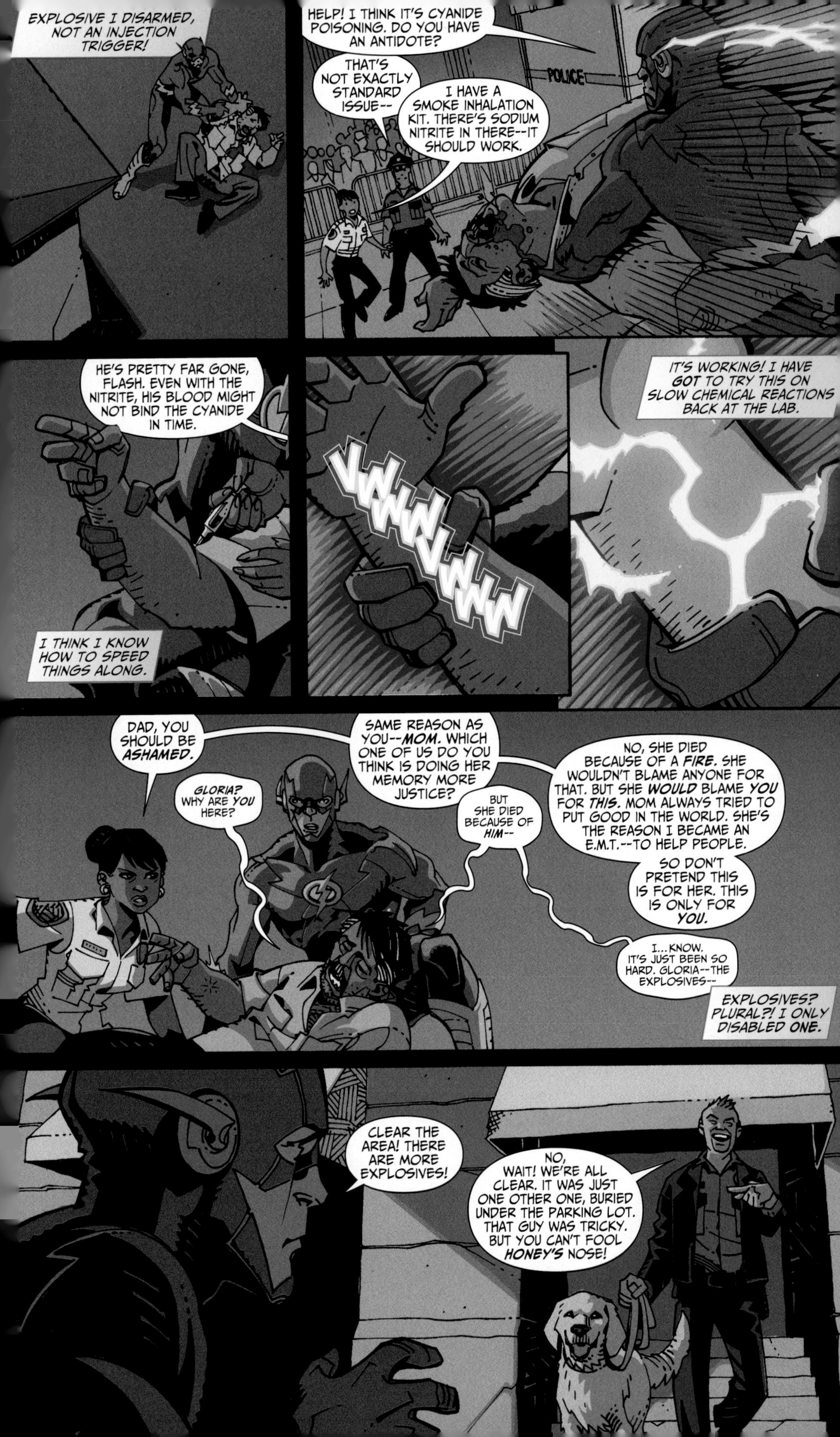
EXPLOSIVE I DISARMED, NOT AN INJECTION TRIGGER!
HELP! I THINK IT'S CYANIDE POISONING. DO YOU HAVE AN ANTIDOTE?
POLICE
THAT'S NOT EXACTLY STANDARD ISSUE--
I HAVE A SMOKE INHALATION KIT. THERE'S SODIUM NITRITE IN THERE--IT SHOULD WORK.
HE'S PRETTY FAR GONE, FLASH. EVEN WITH THE NITRITE, HIS BLOOD MIGHT NOT BIND THE CYANIDE IN TIME.
I THINK I KNOW HOW TO SPEED THINGS ALONG.
VWWWVWWW
IT'S WORKING! I HAVE GOT TO TRY THIS ON SLOW CHEMICAL REACTIONS BACK AT THE LAB.
DAD, YOU SHOULD BE ASHAMED.
GLORIA? WHY ARE YOU HERE?
SAME REASON AS YOU--MOM. WHICH ONE OF US DO YOU THINK IS DOING HER MEMORY MORE JUSTICE?
BUT SHE DIED BECAUSE OF HIM--
NO, SHE DIED BECAUSE OF A FIRE. SHE WOULDN'T BLAME ANYONE FOR THAT. BUT SHE WOULD BLAME YOU FOR THIS. MOM ALWAYS TRIED TO PUT GOOD IN THE WORLD. SHE'S THE REASON I BECAME AN E.M.T.--TO HELP PEOPLE.
SO DON'T PRETEND THIS IS FOR HER. THIS IS ONLY FOR YOU.
I...KNOW. IT'S JUST BEEN SO HARD. GLORIA--THE EXPLOSIVES--
EXPLOSIVES? PLURAL?! I ONLY DISABLED ONE.
CLEAR THE AREA! THERE ARE MORE EXPLOSIVES!
NO, WAIT! WE'RE ALL CLEAR. IT WAS JUST ONE OTHER ONE, BURIED UNDER THE PARKING LOT. THAT GUY WAS TRICKY. BUT YOU CAN'T FOOL HONEY'S NOSE!

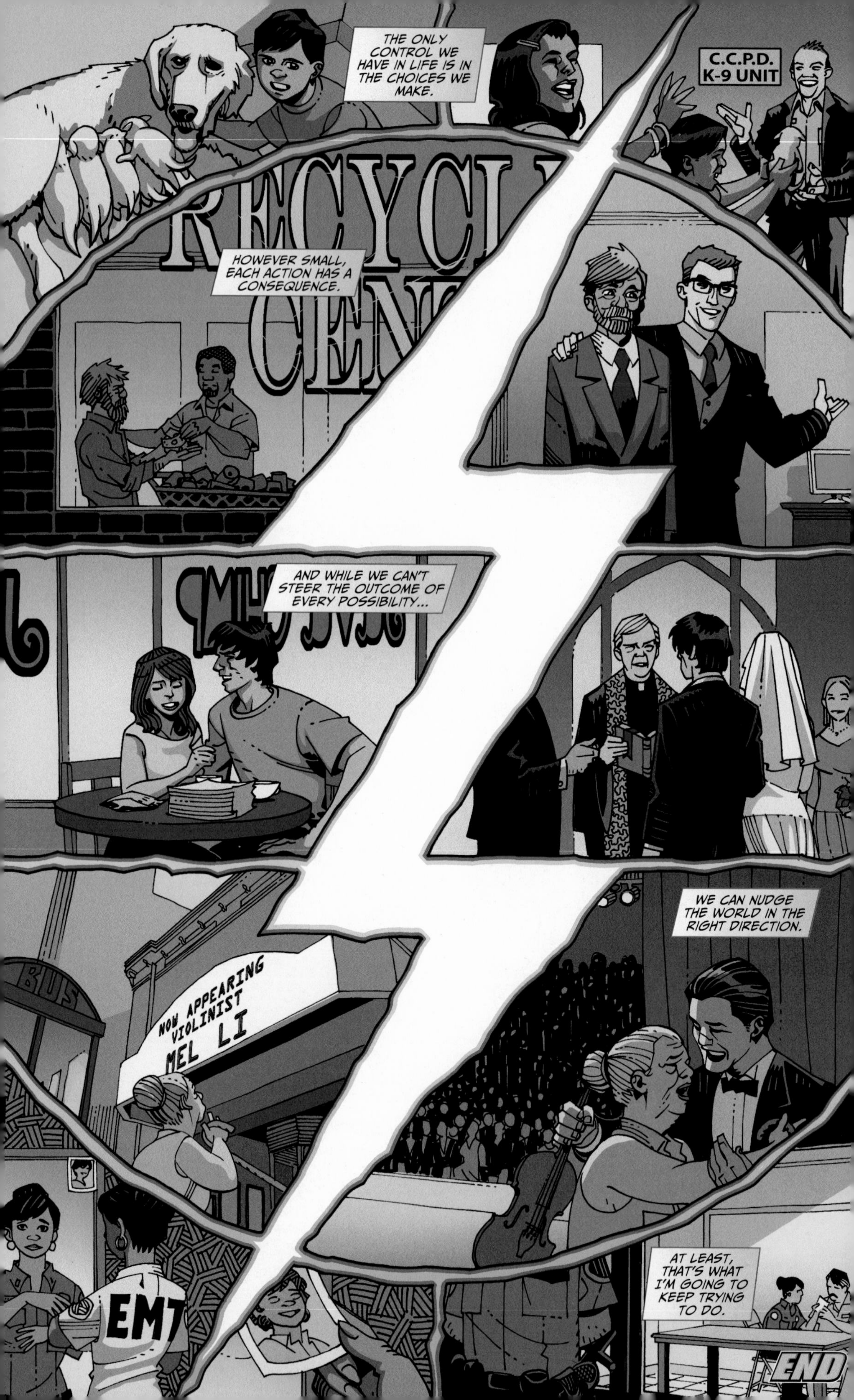
THE ONLY CONTROL WE HAVE IN LIFE IS IN THE CHOICES WE MAKE.
C.C.P.D. K-9 UNIT
RECYCL
CENT
HOWEVER SMALL, EACH ACTION HAS A CONSEQUENCE.
AND WHILE WE CAN'T STEER THE OUTCOME OF EVERY POSSIBILITY...
NOW APPEARING VIOLINIST MEL LI
BUS
WE CAN NUDGE THE WORLD IN THE RIGHT DIRECTION.
EMT
AT LEAST, THAT'S WHAT I'M GOING TO KEEP TRYING TO DO.
END

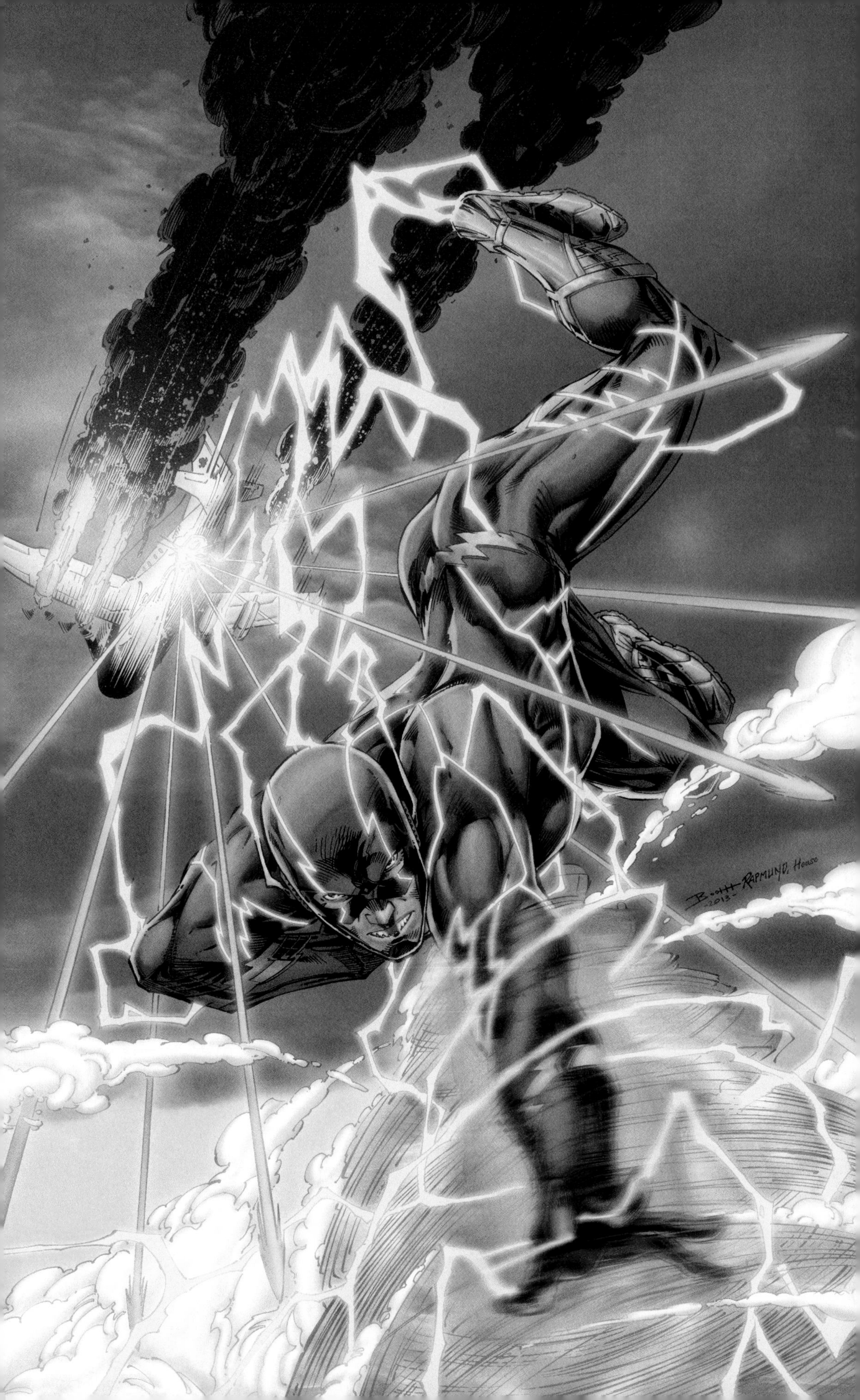
BOOTH RAPMUND, House
-2013-

CHRISTOS N. GAGE writer **NEIL GOOGE** artist cover art by **BRETT BOOTH, NORM RAPMUND & ANDREW DALHOUSE**

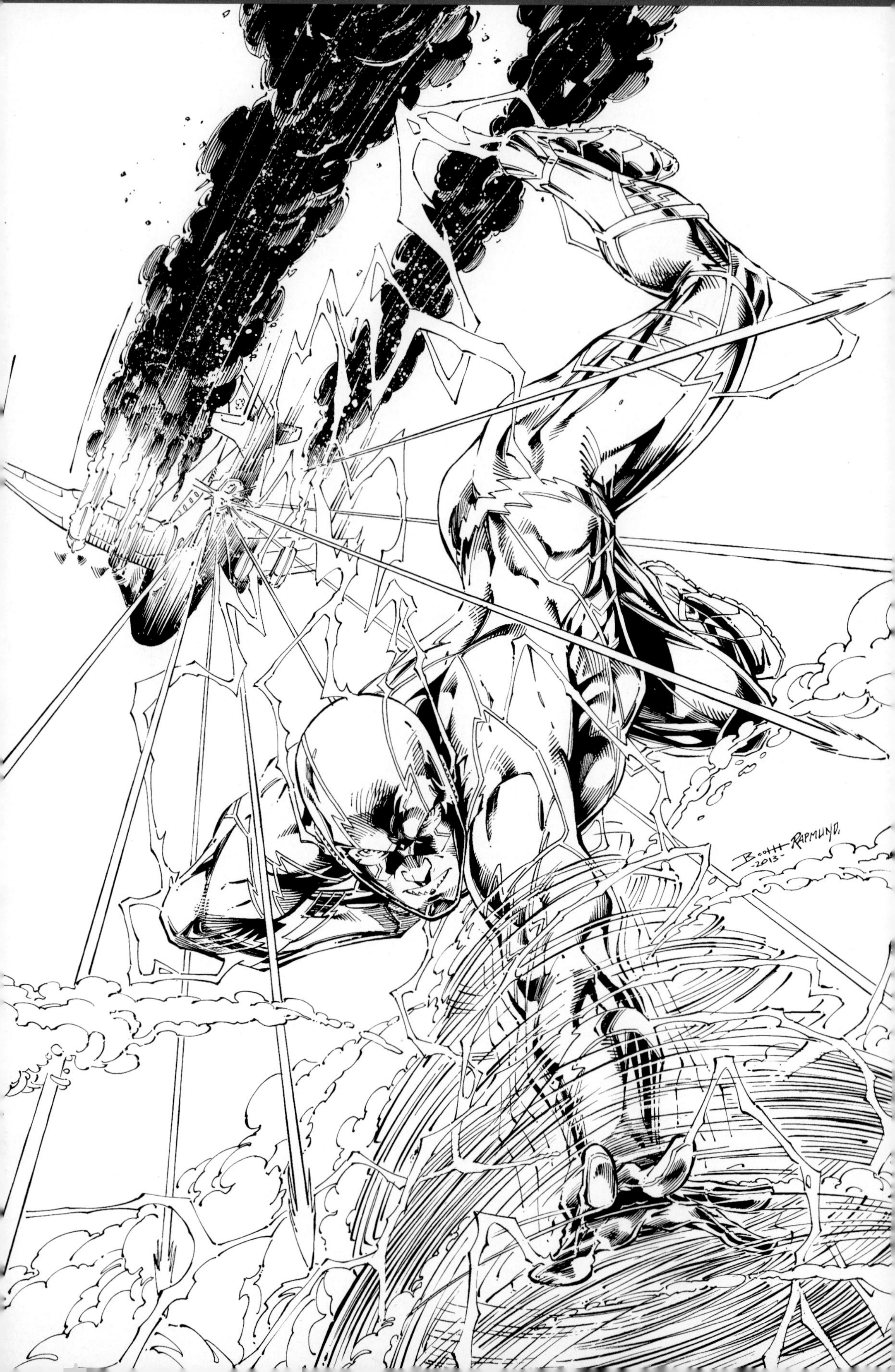

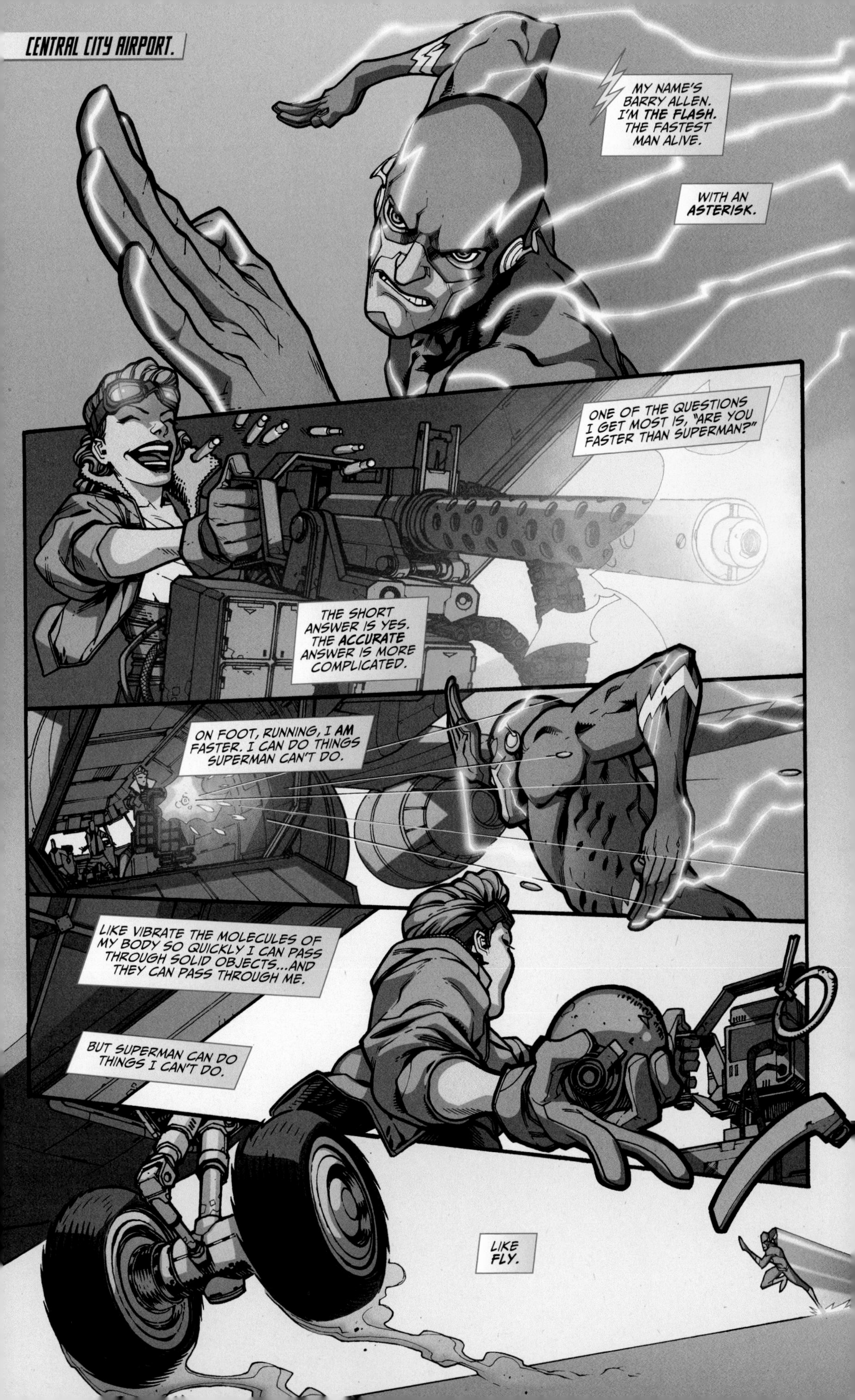
CENTRAL CITY AIRPORT.
MY NAME'S BARRY ALLEN. I'M THE FLASH. THE FASTEST MAN ALIVE.
WITH AN ASTERISK.
ONE OF THE QUESTIONS I GET MOST IS, "ARE YOU FASTER THAN SUPERMAN?"
THE SHORT ANSWER IS YES. THE ACCURATE ANSWER IS MORE COMPLICATED.
ON FOOT, RUNNING, I AM FASTER. I CAN DO THINGS SUPERMAN CAN'T DO.
LIKE VIBRATE THE MOLECULES OF MY BODY SO QUICKLY I CAN PASS THROUGH SOLID OBJECTS...AND THEY CAN PASS THROUGH ME.
BUT SUPERMAN CAN DO THINGS I CAN'T DO.
LIKE FLY.

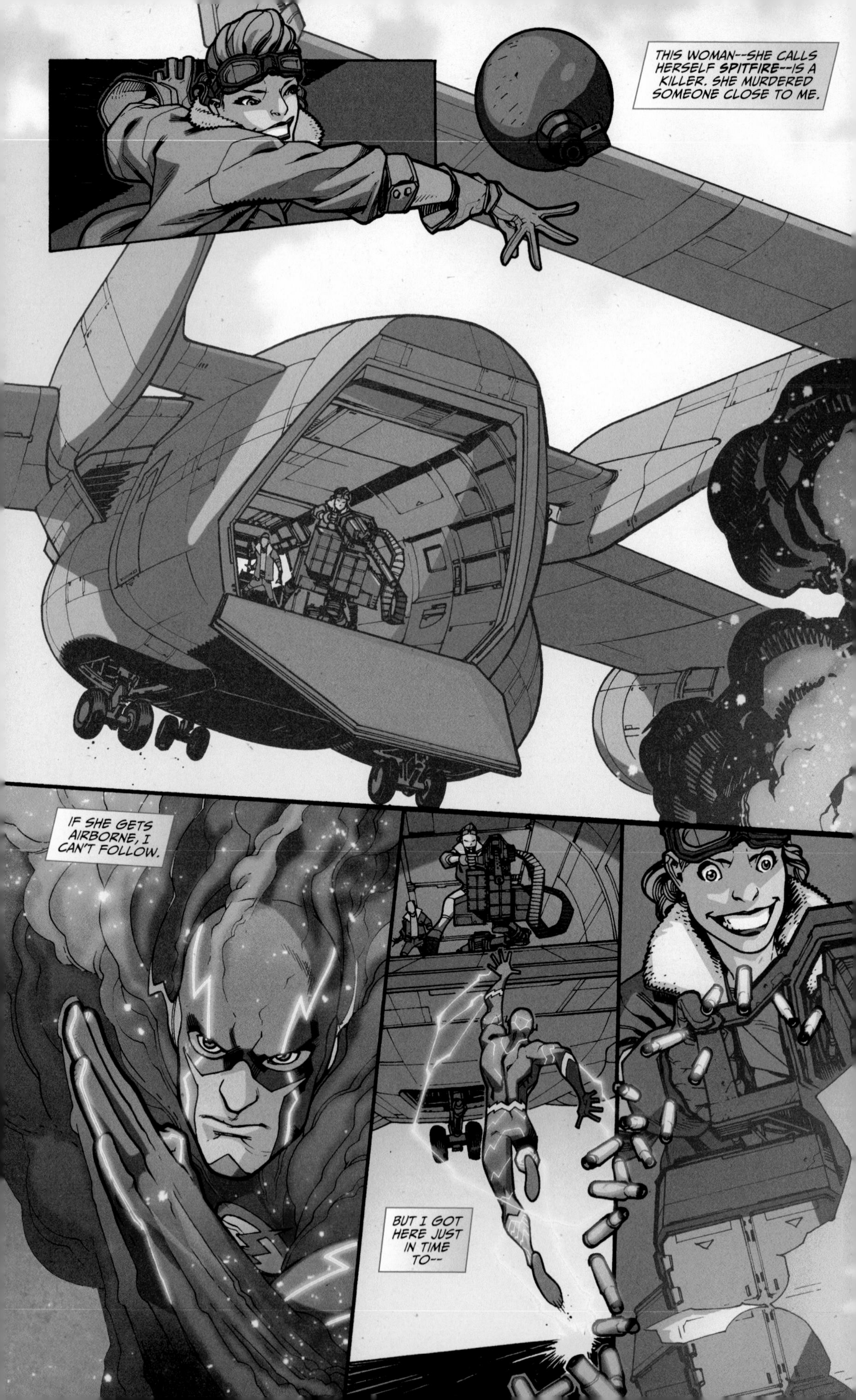
THIS WOMAN--SHE CALLS HERSELF SPITFIRE--IS A KILLER. SHE MURDERED SOMEONE CLOSE TO ME.
IF SHE GETS AIRBORNE, I CAN'T FOLLOW.
BUT I GOT HERE JUST IN TIME TO--

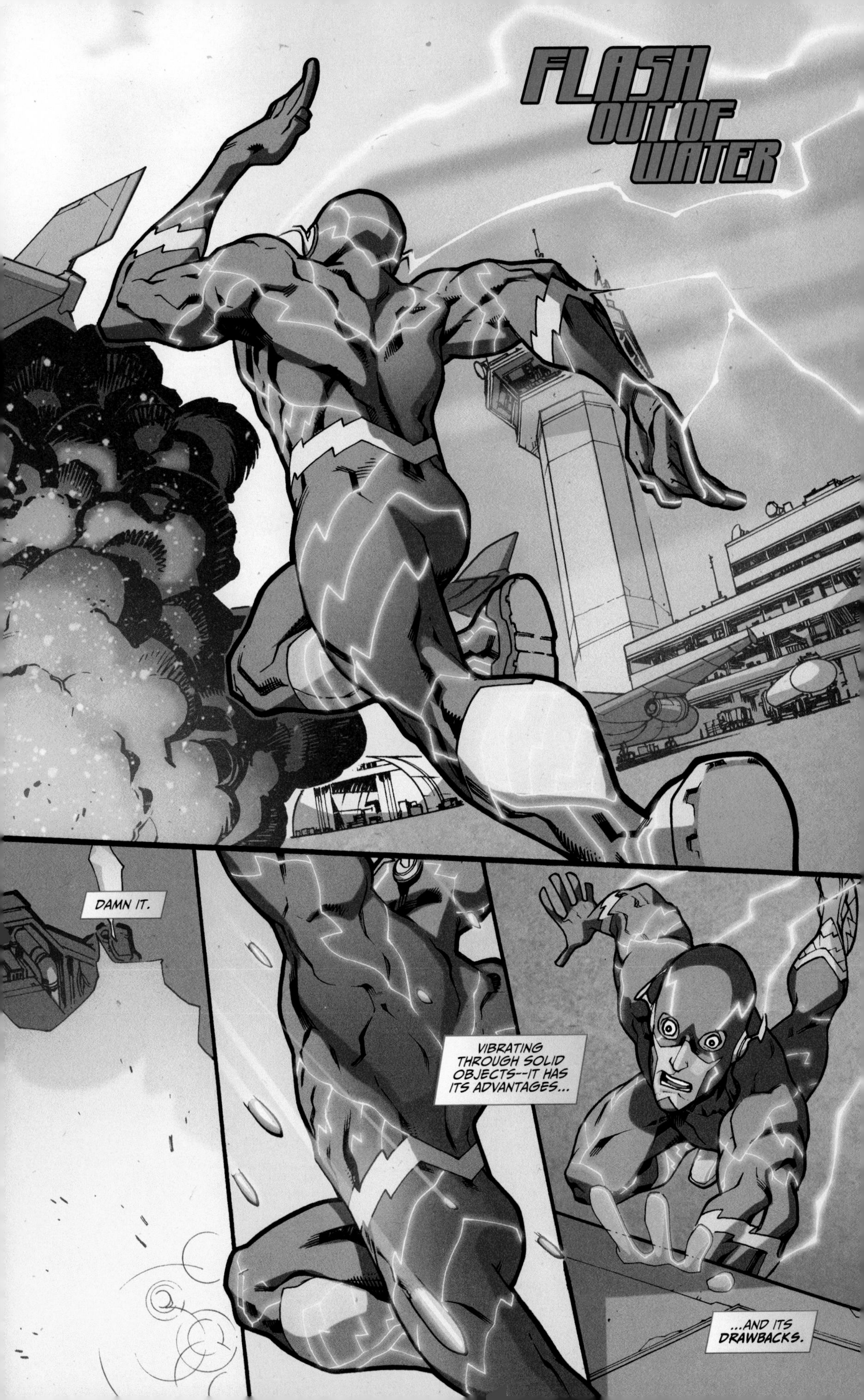
FLASH OUT OF WATER
DAMN IT.
VIBRATING THROUGH SOLID OBJECTS--IT HAS ITS ADVANTAGES...
...AND ITS DRAWBACKS.

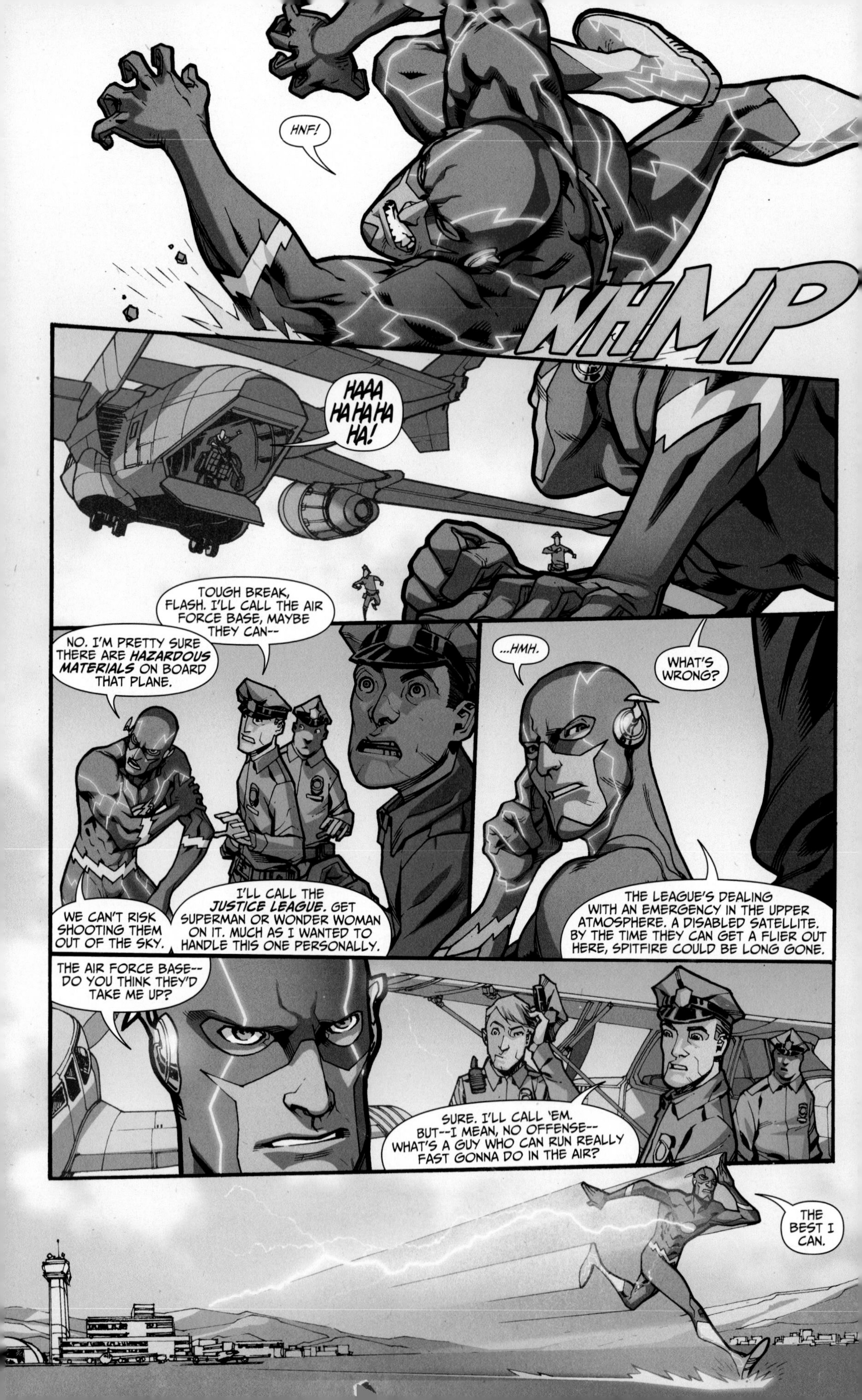
HNF!
WHMP
HAAA HA HA HA HA!
TOUGH BREAK, FLASH. I'LL CALL THE AIR FORCE BASE, MAYBE THEY CAN--
NO. I'M PRETTY SURE THERE ARE HAZARDOUS MATERIALS ON BOARD THAT PLANE.
WE CAN'T RISK SHOOTING THEM OUT OF THE SKY.
I'LL CALL THE JUSTICE LEAGUE. GET SUPERMAN OR WONDER WOMAN ON IT. MUCH AS I WANTED TO HANDLE THIS ONE PERSONALLY.
...HMH.
WHAT'S WRONG?
THE LEAGUE'S DEALING WITH AN EMERGENCY IN THE UPPER ATMOSPHERE. A DISABLED SATELLITE. BY THE TIME THEY CAN GET A FLIER OUT HERE, SPITFIRE COULD BE LONG GONE.
THE AIR FORCE BASE-- DO YOU THINK THEY'D TAKE ME UP?
SURE. I'LL CALL 'EM. BUT--I MEAN, NO OFFENSE-- WHAT'S A GUY WHO CAN RUN REALLY FAST GONNA DO IN THE AIR?
THE BEST I CAN.

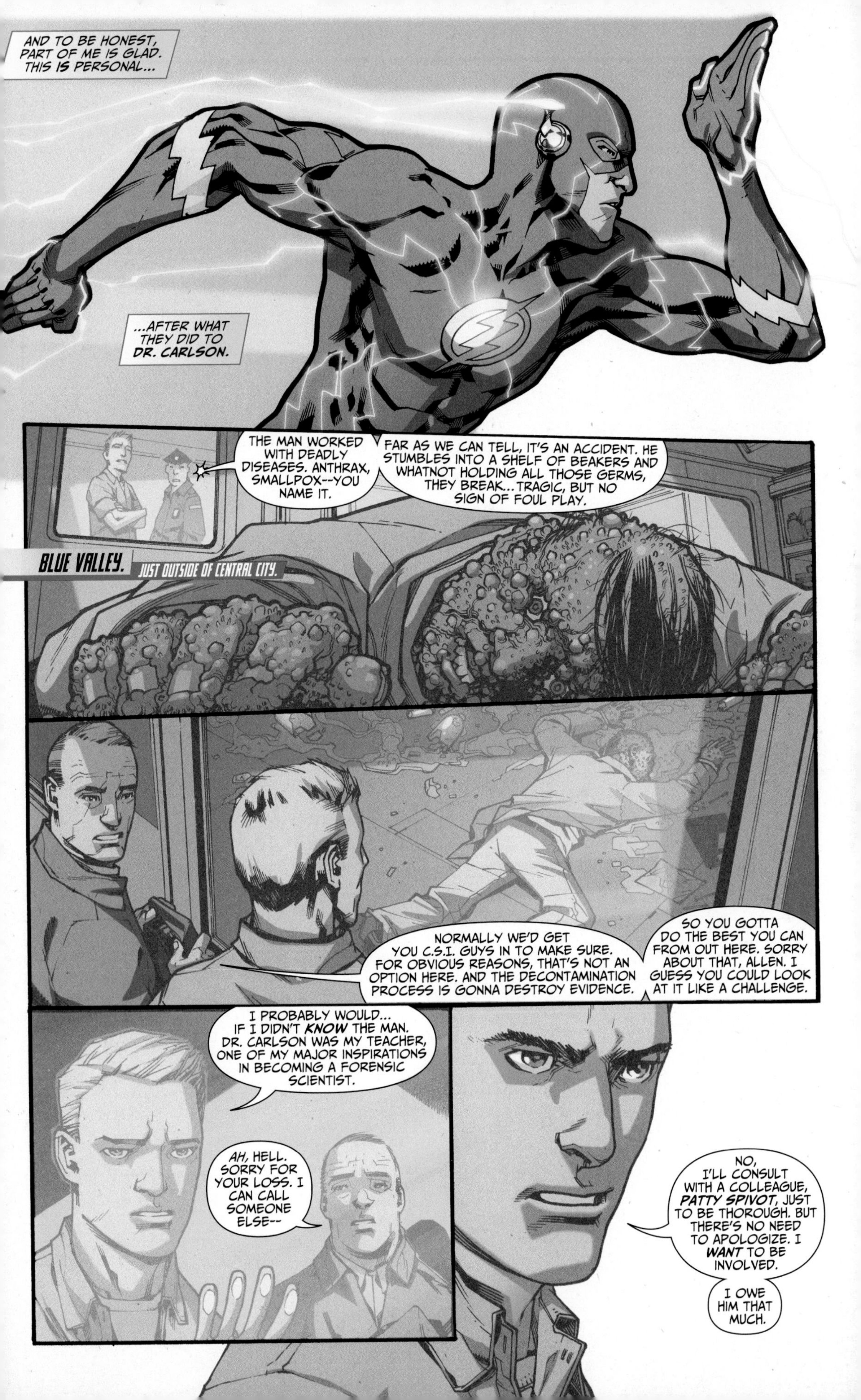
AND TO BE HONEST, PART OF ME IS GLAD. THIS IS PERSONAL...
...AFTER WHAT THEY DID TO DR. CARLSON.
THE MAN WORKED WITH DEADLY DISEASES. ANTHRAX, SMALLPOX--YOU NAME IT.
FAR AS WE CAN TELL, IT'S AN ACCIDENT. HE STUMBLES INTO A SHELF OF BEAKERS AND WHATNOT HOLDING ALL THOSE GERMS, THEY BREAK...TRAGIC, BUT NO SIGN OF FOUL PLAY.
BLUE VALLEY.
JUST OUTSIDE OF CENTRAL CITY.
NORMALLY WE'D GET YOU C.S.I. GUYS IN TO MAKE SURE. FOR OBVIOUS REASONS, THAT'S NOT AN OPTION HERE. AND THE DECONTAMINATION PROCESS IS GONNA DESTROY EVIDENCE.
SO YOU GOTTA DO THE BEST YOU CAN FROM OUT HERE. SORRY ABOUT THAT, ALLEN. I GUESS YOU COULD LOOK AT IT LIKE A CHALLENGE.
I PROBABLY WOULD... IF I DIDN'T KNOW THE MAN. DR. CARLSON WAS MY TEACHER, ONE OF MY MAJOR INSPIRATIONS IN BECOMING A FORENSIC SCIENTIST.
AH, HELL. SORRY FOR YOUR LOSS. I CAN CALL SOMEONE ELSE--
NO, I'LL CONSULT WITH A COLLEAGUE, PATTY SPIVOT, JUST TO BE THOROUGH. BUT THERE'S NO NEED TO APOLOGIZE. I WANT TO BE INVOLVED.
I OWE HIM THAT MUCH.

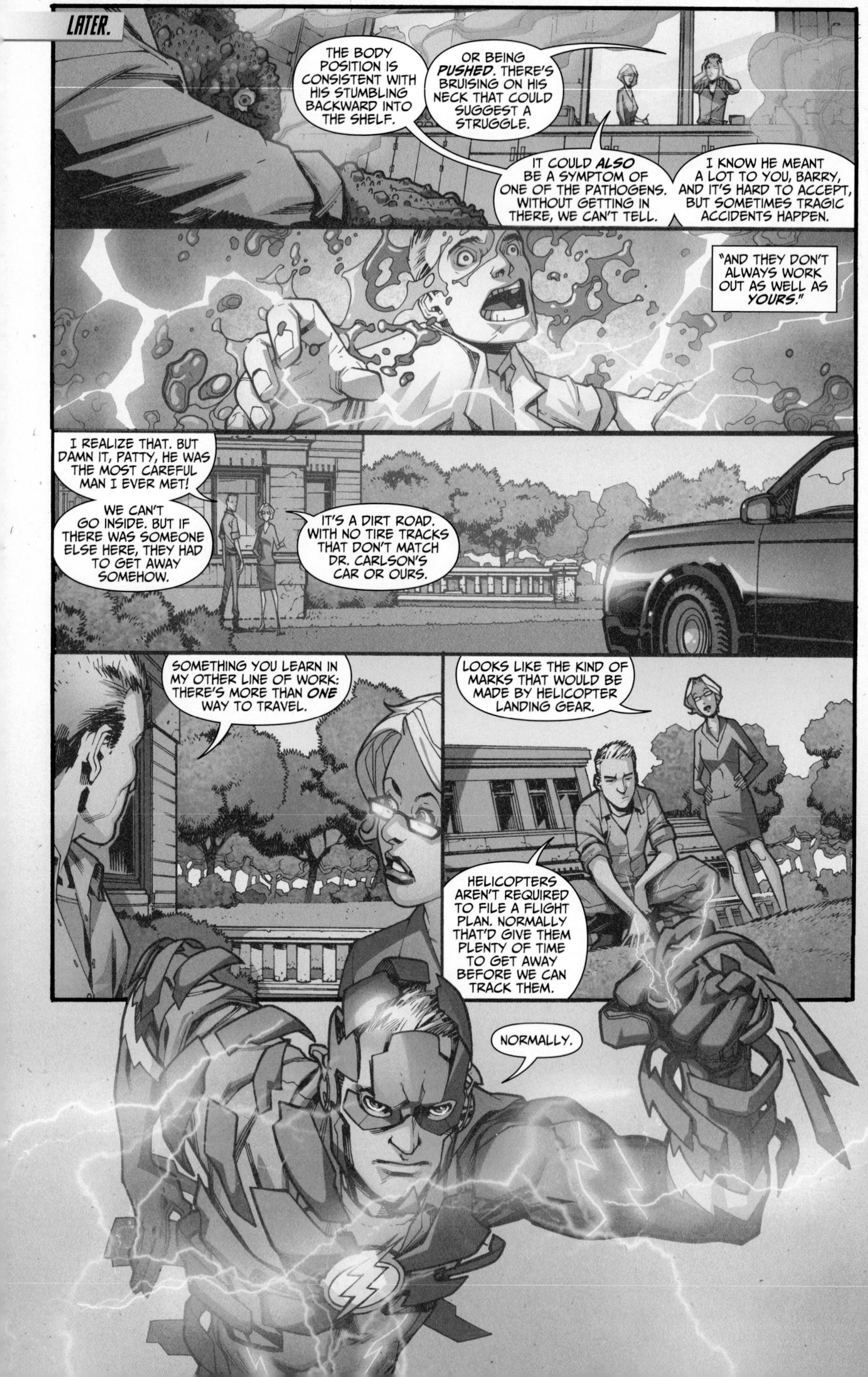
LATER.
THE BODY POSITION IS CONSISTENT WITH HIS STUMBLING BACKWARD INTO THE SHELF.
OR BEING PUSHED. THERE'S BRUISING ON HIS NECK THAT COULD SUGGEST A STRUGGLE.
IT COULD ALSO BE A SYMPTOM OF ONE OF THE PATHOGENS. WITHOUT GETTING IN THERE, WE CAN'T TELL.
I KNOW HE MEANT A LOT TO YOU, BARRY, AND IT'S HARD TO ACCEPT, BUT SOMETIMES TRAGIC ACCIDENTS HAPPEN.
"AND THEY DON'T ALWAYS WORK OUT AS WELL AS YOURS."
I REALIZE THAT. BUT DAMN IT, PATTY, HE WAS THE MOST CAREFUL MAN I EVER MET!
WE CAN'T GO INSIDE. BUT IF THERE WAS SOMEONE ELSE HERE, THEY HAD TO GET AWAY SOMEHOW.
IT'S A DIRT ROAD. WITH NO TIRE TRACKS THAT DON'T MATCH DR. CARLSON'S CAR OR OURS.
SOMETHING YOU LEARN IN MY OTHER LINE OF WORK: THERE'S MORE THAN ONE WAY TO TRAVEL.
LOOKS LIKE THE KIND OF MARKS THAT WOULD BE MADE BY HELICOPTER LANDING GEAR.
HELICOPTERS AREN'T REQUIRED TO FILE A FLIGHT PLAN. NORMALLY THAT'D GIVE THEM PLENTY OF TIME TO GET AWAY BEFORE WE CAN TRACK THEM.
NORMALLY.

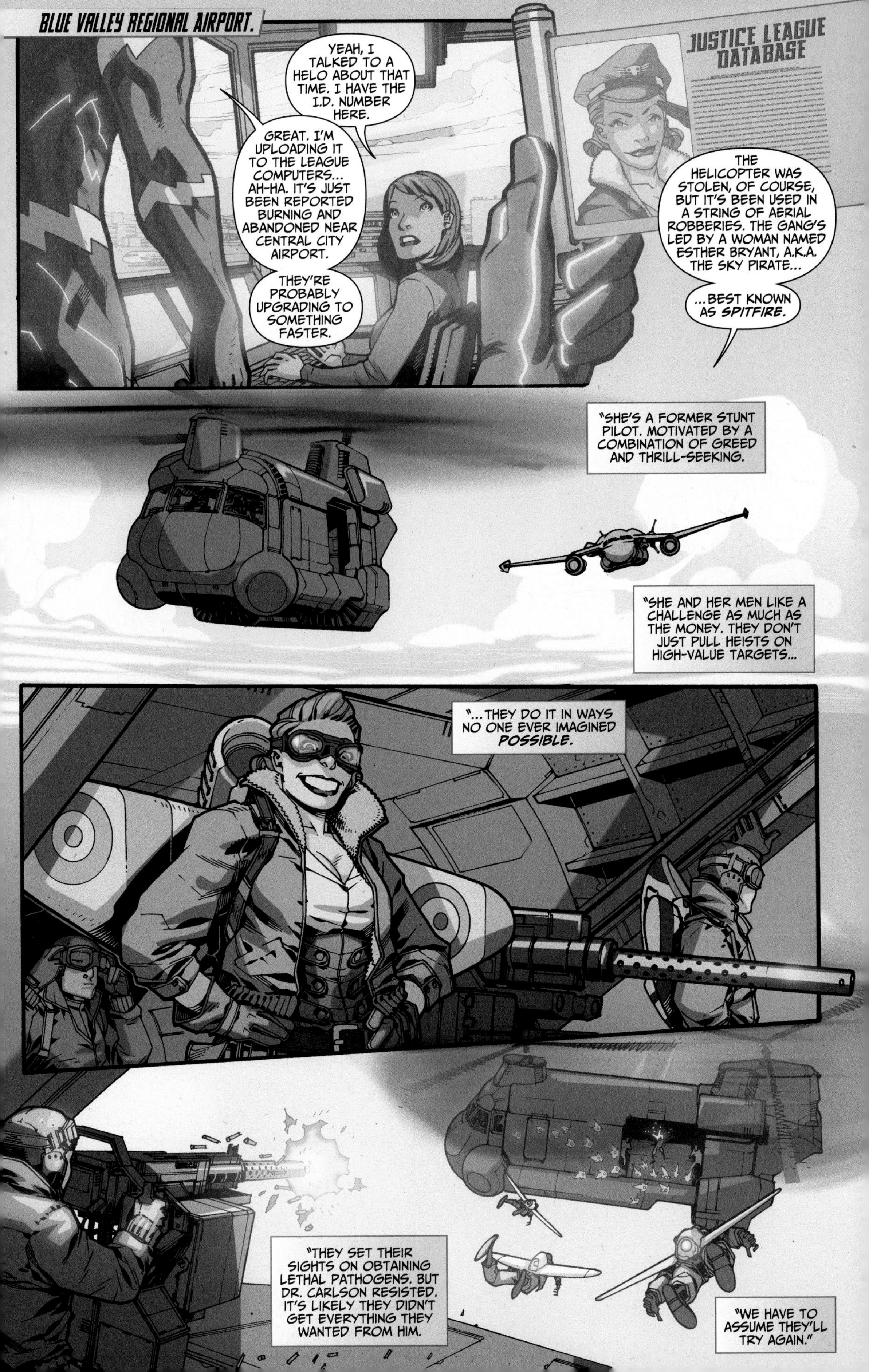
BLUE VALLEY REGIONAL AIRPORT.
JUSTICE LEAGUE DATABASE
YEAH, I TALKED TO A HELO ABOUT THAT TIME. I HAVE THE I.D. NUMBER HERE.
GREAT. I'M UPLOADING IT TO THE LEAGUE COMPUTERS... AH-HA. IT'S JUST BEEN REPORTED BURNING AND ABANDONED NEAR CENTRAL CITY AIRPORT.
THEY'RE PROBABLY UPGRADING TO SOMETHING FASTER.
THE HELICOPTER WAS STOLEN, OF COURSE, BUT IT'S BEEN USED IN A STRING OF AERIAL ROBBERIES. THE GANG'S LED BY A WOMAN NAMED ESTHER BRYANT, A.K.A. THE SKY PIRATE...
...BEST KNOWN AS *SPITFIRE.*
"SHE'S A FORMER STUNT PILOT. MOTIVATED BY A COMBINATION OF GREED AND THRILL-SEEKING.
"SHE AND HER MEN LIKE A CHALLENGE AS MUCH AS THE MONEY. THEY DON'T JUST PULL HEISTS ON HIGH-VALUE TARGETS...
"...THEY DO IT IN WAYS NO ONE EVER IMAGINED *POSSIBLE.*
"THEY SET THEIR SIGHTS ON OBTAINING LETHAL PATHOGENS. BUT DR. CARLSON RESISTED. IT'S LIKELY THEY DIDN'T GET EVERYTHING THEY WANTED FROM HIM.
"WE HAVE TO ASSUME THEY'LL TRY AGAIN."

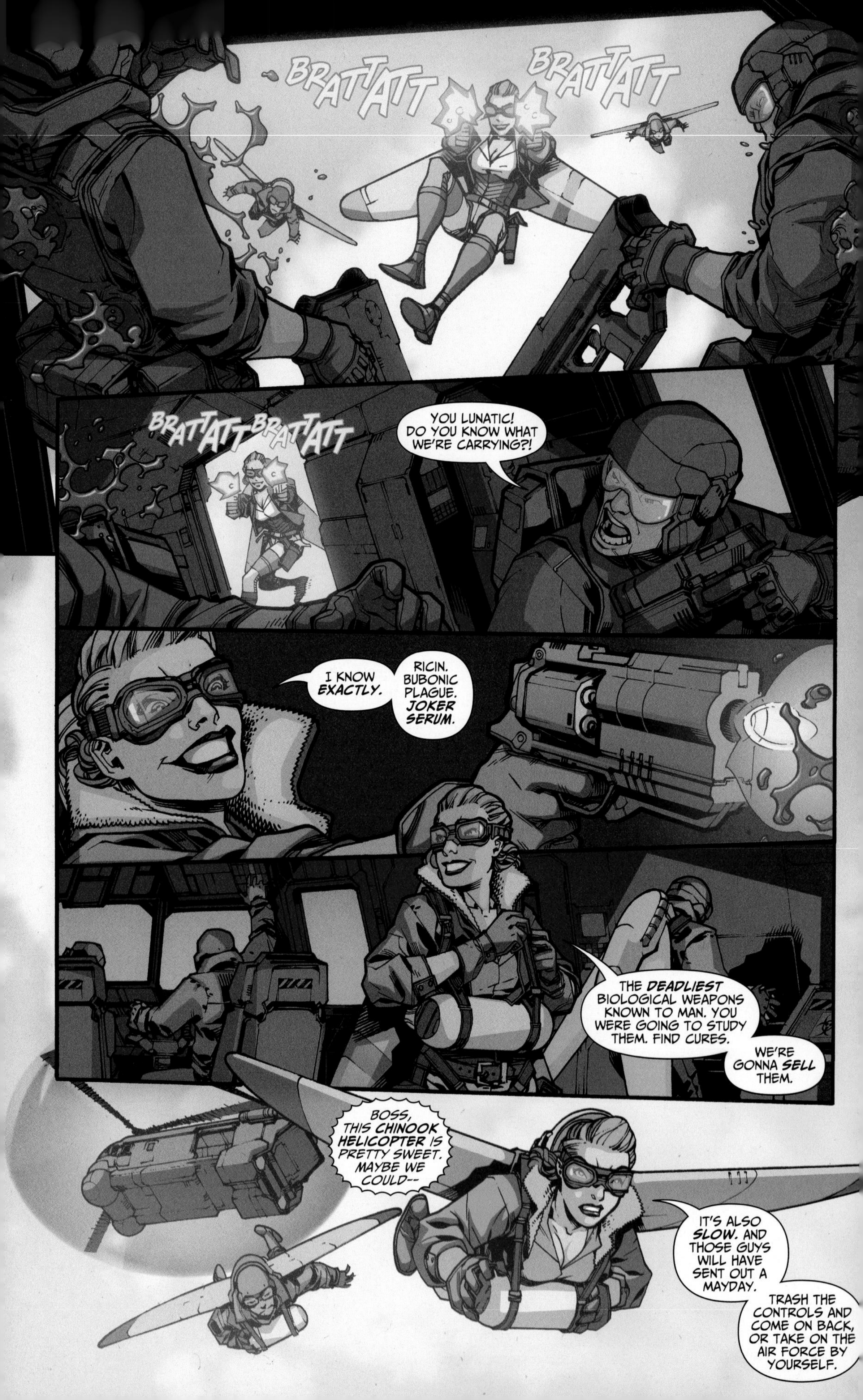
BRATTATT
BRATTATT
BRATTATT BRATTATT
YOU LUNATIC! DO YOU KNOW WHAT WE'RE CARRYING?!
I KNOW EXACTLY.
RICIN. BUBONIC PLAGUE. JOKER SERUM.
THE DEADLIEST BIOLOGICAL WEAPONS KNOWN TO MAN. YOU WERE GOING TO STUDY THEM. FIND CURES.
WE'RE GONNA SELL THEM.
BOSS, THIS CHINOOK HELICOPTER IS PRETTY SWEET. MAYBE WE COULD--
IT'S ALSO SLOW. AND THOSE GUYS WILL HAVE SENT OUT A MAYDAY.
TRASH THE CONTROLS AND COME ON BACK, OR TAKE ON THE AIR FORCE BY YOURSELF.

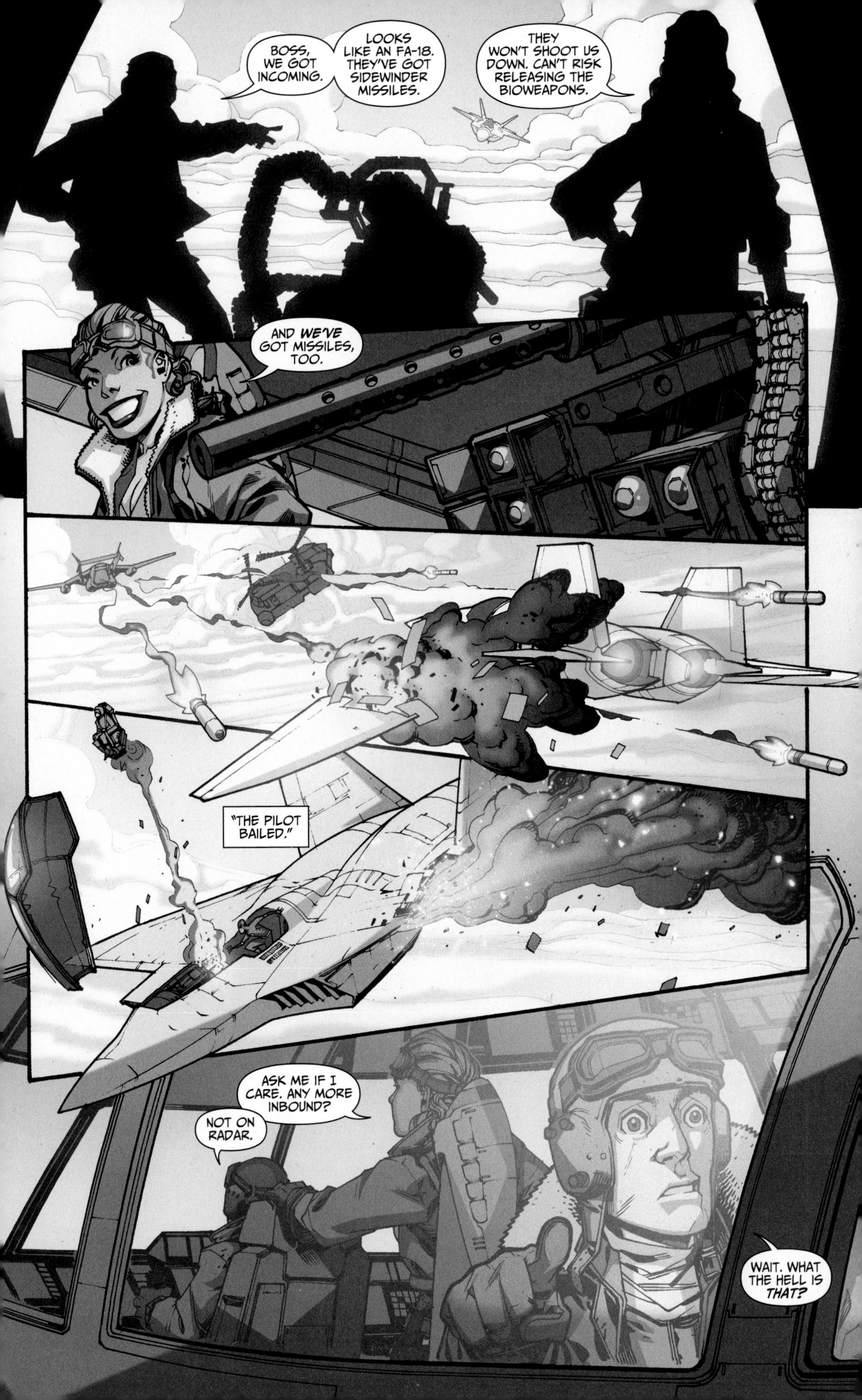
BOSS, WE GOT INCOMING.
LOOKS LIKE AN FA-18. THEY'VE GOT SIDEWINDER MISSILES.
THEY WON'T SHOOT US DOWN. CAN'T RISK RELEASING THE BIOWEAPONS.
AND *WE'VE* GOT MISSILES, TOO.
"THE PILOT BAILED."
ASK ME IF I CARE. ANY MORE INBOUND?
NOT ON RADAR.
WAIT. WHAT THE HELL IS *THAT?*

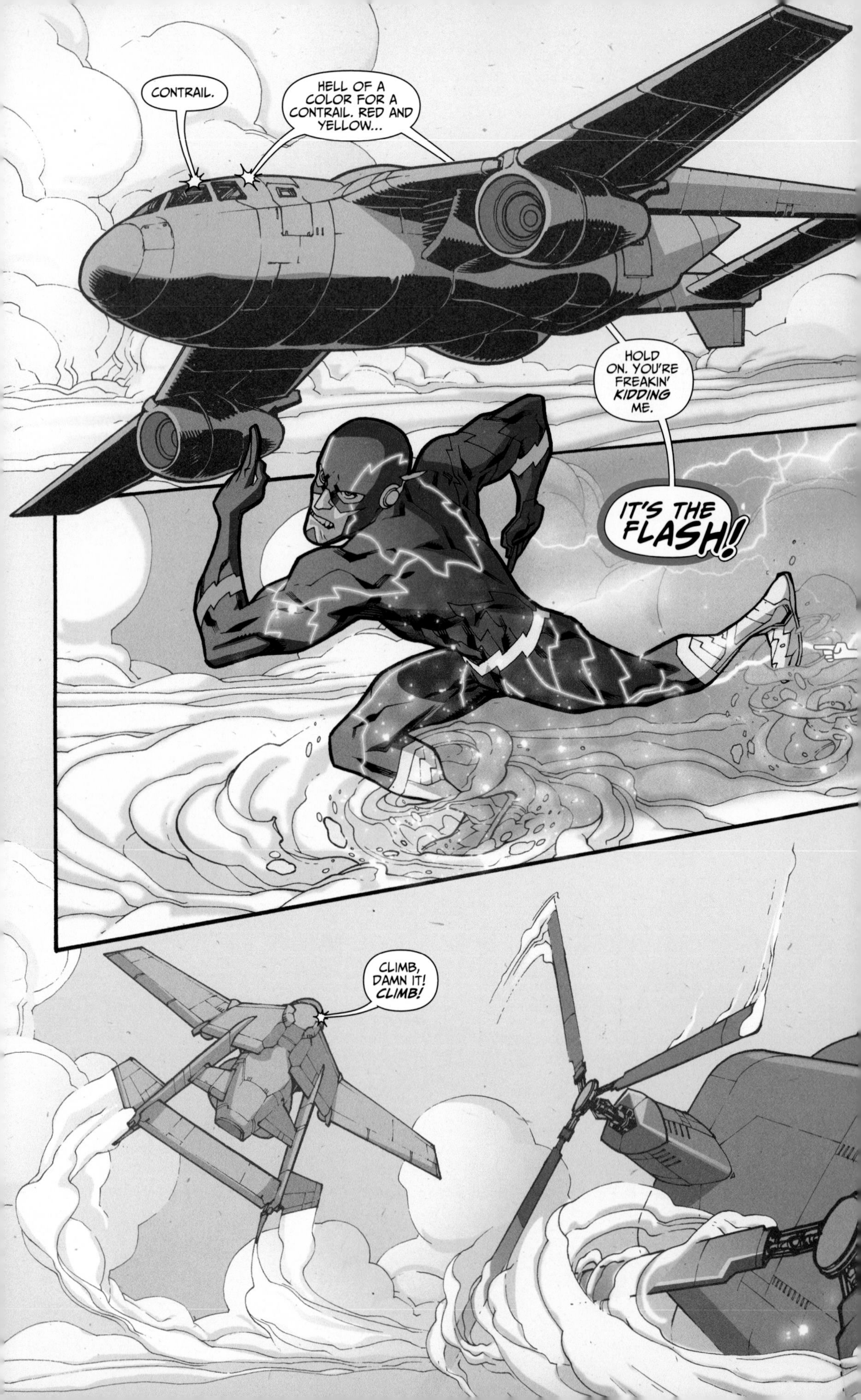
CONTRAIL.
HELL OF A COLOR FOR A CONTRAIL. RED AND YELLOW...
HOLD ON. YOU'RE FREAKIN' *KIDDING* ME.
IT'S THE FLASH!
CLIMB, DAMN IT! *CLIMB!*

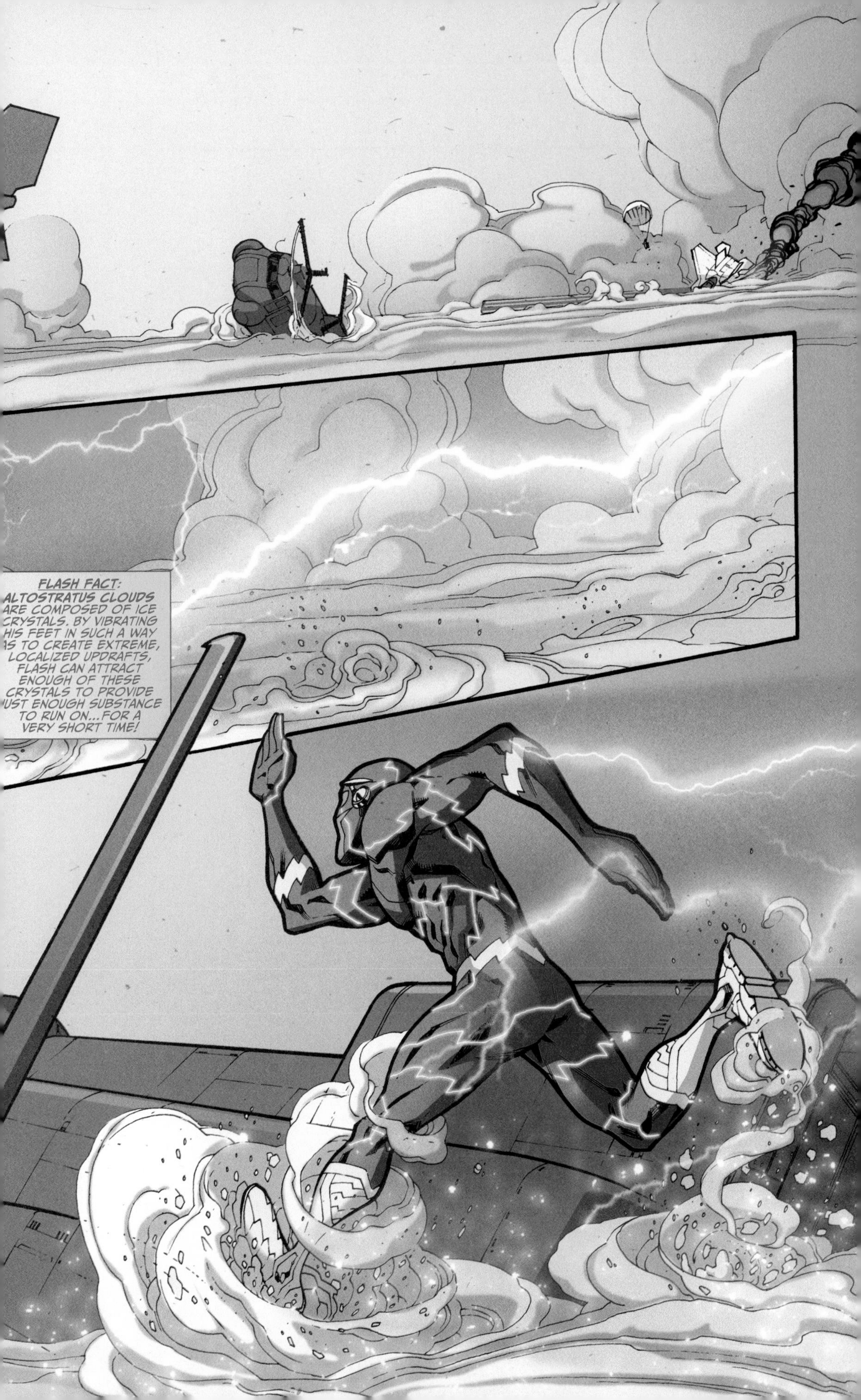
FLASH FACT:
ALTOSTRATUS CLOUDS ARE COMPOSED OF ICE CRYSTALS. BY VIBRATING HIS FEET IN SUCH A WAY AS TO CREATE EXTREME, LOCALIZED UPDRAFTS, FLASH CAN ATTRACT ENOUGH OF THESE CRYSTALS TO PROVIDE JUST ENOUGH SUBSTANCE TO RUN ON...FOR A VERY SHORT TIME!

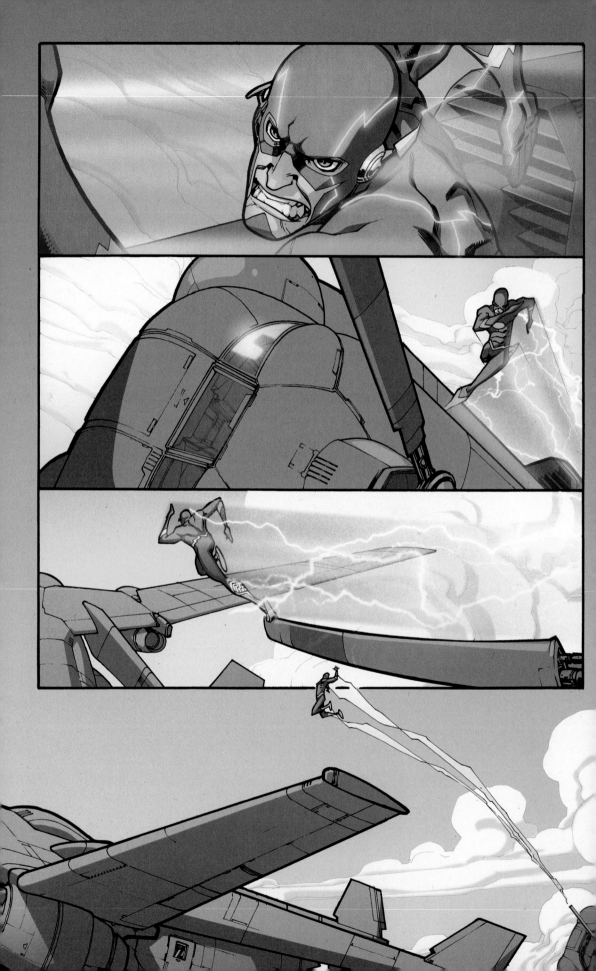

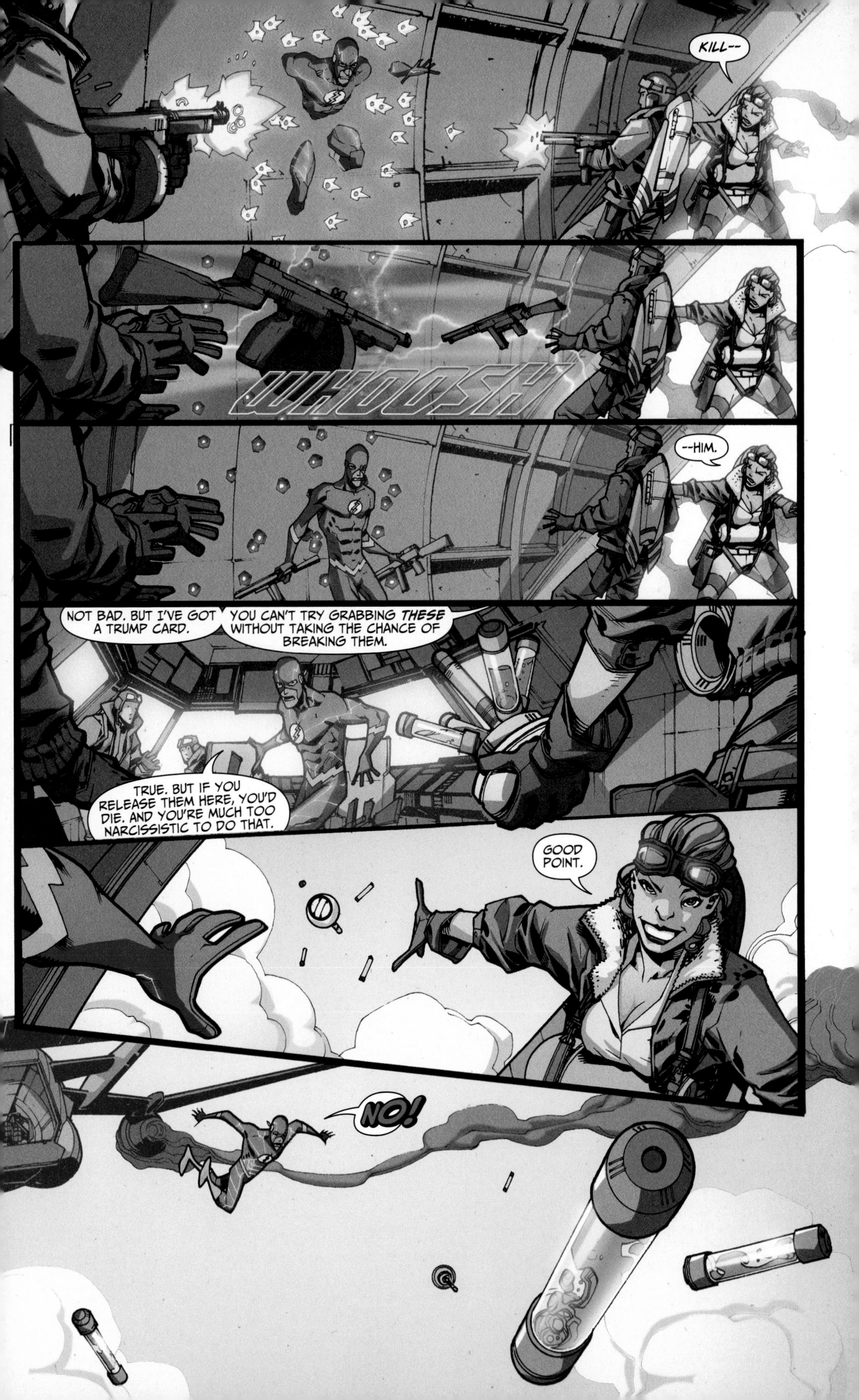
KILL--
WHOOSH
--HIM.
NOT BAD. BUT I'VE GOT A TRUMP CARD.
YOU CAN'T TRY GRABBING *THESE* WITHOUT TAKING THE CHANCE OF BREAKING THEM.
TRUE. BUT IF YOU RELEASE THEM HERE, YOU'D DIE. AND YOU'RE MUCH TOO NARCISSISTIC TO DO THAT.
GOOD POINT.
NO!

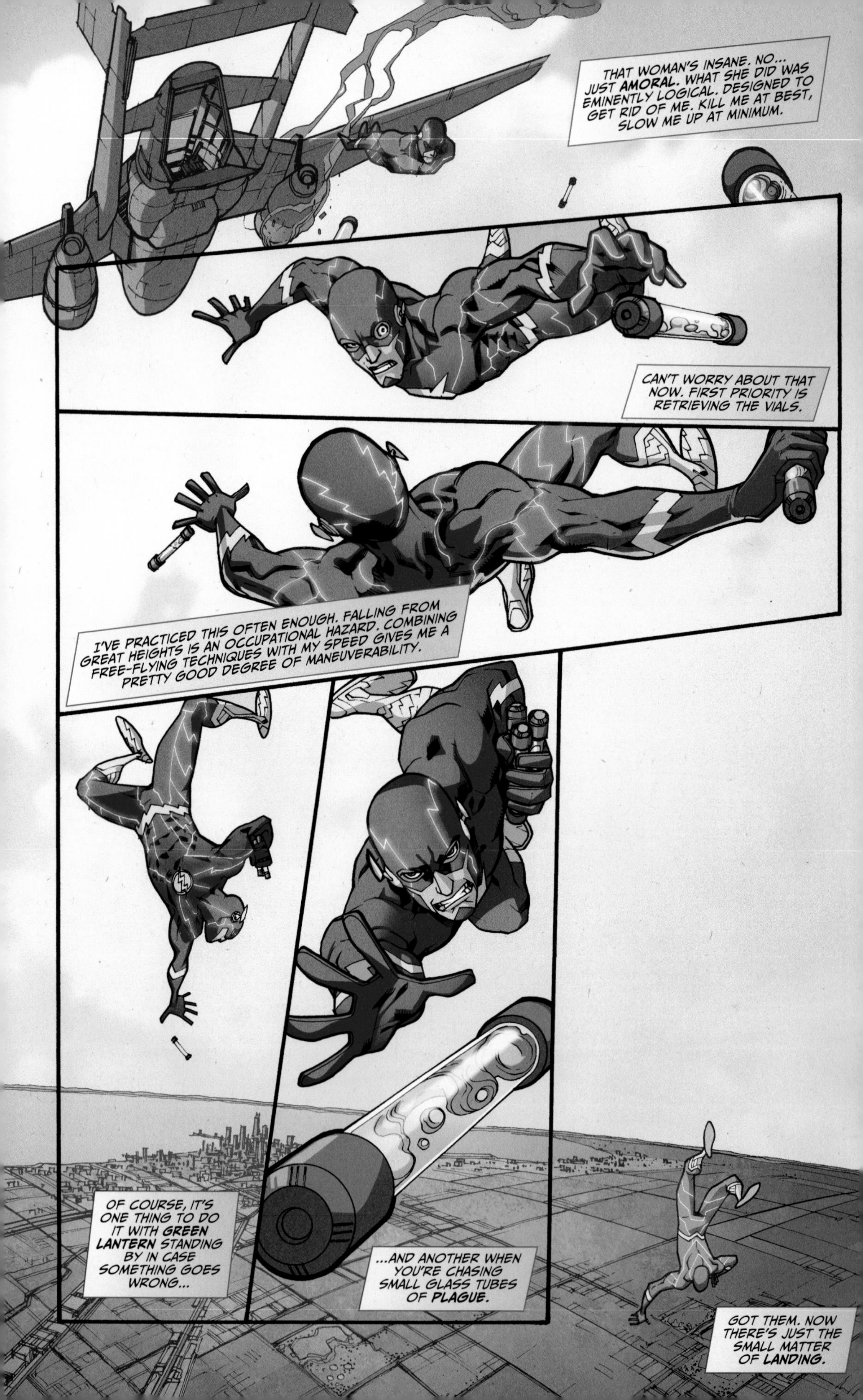
THAT WOMAN'S INSANE. NO... JUST AMORAL. WHAT SHE DID WAS EMINENTLY LOGICAL. DESIGNED TO GET RID OF ME. KILL ME AT BEST, SLOW ME UP AT MINIMUM.
CAN'T WORRY ABOUT THAT NOW. FIRST PRIORITY IS RETRIEVING THE VIALS.
I'VE PRACTICED THIS OFTEN ENOUGH. FALLING FROM GREAT HEIGHTS IS AN OCCUPATIONAL HAZARD. COMBINING FREE-FLYING TECHNIQUES WITH MY SPEED GIVES ME A PRETTY GOOD DEGREE OF MANEUVERABILITY.
OF COURSE, IT'S ONE THING TO DO IT WITH GREEN LANTERN STANDING BY IN CASE SOMETHING GOES WRONG...
...AND ANOTHER WHEN YOU'RE CHASING SMALL GLASS TUBES OF PLAGUE.
GOT THEM. NOW THERE'S JUST THE SMALL MATTER OF LANDING.

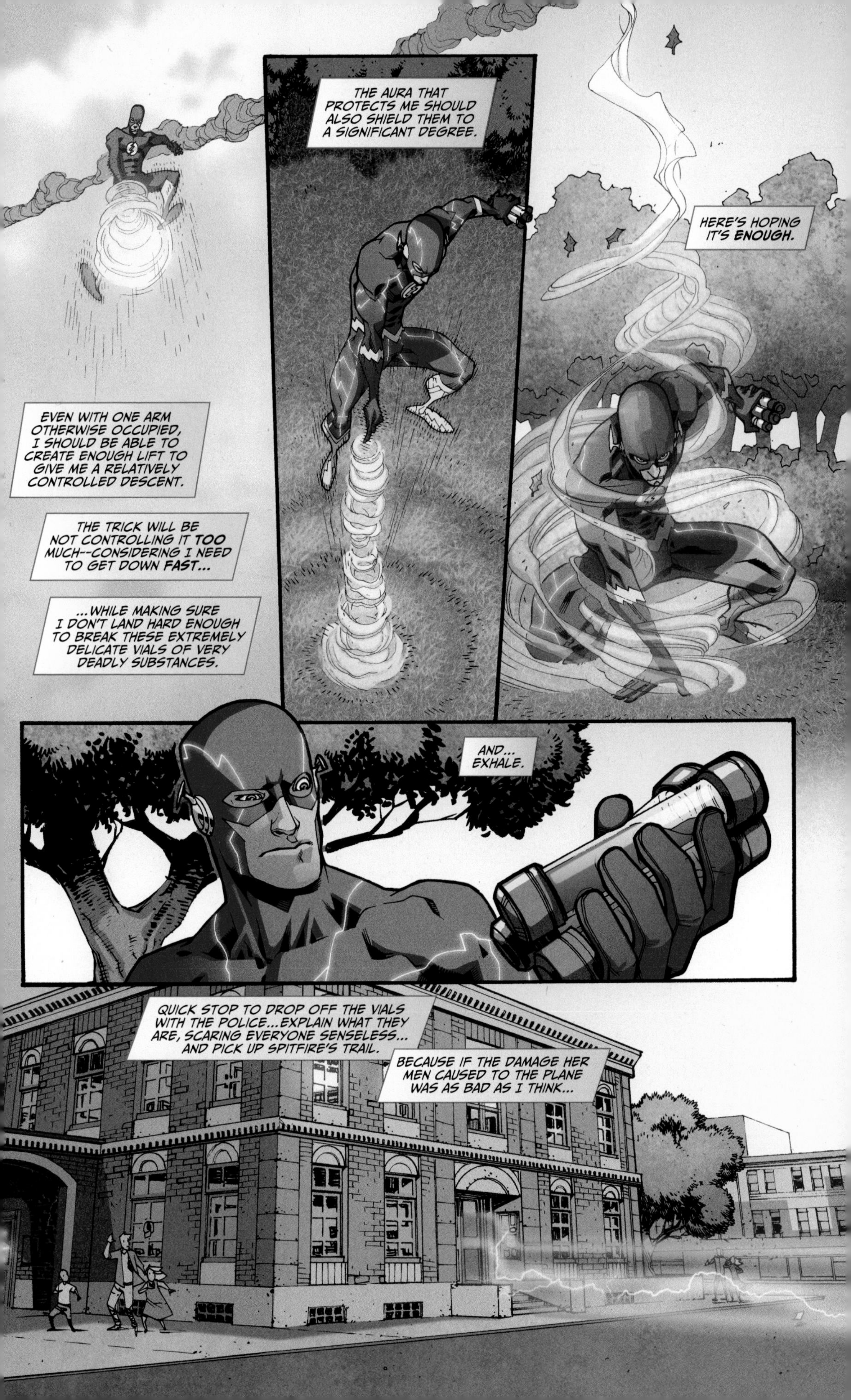
THE AURA THAT PROTECTS ME SHOULD ALSO SHIELD THEM TO A SIGNIFICANT DEGREE.
HERE'S HOPING IT'S ENOUGH.
EVEN WITH ONE ARM OTHERWISE OCCUPIED, I SHOULD BE ABLE TO CREATE ENOUGH LIFT TO GIVE ME A RELATIVELY CONTROLLED DESCENT.
THE TRICK WILL BE NOT CONTROLLING IT TOO MUCH--CONSIDERING I NEED TO GET DOWN FAST...
...WHILE MAKING SURE I DON'T LAND HARD ENOUGH TO BREAK THESE EXTREMELY DELICATE VIALS OF VERY DEADLY SUBSTANCES.
AND... EXHALE.
QUICK STOP TO DROP OFF THE VIALS WITH THE POLICE...EXPLAIN WHAT THEY ARE, SCARING EVERYONE SENSELESS... AND PICK UP SPITFIRE'S TRAIL.
BECAUSE IF THE DAMAGE HER MEN CAUSED TO THE PLANE WAS AS BAD AS I THINK...

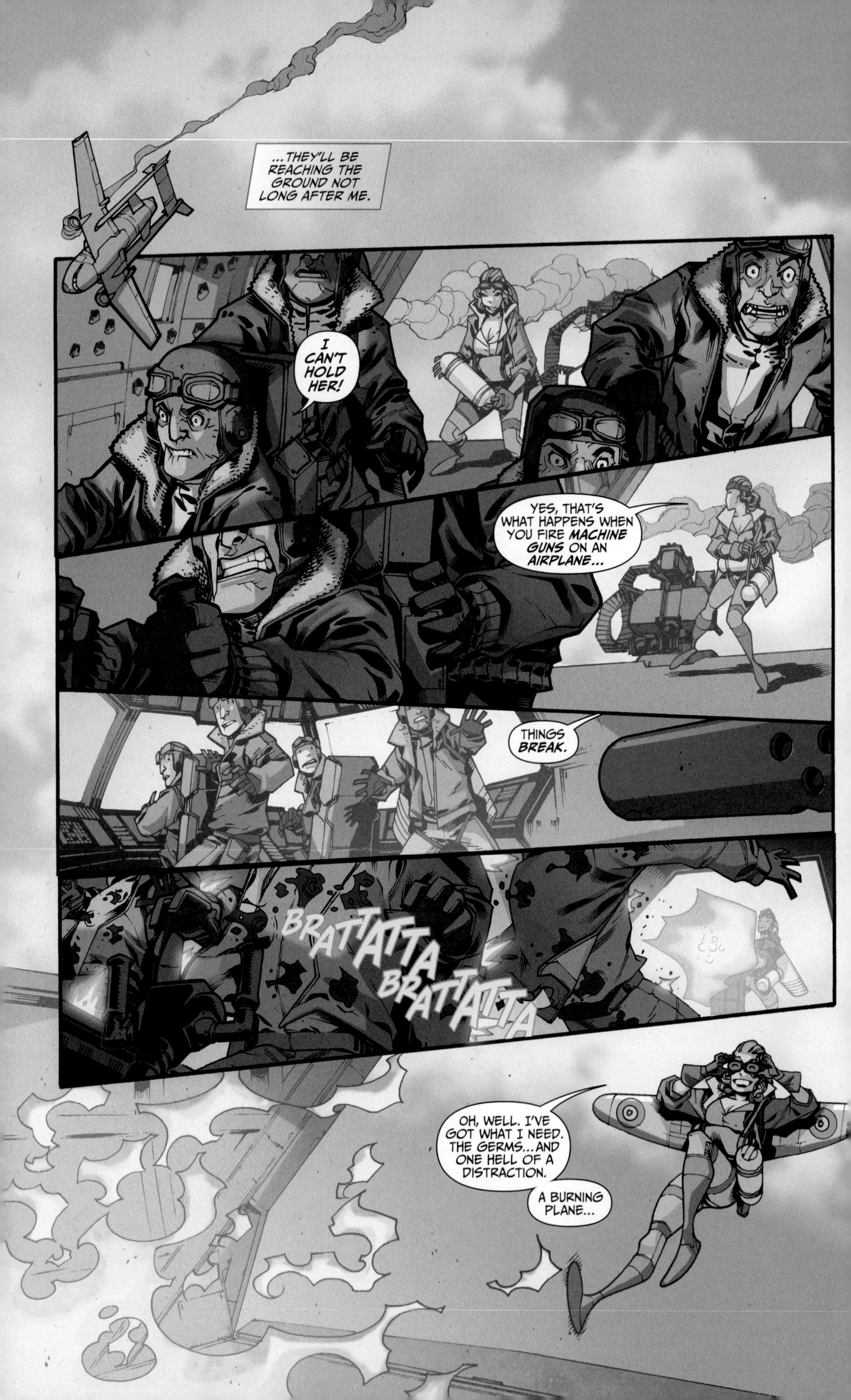
...THEY'LL BE REACHING THE GROUND NOT LONG AFTER ME.
I CAN'T HOLD HER!
YES, THAT'S WHAT HAPPENS WHEN YOU FIRE MACHINE GUNS ON AN AIRPLANE...
THINGS BREAK.
BRATTATTA BRATTATTA
OH, WELL. I'VE GOT WHAT I NEED. THE GERMS...AND ONE HELL OF A DISTRACTION.
A BURNING PLANE...

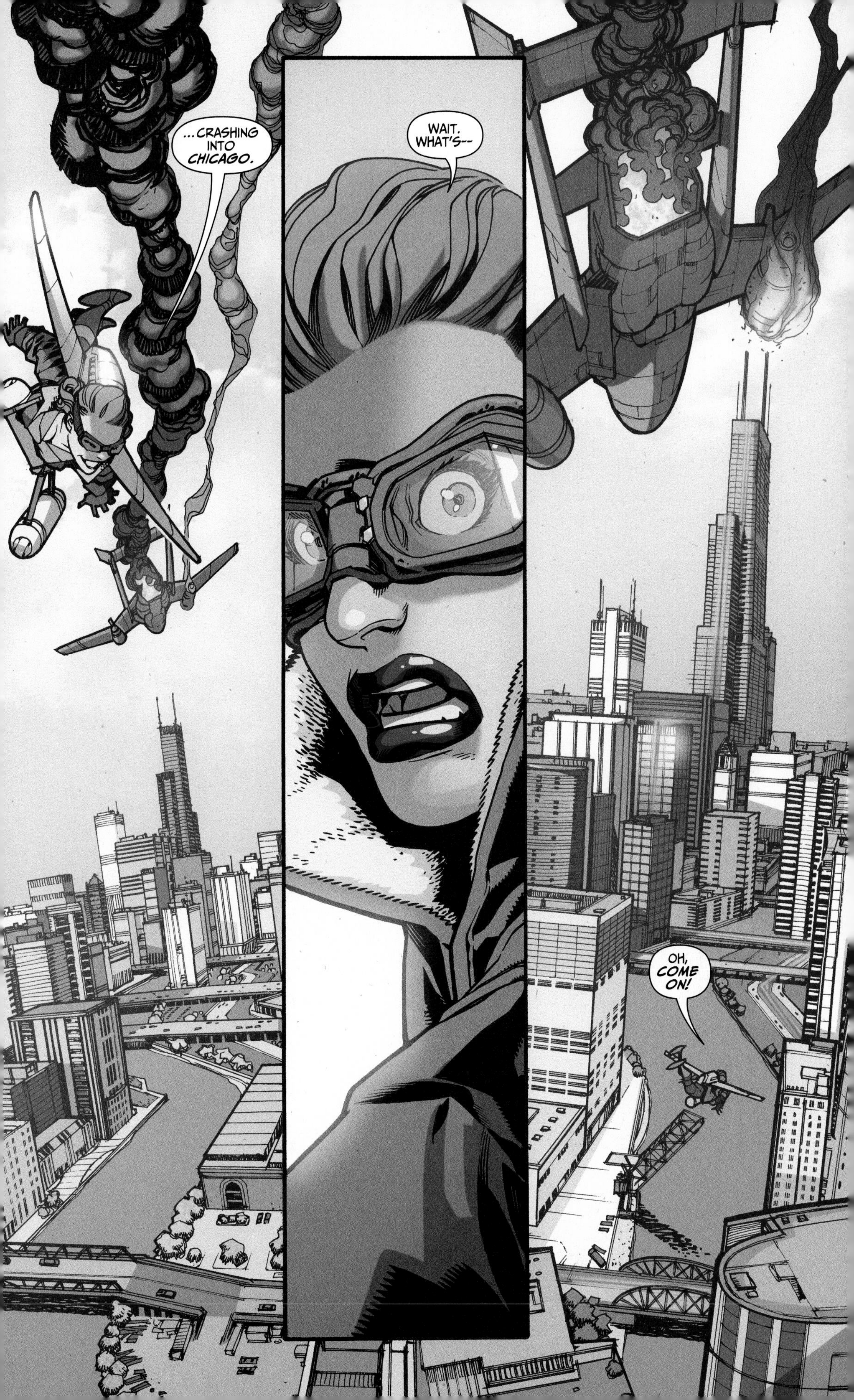
...CRASHING INTO CHICAGO.
WAIT. WHAT'S--
OH, COME ON!

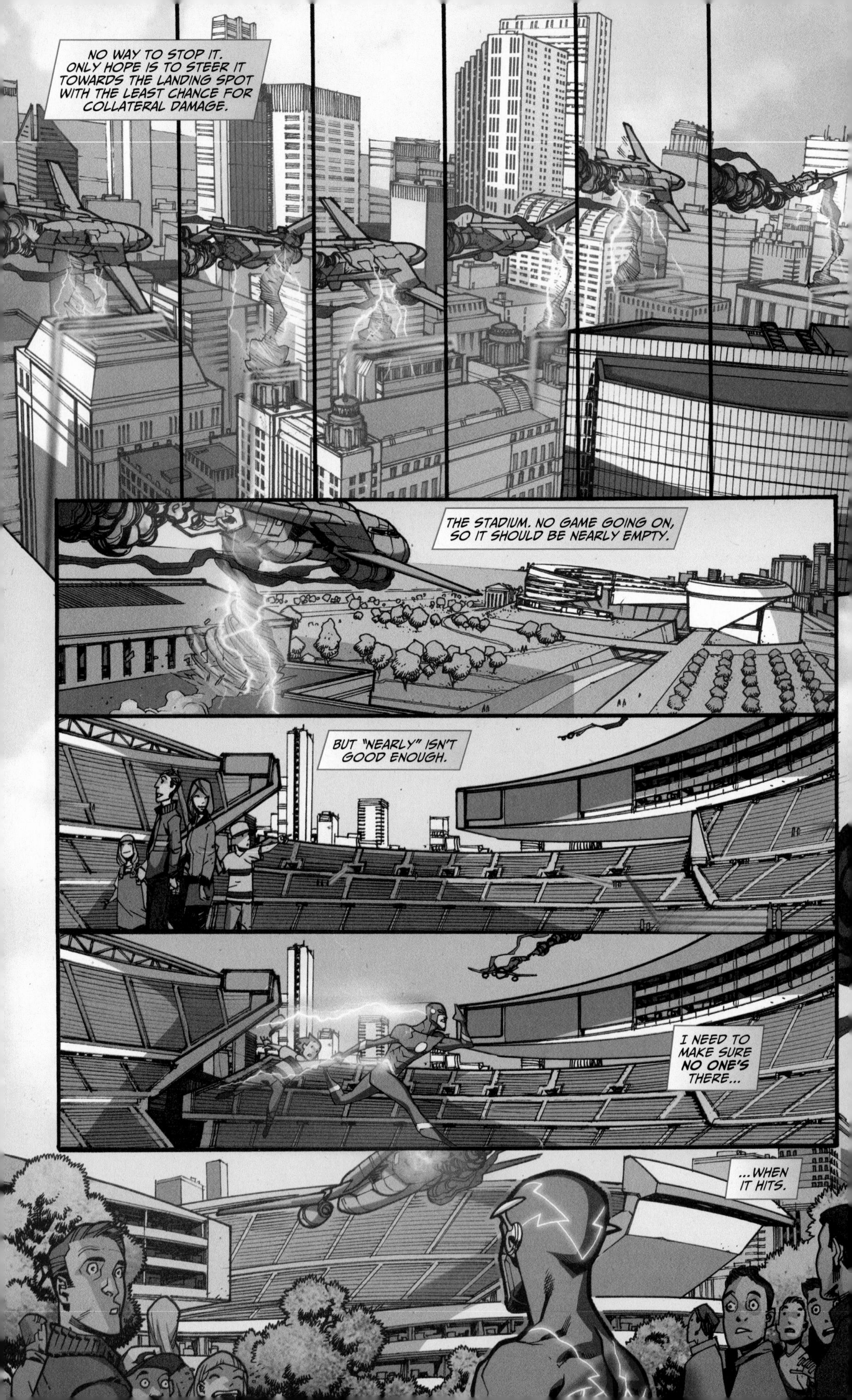
NO WAY TO STOP IT. ONLY HOPE IS TO STEER IT TOWARDS THE LANDING SPOT WITH THE LEAST CHANCE FOR COLLATERAL DAMAGE.
THE STADIUM. NO GAME GOING ON, SO IT SHOULD BE NEARLY EMPTY.
BUT "NEARLY" ISN'T GOOD ENOUGH.
I NEED TO MAKE SURE NO ONE'S THERE...
...WHEN IT HITS.

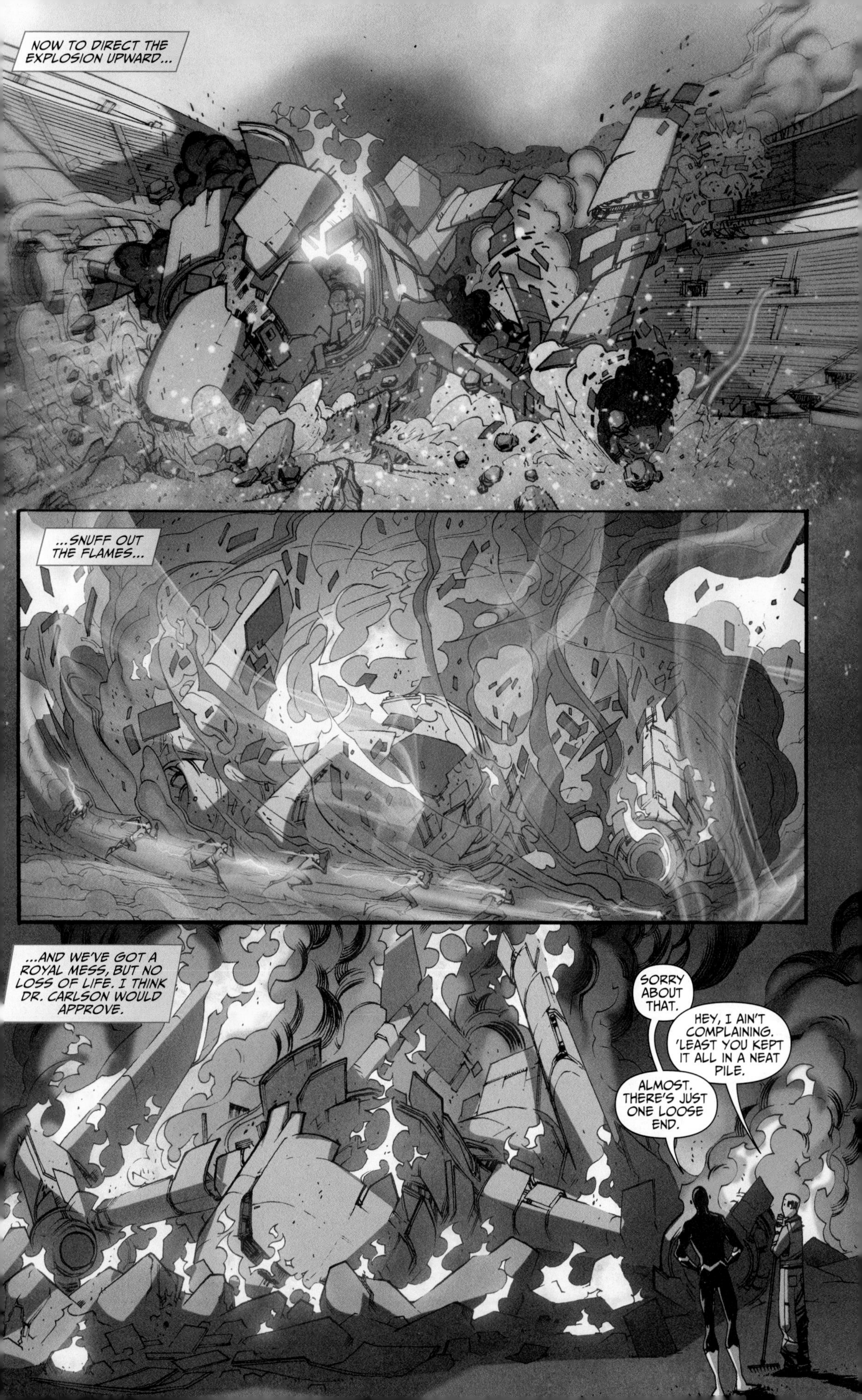
NOW TO DIRECT THE EXPLOSION UPWARD...
...SNUFF OUT THE FLAMES...
...AND WE'VE GOT A ROYAL MESS, BUT NO LOSS OF LIFE. I THINK DR. CARLSON WOULD APPROVE.
SORRY ABOUT THAT.
HEY, I AIN'T COMPLAINING. 'LEAST YOU KEPT IT ALL IN A NEAT PILE.
ALMOST. THERE'S JUST ONE LOOSE END.

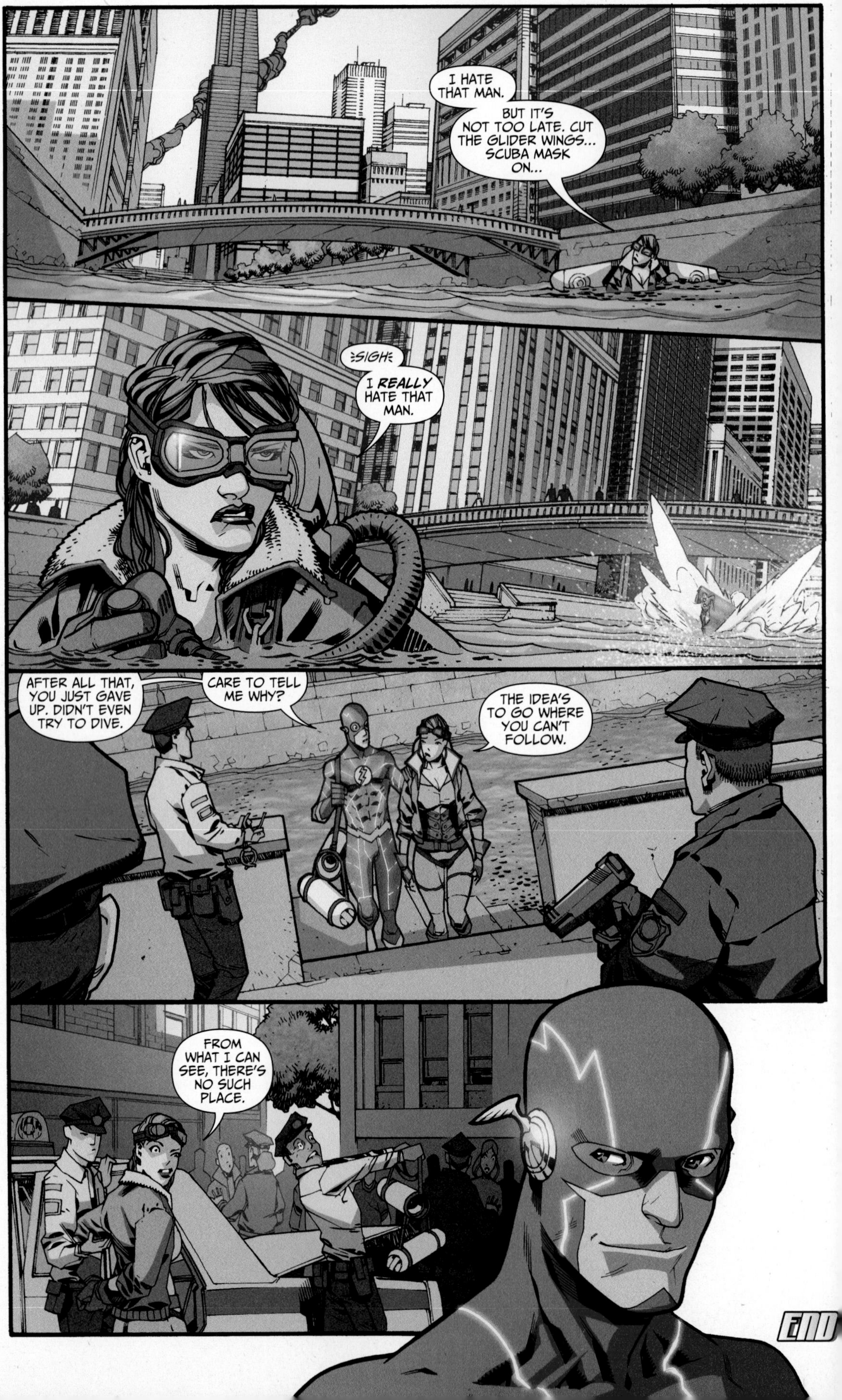
I HATE THAT MAN.
BUT IT'S NOT TOO LATE. CUT THE GLIDER WINGS... SCUBA MASK ON...
SIGH
I REALLY HATE THAT MAN.
AFTER ALL THAT, YOU JUST GAVE UP. DIDN'T EVEN TRY TO DIVE.
CARE TO TELL ME WHY?
THE IDEA'S TO GO WHERE YOU CAN'T FOLLOW.
FROM WHAT I CAN SEE, THERE'S NO SUCH PLACE.
END

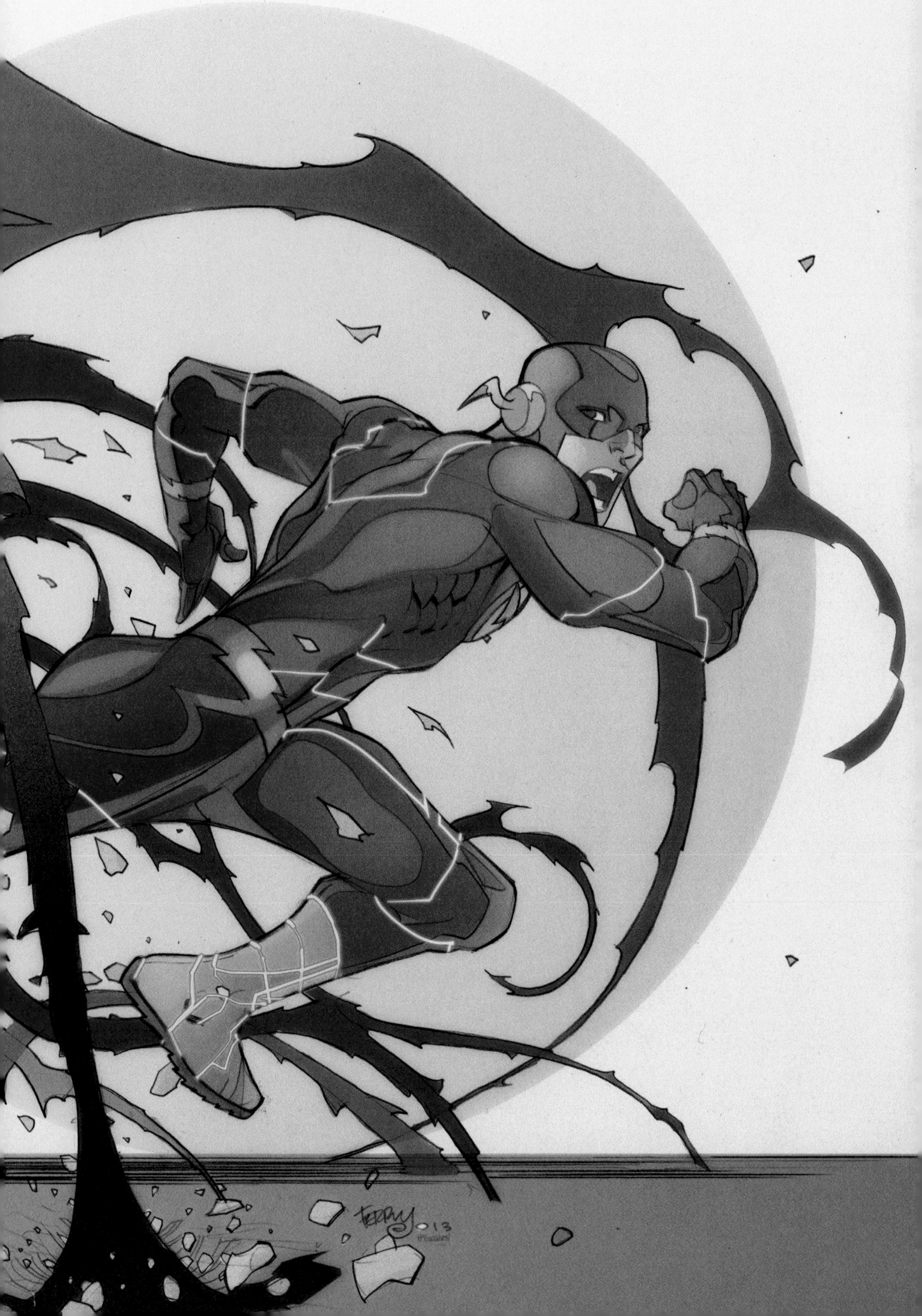

BRIAN BUCCELLATO writer **PATRICK ZIRCHER** artist cover art by **PASQUAL FERRY & MATT HOLLINGSWORTH**

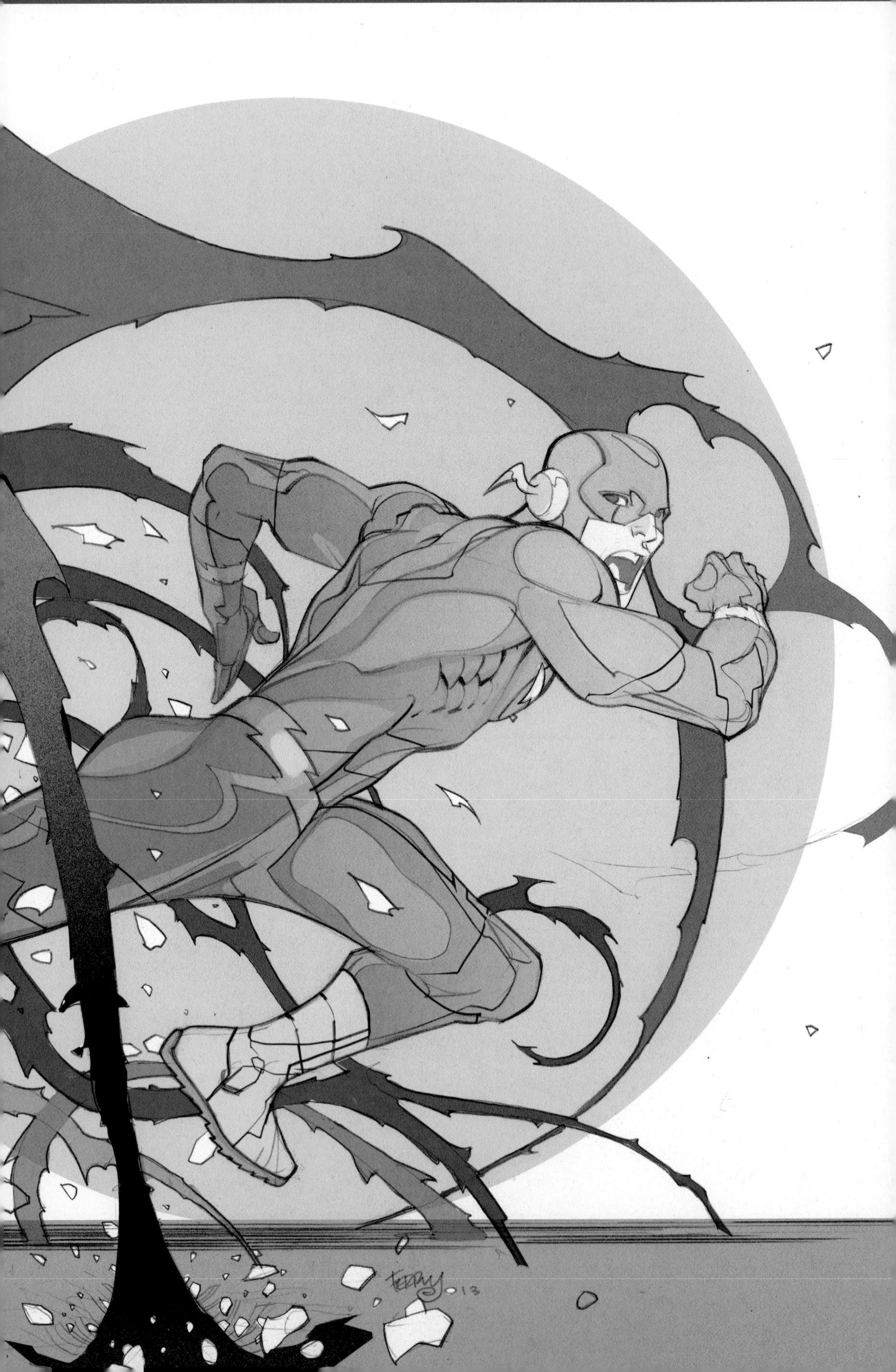

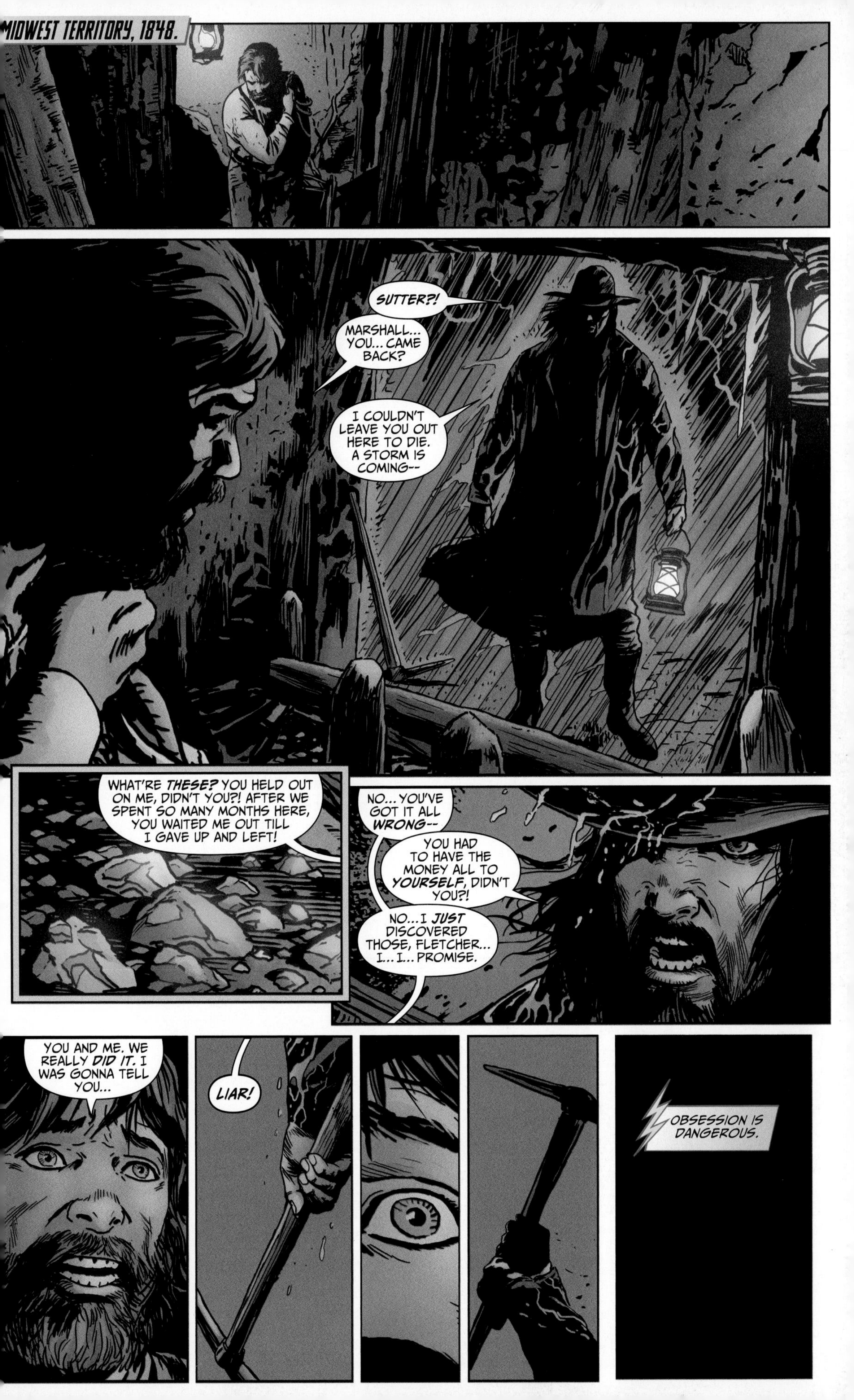

MIDWEST TERRITORY, 1848.
SUTTER?!
MARSHALL... YOU... CAME BACK?
I COULDN'T LEAVE YOU OUT HERE TO DIE. A STORM IS COMING--
WHAT'RE THESE? YOU HELD OUT ON ME, DIDN'T YOU?! AFTER WE SPENT SO MANY MONTHS HERE, YOU WAITED ME OUT TILL I GAVE UP AND LEFT!
NO... YOU'VE GOT IT ALL WRONG--
YOU HAD TO HAVE THE MONEY ALL TO YOURSELF, DIDN'T YOU?!
NO... I JUST DISCOVERED THOSE, FLETCHER... I... I... PROMISE.
YOU AND ME. WE REALLY DID IT. I WAS GONNA TELL YOU...
LIAR!
OBSESSION IS DANGEROUS.

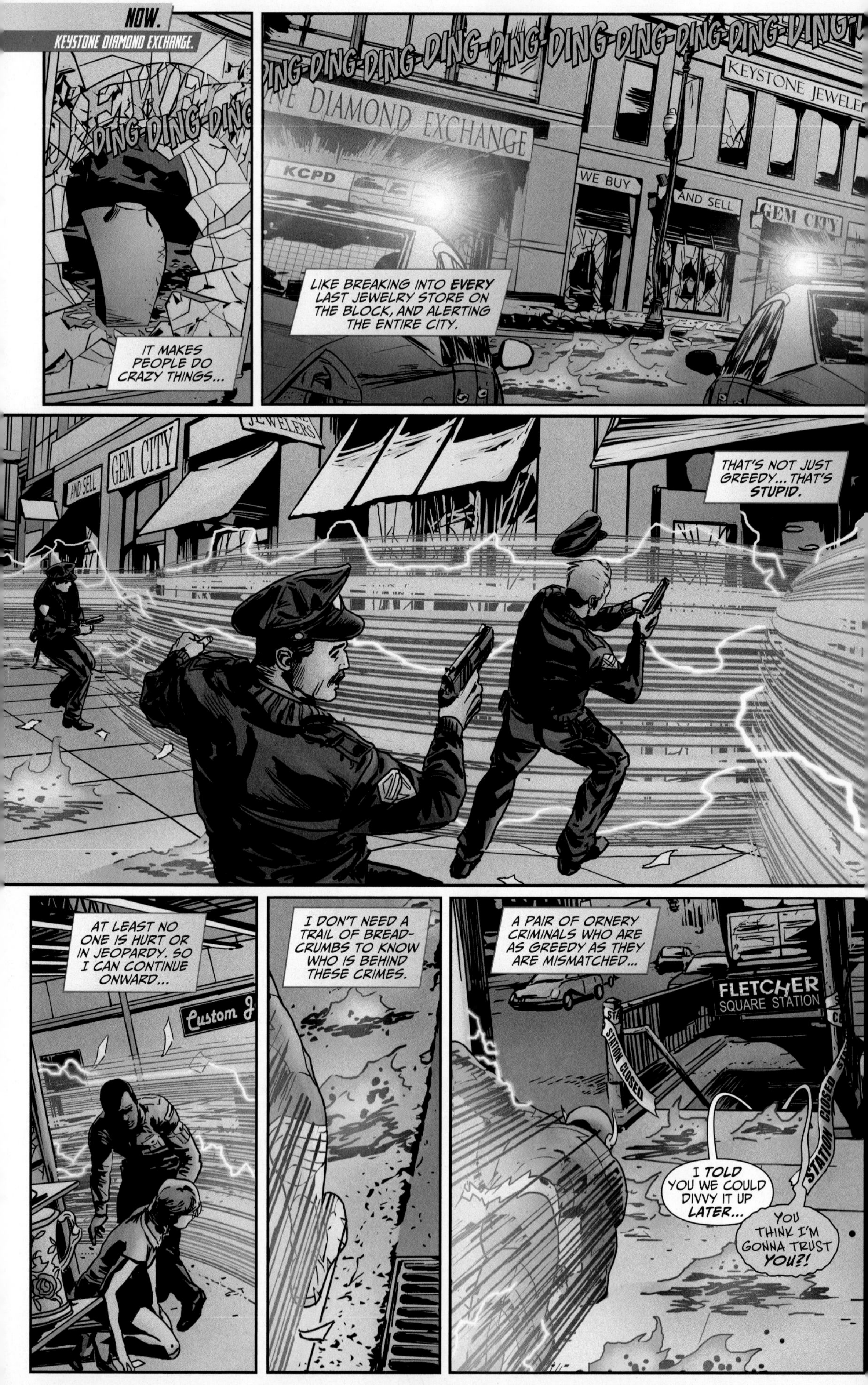
NOW.
KEYSTONE DIAMOND EXCHANGE.
DING-DING-DING
IT MAKES PEOPLE DO CRAZY THINGS...
DING-DING-DING-DING-DING-DING-DING-DING-DING!
KEYSTONE JEWELE
DIAMOND EXCHANGE
KCPD
WE BUY
AND SELL
GEM CITY
LIKE BREAKING INTO EVERY LAST JEWELRY STORE ON THE BLOCK, AND ALERTING THE ENTIRE CITY.
AND SELL
GEM CITY
JEWELERS
THAT'S NOT JUST GREEDY... THAT'S STUPID.
AT LEAST NO ONE IS HURT OR IN JEOPARDY. SO I CAN CONTINUE ONWARD...
Custom J
I DON'T NEED A TRAIL OF BREAD-CRUMBS TO KNOW WHO IS BEHIND THESE CRIMES.
A PAIR OF ORNERY CRIMINALS WHO ARE AS GREEDY AS THEY ARE MISMATCHED...
FLETCHER
SQUARE STATION
STATION CLOSED
I TOLD YOU WE COULD DIVVY IT UP LATER...
YOU THINK I'M GONNA TRUST YOU?!

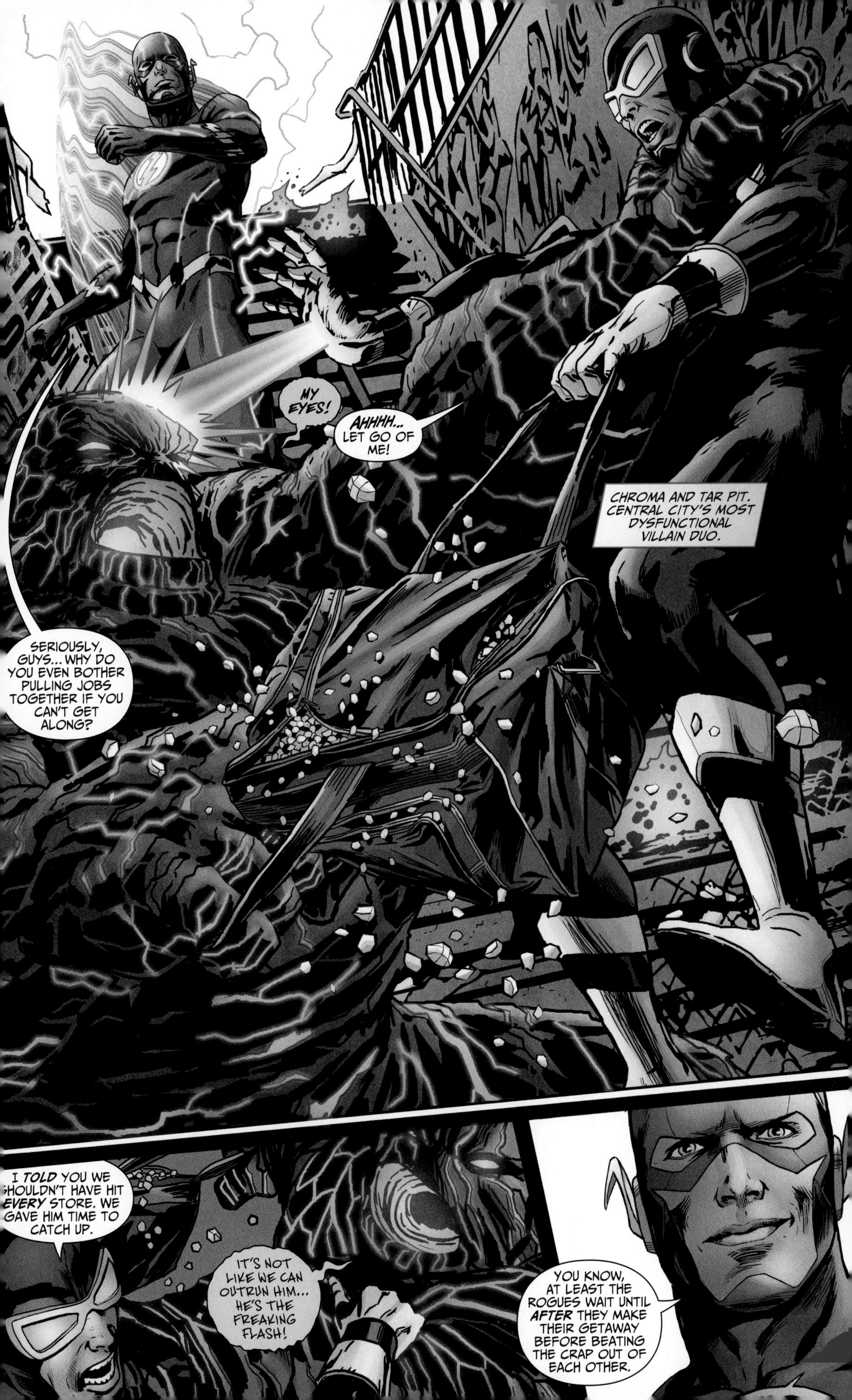
MY EYES!
AHHHH... LET GO OF ME!
CHROMA AND TAR PIT. CENTRAL CITY'S MOST DYSFUNCTIONAL VILLAIN DUO.
SERIOUSLY, GUYS... WHY DO YOU EVEN BOTHER PULLING JOBS TOGETHER IF YOU CAN'T GET ALONG?
I TOLD YOU WE SHOULDN'T HAVE HIT EVERY STORE. WE GAVE HIM TIME TO CATCH UP.
IT'S NOT LIKE WE CAN OUTRUN HIM... HE'S THE FREAKING FLASH!
YOU KNOW, AT LEAST THE ROGUES WAIT UNTIL AFTER THEY MAKE THEIR GETAWAY BEFORE BEATING THE CRAP OUT OF EACH OTHER.

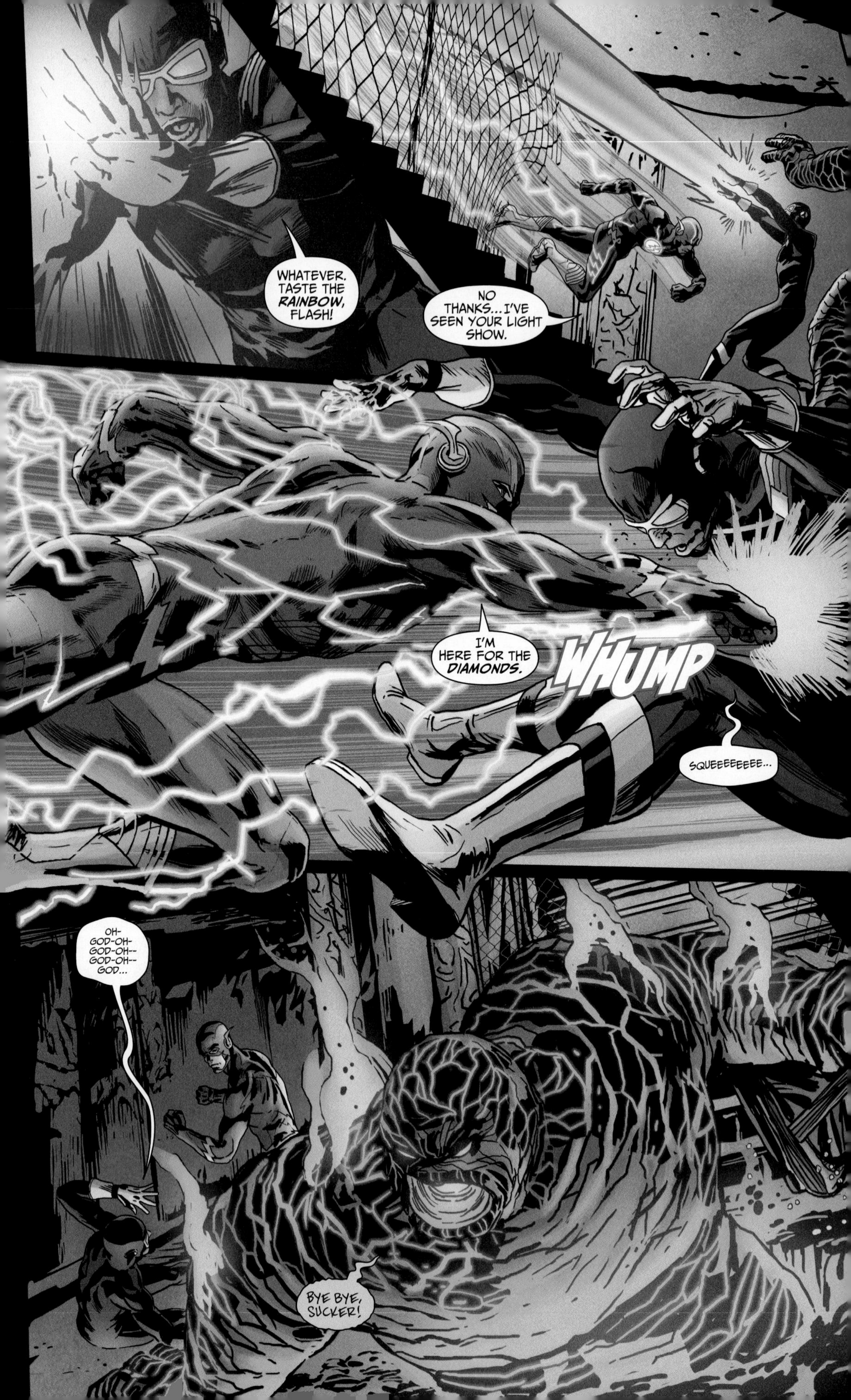
WHATEVER. TASTE THE RAINBOW, FLASH!
NO THANKS... I'VE SEEN YOUR LIGHT SHOW.
I'M HERE FOR THE DIAMONDS.
WHUMP
SQUEEEEEEEE...
OH- GOD-OH- GOD-OH-- GOD-OH-- GOD...
BYE BYE, SUCKER!

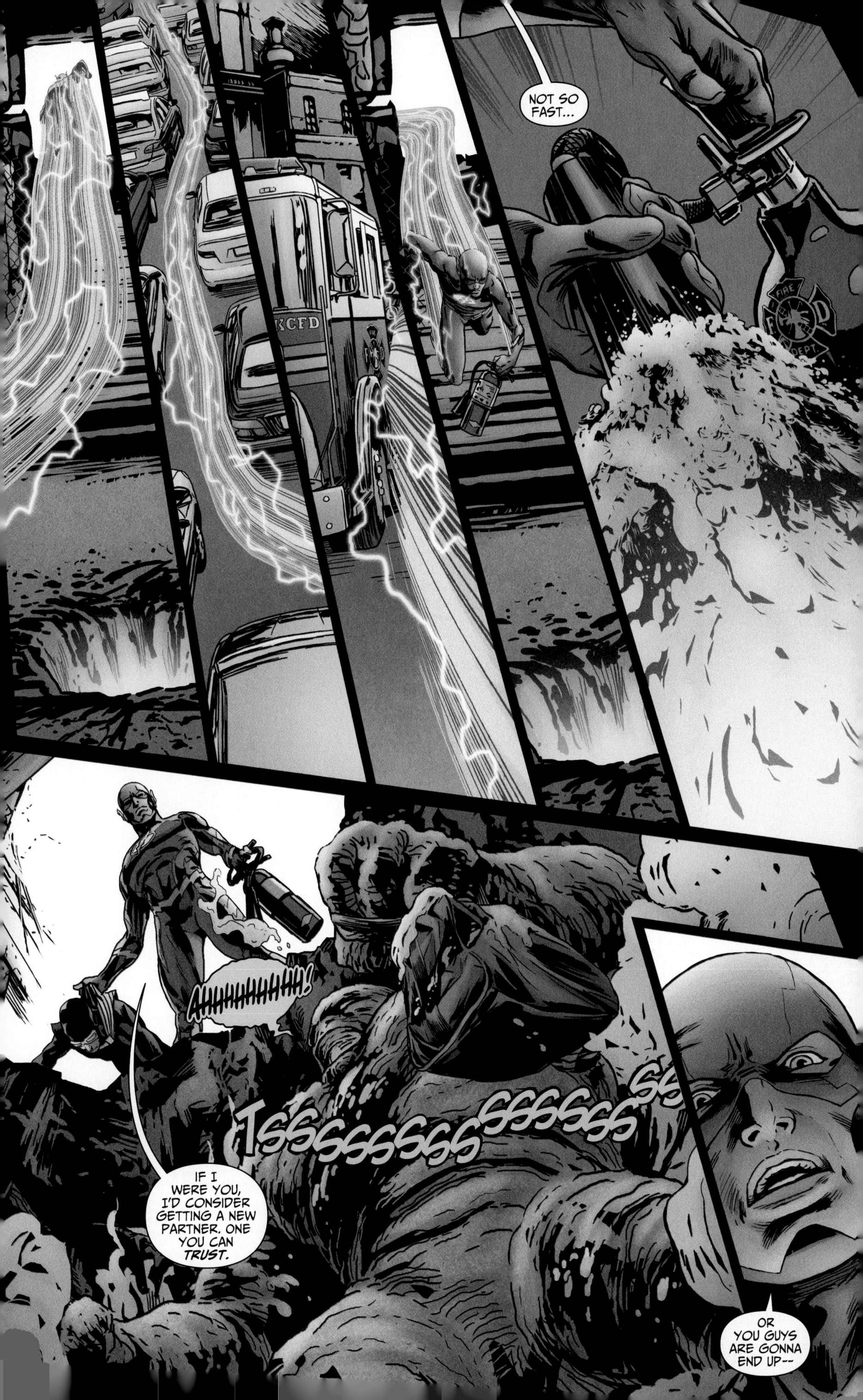

NOT SO FAST...
KCFD
AHHHHHHHHH!
TSSSSSSSSSSSSSSSSS
IF I WERE YOU, I'D CONSIDER GETTING A NEW PARTNER. ONE YOU CAN *TRUST*.
OR YOU GUYS ARE GONNA END UP--

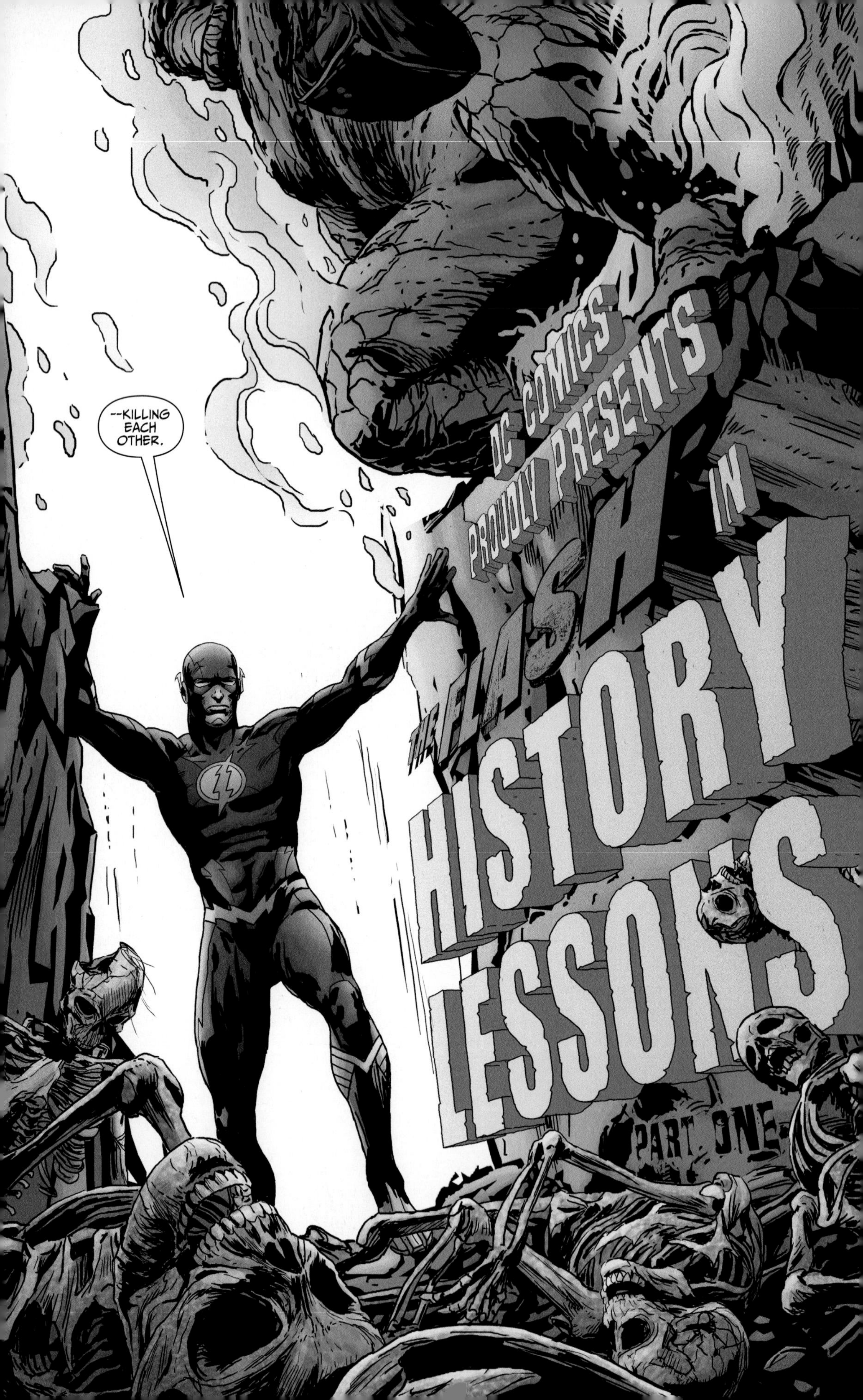
--KILLING EACH OTHER.
DC COMICS PROUDLY PRESENTS
THE FLASH IN
HISTORY LESSONS
PART ONE

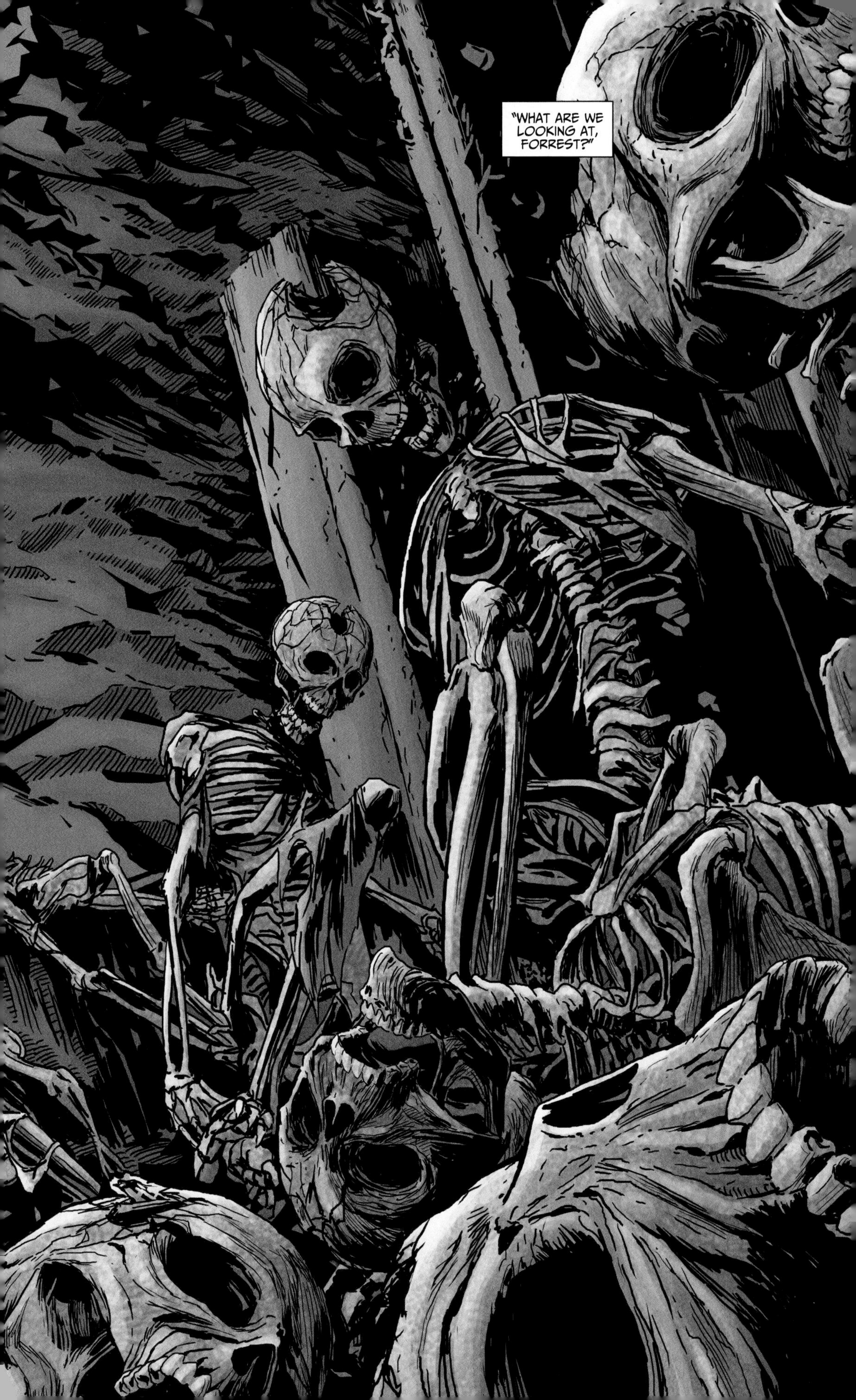
"WHAT ARE WE LOOKING AT, FORREST?"

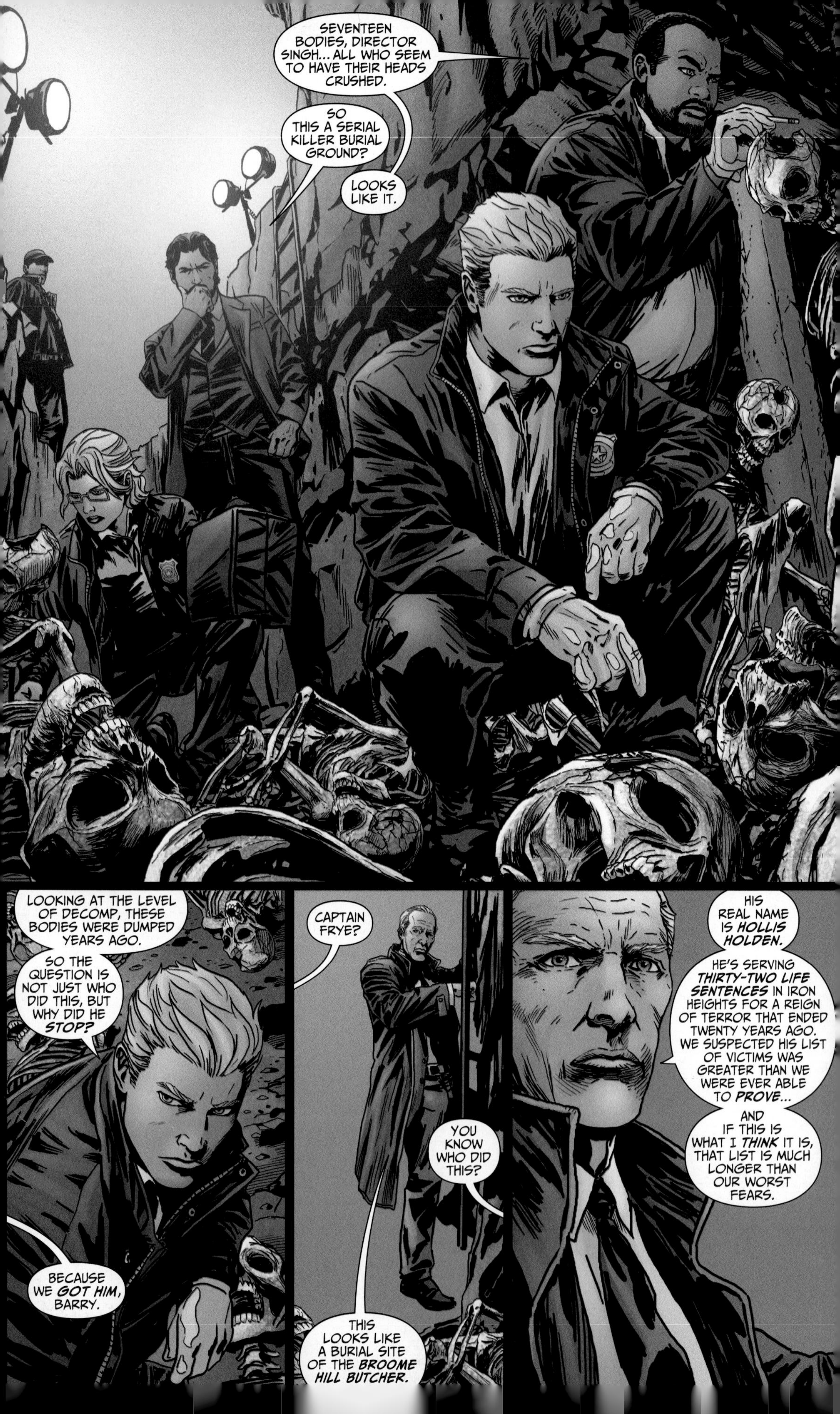

SEVENTEEN BODIES, DIRECTOR SINGH... ALL WHO SEEM TO HAVE THEIR HEADS CRUSHED.
SO THIS A SERIAL KILLER BURIAL GROUND?
LOOKS LIKE IT.
LOOKING AT THE LEVEL OF DECOMP, THESE BODIES WERE DUMPED YEARS AGO.
SO THE QUESTION IS NOT JUST WHO DID THIS, BUT WHY DID HE *STOP?*
BECAUSE WE ***GOT HIM***, BARRY.
CAPTAIN FRYE?
YOU KNOW WHO DID THIS?
THIS LOOKS LIKE A BURIAL SITE OF THE ***BROOME HILL BUTCHER.***
HIS REAL NAME IS ***HOLLIS HOLDEN.***
HE'S SERVING ***THIRTY-TWO LIFE SENTENCES*** IN IRON HEIGHTS FOR A REIGN OF TERROR THAT ENDED TWENTY YEARS AGO. WE SUSPECTED HIS LIST OF VICTIMS WAS GREATER THAN WE WERE EVER ABLE TO ***PROVE...***
AND IF THIS IS WHAT I *THINK* IT IS, THAT LIST IS MUCH LONGER THAN OUR WORST FEARS.

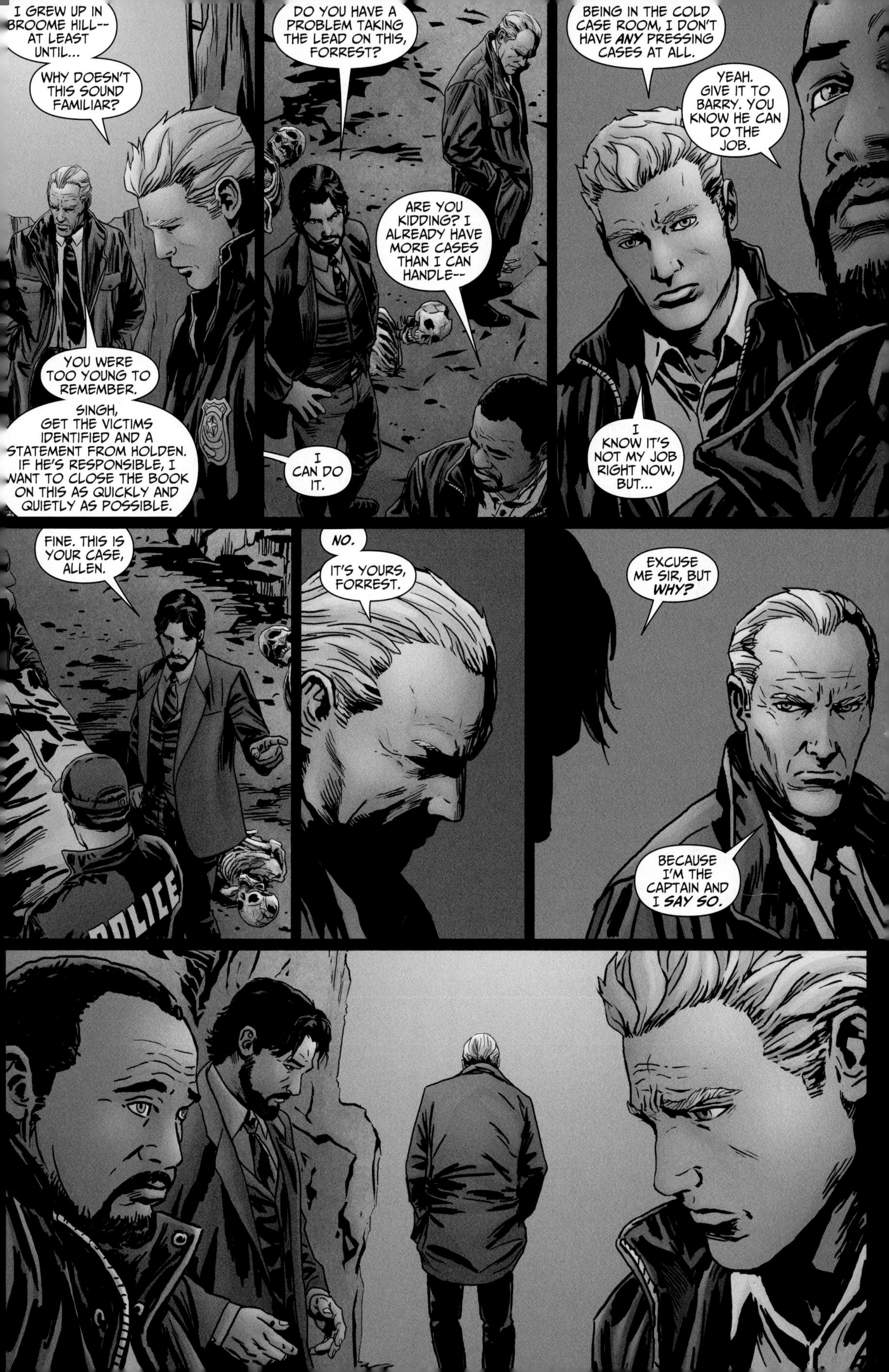
I GREW UP IN BROOME HILL-- AT LEAST UNTIL...
WHY DOESN'T THIS SOUND FAMILIAR?
YOU WERE TOO YOUNG TO REMEMBER.
SINGH, GET THE VICTIMS IDENTIFIED AND A STATEMENT FROM HOLDEN. IF HE'S RESPONSIBLE, I WANT TO CLOSE THE BOOK ON THIS AS QUICKLY AND QUIETLY AS POSSIBLE.
DO YOU HAVE A PROBLEM TAKING THE LEAD ON THIS, FORREST?
ARE YOU KIDDING? I ALREADY HAVE MORE CASES THAN I CAN HANDLE--
I CAN DO IT.
BEING IN THE COLD CASE ROOM, I DON'T HAVE ANY PRESSING CASES AT ALL.
YEAH. GIVE IT TO BARRY. YOU KNOW HE CAN DO THE JOB.
I KNOW IT'S NOT MY JOB RIGHT NOW, BUT...
FINE. THIS IS YOUR CASE, ALLEN.
NO.
IT'S YOURS, FORREST.
EXCUSE ME SIR, BUT WHY?
BECAUSE I'M THE CAPTAIN AND I SAY SO.
POLICE

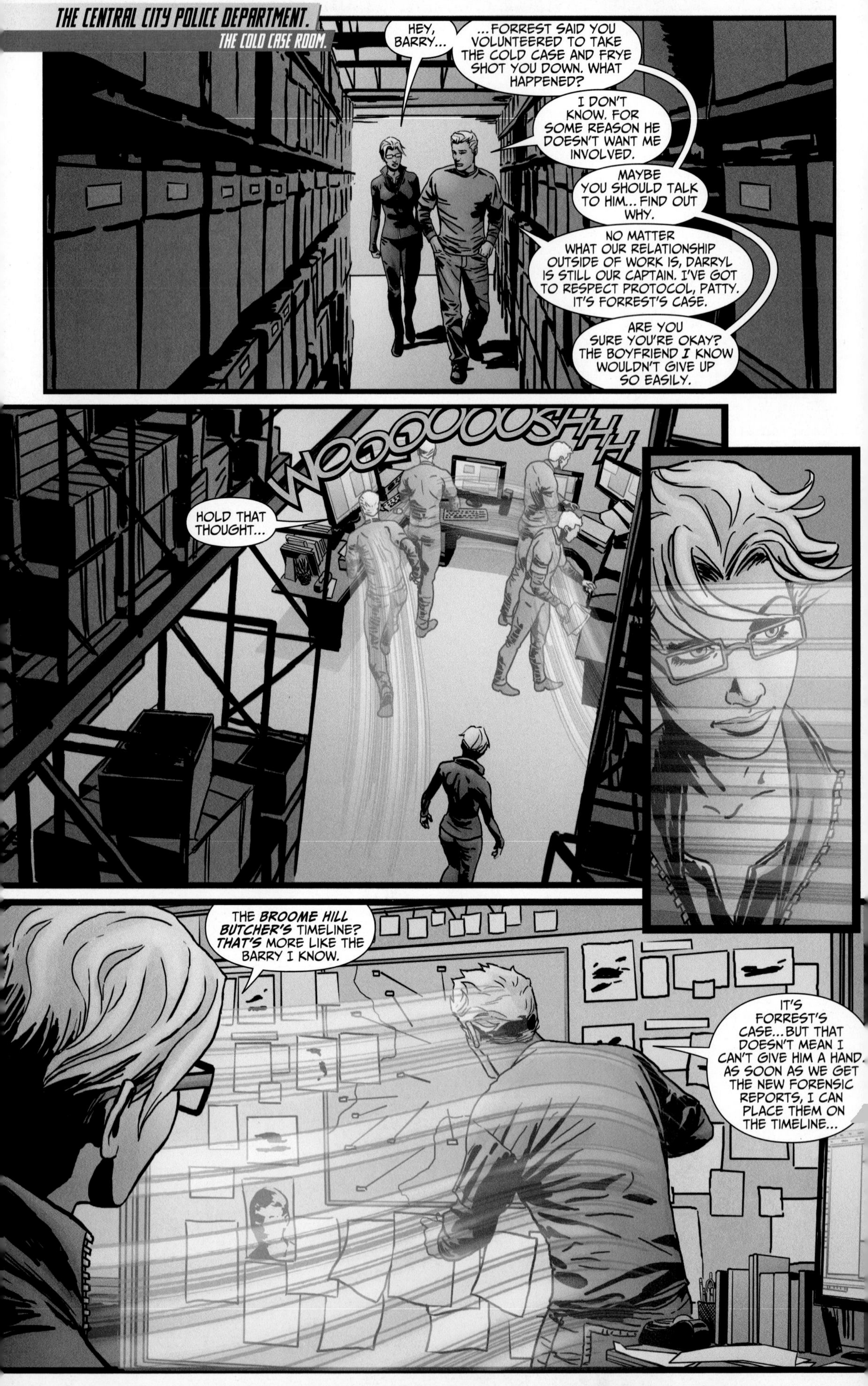
THE CENTRAL CITY POLICE DEPARTMENT.
THE COLD CASE ROOM.
HEY, BARRY...
...FORREST SAID YOU VOLUNTEERED TO TAKE THE COLD CASE AND FRYE SHOT YOU DOWN. WHAT HAPPENED?
I DON'T KNOW. FOR SOME REASON HE DOESN'T WANT ME INVOLVED.
MAYBE YOU SHOULD TALK TO HIM... FIND OUT WHY.
NO MATTER WHAT OUR RELATIONSHIP OUTSIDE OF WORK IS, DARRYL IS STILL OUR CAPTAIN. I'VE GOT TO RESPECT PROTOCOL, PATTY. IT'S FORREST'S CASE.
ARE YOU SURE YOU'RE OKAY? THE BOYFRIEND I KNOW WOULDN'T GIVE UP SO EASILY.
WOOOOOOOUSHHH
HOLD THAT THOUGHT...
THE BROOME HILL BUTCHER'S TIMELINE? THAT'S MORE LIKE THE BARRY I KNOW.
IT'S FORREST'S CASE...BUT THAT DOESN'T MEAN I CAN'T GIVE HIM A HAND. AS SOON AS WE GET THE NEW FORENSIC REPORTS, I CAN PLACE THEM ON THE TIMELINE...

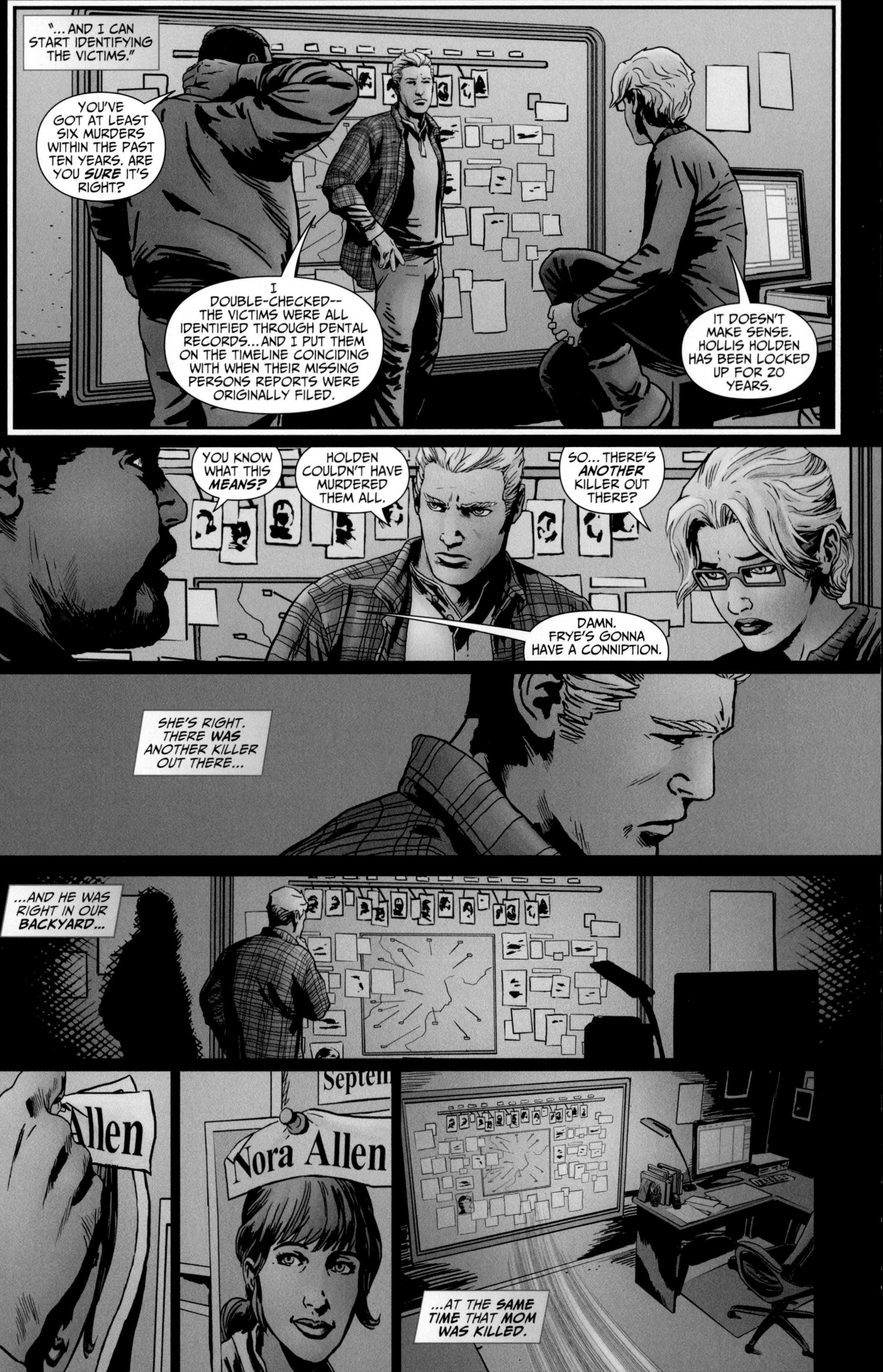
"...AND I CAN START IDENTIFYING THE VICTIMS."
YOU'VE GOT AT LEAST SIX MURDERS WITHIN THE PAST TEN YEARS. ARE YOU SURE IT'S RIGHT?
I DOUBLE-CHECKED-- THE VICTIMS WERE ALL IDENTIFIED THROUGH DENTAL RECORDS...AND I PUT THEM ON THE TIMELINE COINCIDING WITH WHEN THEIR MISSING PERSONS REPORTS WERE ORIGINALLY FILED.
IT DOESN'T MAKE SENSE. HOLLIS HOLDEN HAS BEEN LOCKED UP FOR 20 YEARS.
YOU KNOW WHAT THIS MEANS?
HOLDEN COULDN'T HAVE MURDERED THEM ALL.
SO... THERE'S ANOTHER KILLER OUT THERE?
DAMN. FRYE'S GONNA HAVE A CONNIPTION.
SHE'S RIGHT. THERE WAS ANOTHER KILLER OUT THERE...
...AND HE WAS RIGHT IN OUR BACKYARD...
Allen
Septem
Nora Allen
...AT THE SAME TIME THAT MOM WAS KILLED.

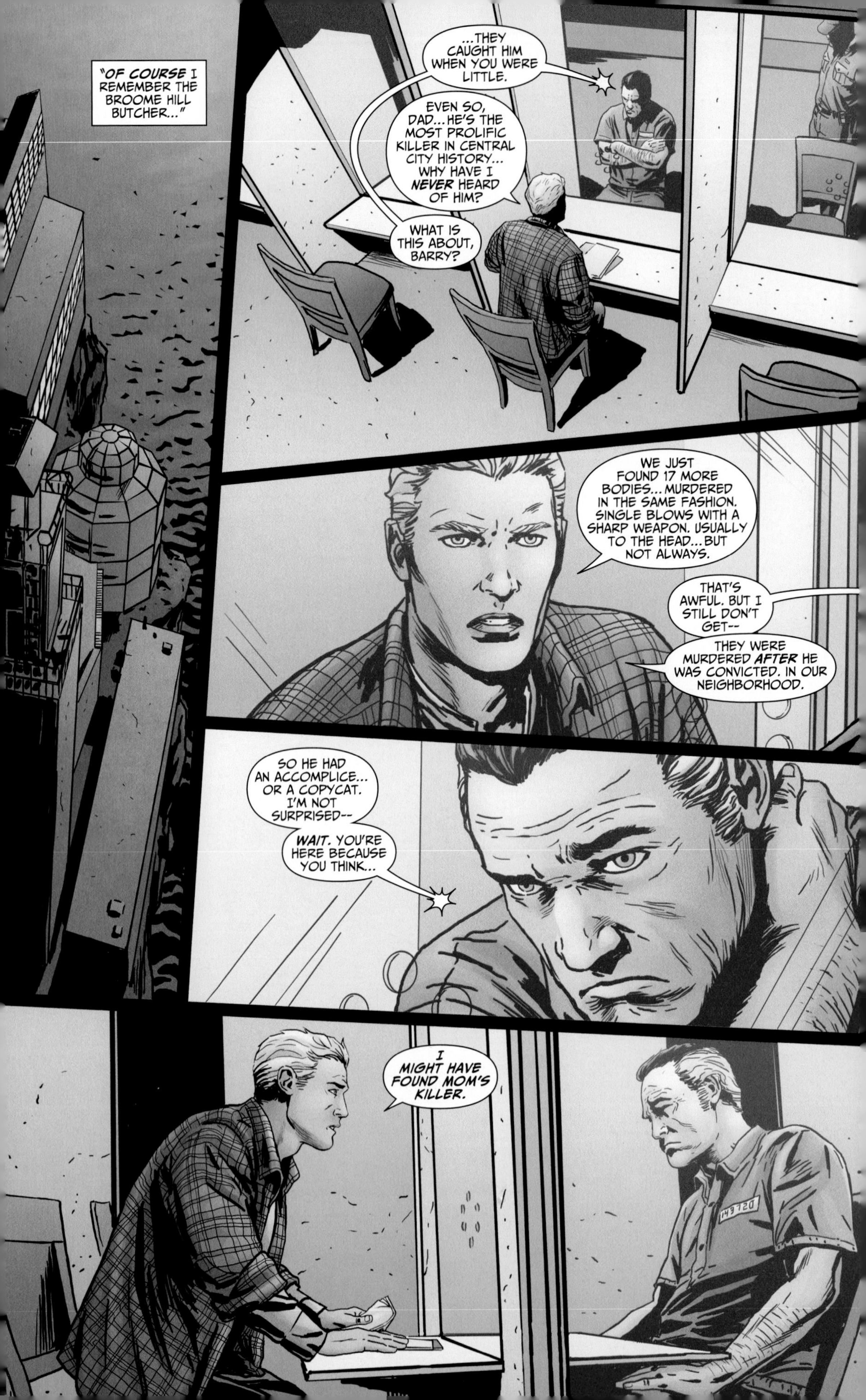
"OF COURSE I REMEMBER THE BROOME HILL BUTCHER..."
...THEY CAUGHT HIM WHEN YOU WERE LITTLE.
EVEN SO, DAD... HE'S THE MOST PROLIFIC KILLER IN CENTRAL CITY HISTORY... WHY HAVE I NEVER HEARD OF HIM?
WHAT IS THIS ABOUT, BARRY?
WE JUST FOUND 17 MORE BODIES... MURDERED IN THE SAME FASHION. SINGLE BLOWS WITH A SHARP WEAPON. USUALLY TO THE HEAD... BUT NOT ALWAYS.
THAT'S AWFUL. BUT I STILL DON'T GET--
THEY WERE MURDERED AFTER HE WAS CONVICTED. IN OUR NEIGHBORHOOD.
SO HE HAD AN ACCOMPLICE... OR A COPYCAT. I'M NOT SURPRISED--
WAIT. YOU'RE HERE BECAUSE YOU THINK...
I MIGHT HAVE FOUND MOM'S KILLER.

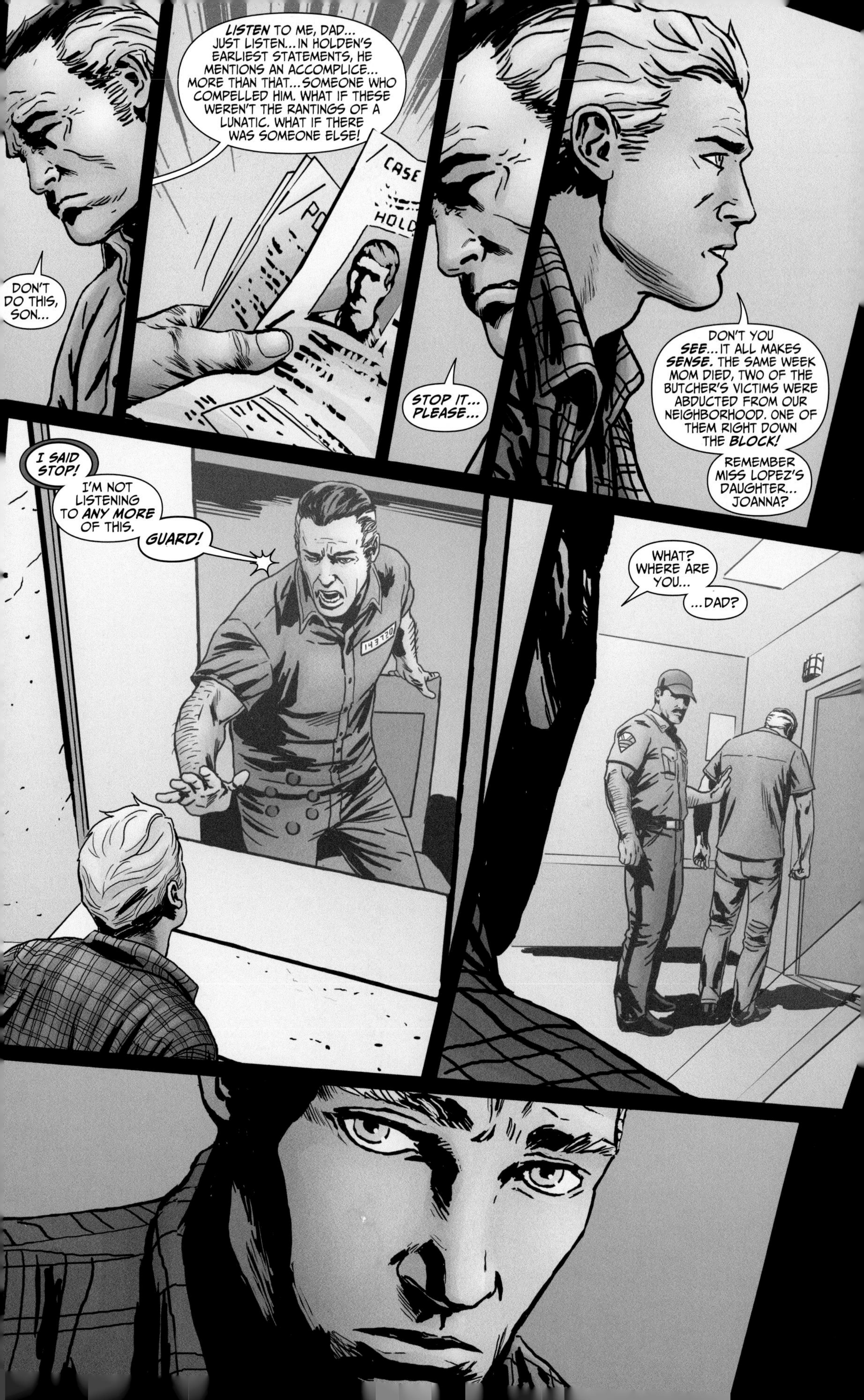
LISTEN TO ME, DAD... JUST LISTEN...IN HOLDEN'S EARLIEST STATEMENTS, HE MENTIONS AN ACCOMPLICE... MORE THAN THAT...SOMEONE WHO COMPELLED HIM. WHAT IF THESE WEREN'T THE RANTINGS OF A LUNATIC. WHAT IF THERE WAS SOMEONE ELSE!
DON'T DO THIS, SON...
CASE
HOLD
STOP IT... PLEASE...
DON'T YOU SEE...IT ALL MAKES SENSE. THE SAME WEEK MOM DIED, TWO OF THE BUTCHER'S VICTIMS WERE ABDUCTED FROM OUR NEIGHBORHOOD. ONE OF THEM RIGHT DOWN THE BLOCK!
REMEMBER MISS LOPEZ'S DAUGHTER... JOANNA?
I SAID STOP!
I'M NOT LISTENING TO ANY MORE OF THIS.
GUARD!
143720
WHAT? WHERE ARE YOU...
...DAD?

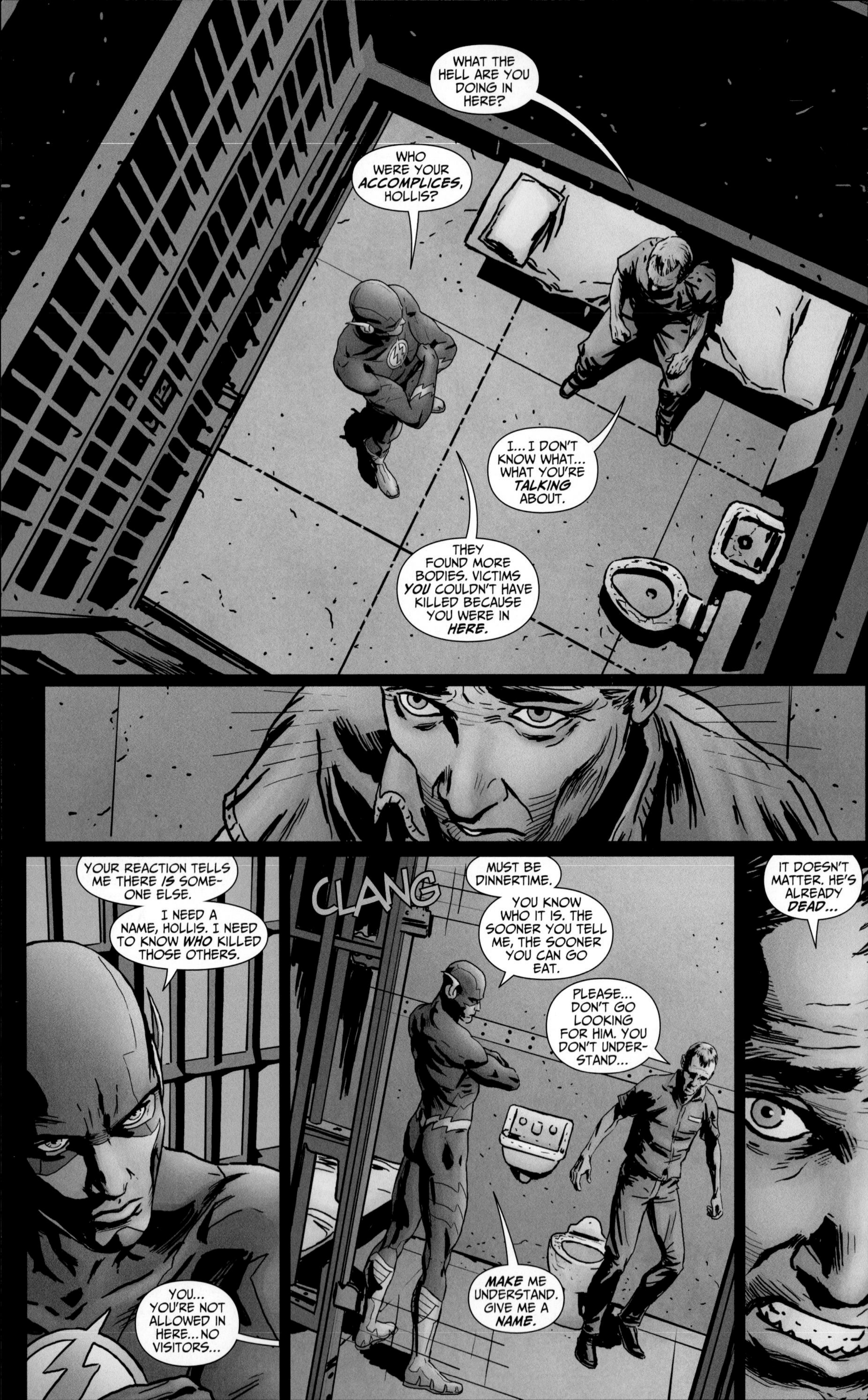
WHAT THE HELL ARE YOU DOING IN HERE?
WHO WERE YOUR ACCOMPLICES, HOLLIS?
I... I DON'T KNOW WHAT... WHAT YOU'RE TALKING ABOUT.
THEY FOUND MORE BODIES. VICTIMS YOU COULDN'T HAVE KILLED BECAUSE YOU WERE IN HERE.
YOUR REACTION TELLS ME THERE IS SOME-ONE ELSE.
I NEED A NAME, HOLLIS. I NEED TO KNOW WHO KILLED THOSE OTHERS.
YOU... YOU'RE NOT ALLOWED IN HERE... NO VISITORS...
CLANG
MUST BE DINNERTIME.
YOU KNOW WHO IT IS. THE SOONER YOU TELL ME, THE SOONER YOU CAN GO EAT.
PLEASE... DON'T GO LOOKING FOR HIM. YOU DON'T UNDER-STAND...
MAKE ME UNDERSTAND. GIVE ME A NAME.
IT DOESN'T MATTER. HE'S ALREADY DEAD...

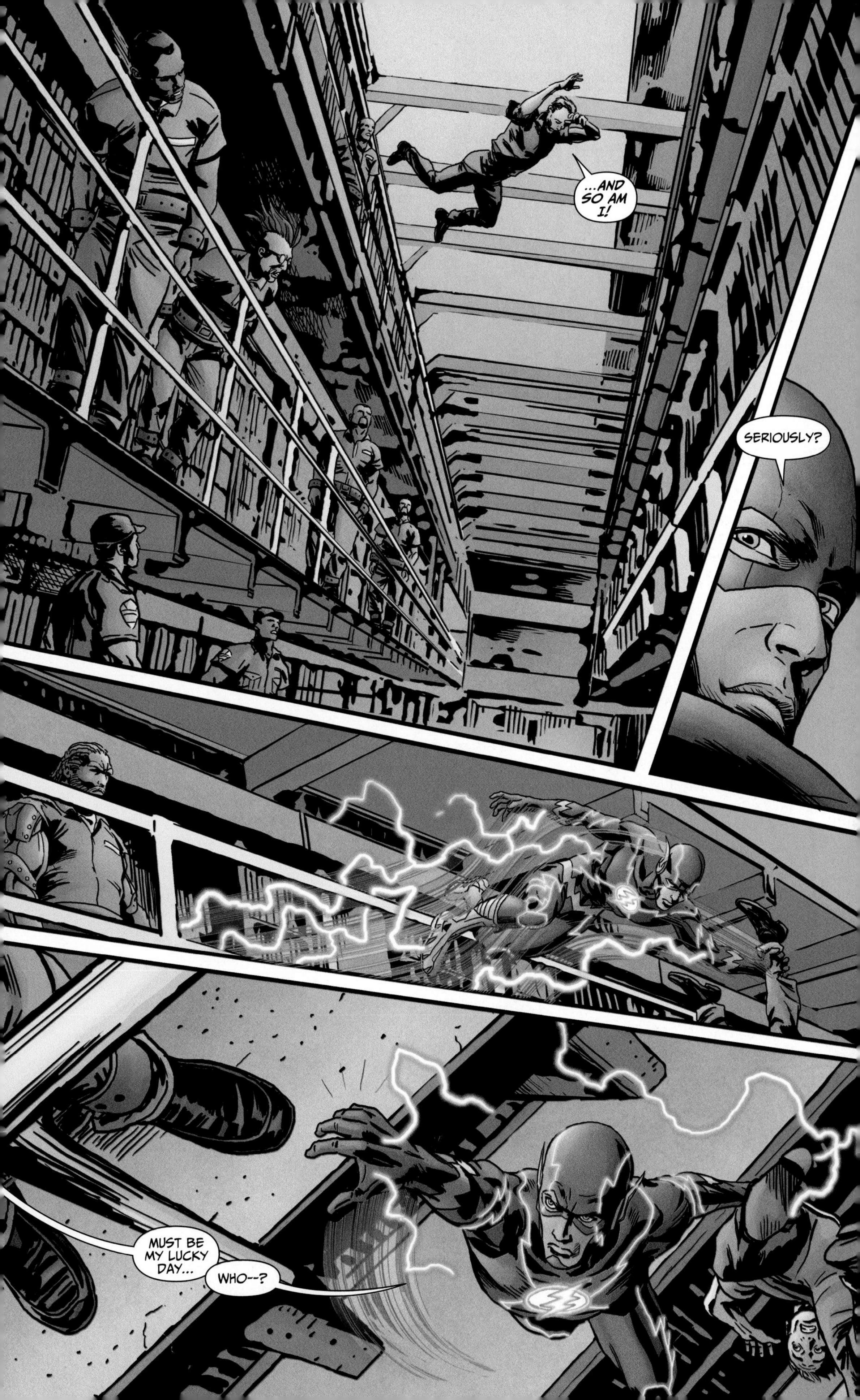
...AND SO AM I!
SERIOUSLY?
MUST BE MY LUCKY DAY...
WHO--?

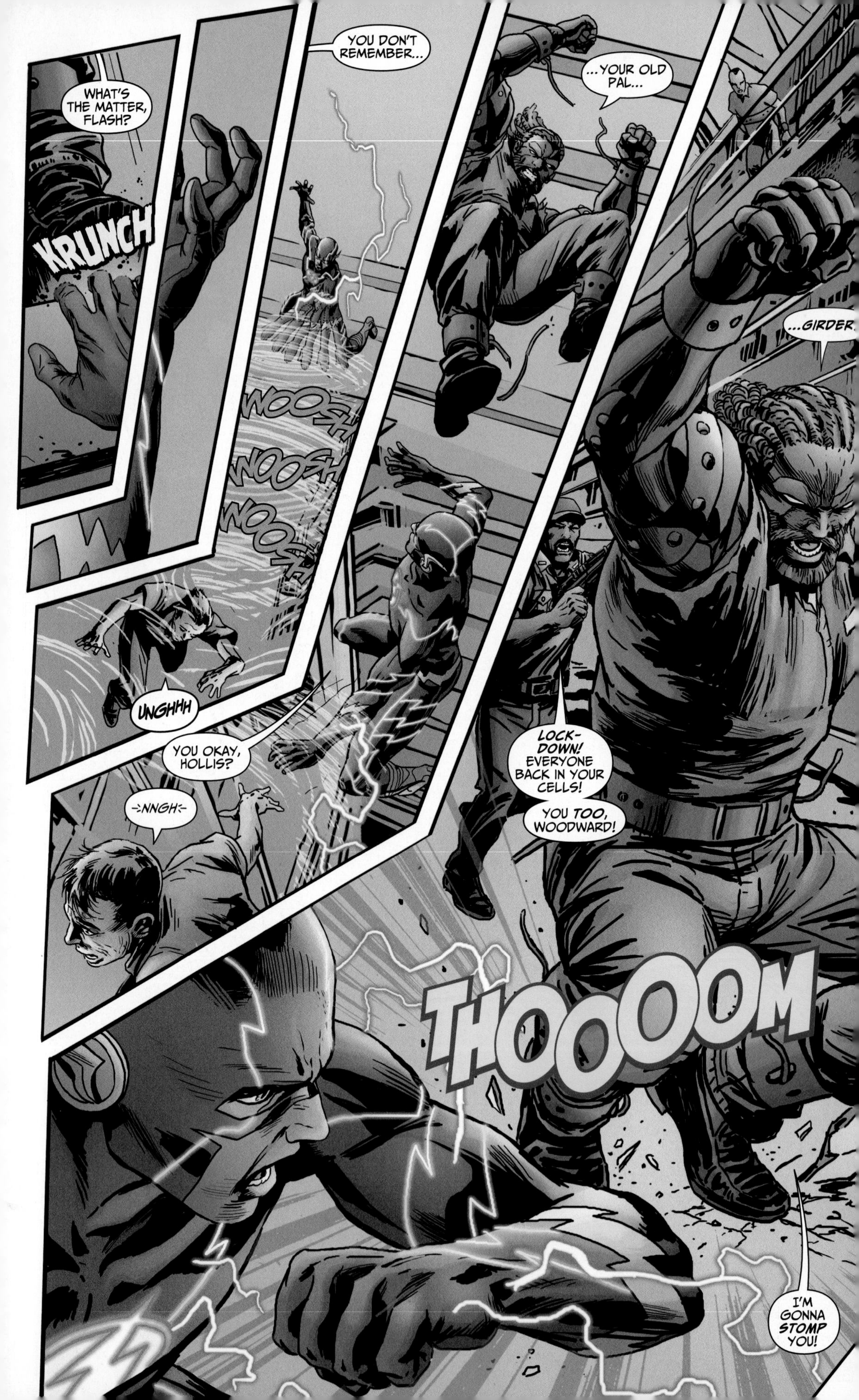
WHAT'S THE MATTER, FLASH?
KRUNCH
YOU DON'T REMEMBER...
...YOUR OLD PAL...
...GIRDER.
WOOSH
WOOSH
WOOSH
UNGHHH
YOU OKAY, HOLLIS?
-NNGH-
LOCK-DOWN! EVERYONE BACK IN YOUR CELLS!
YOU TOO, WOODWARD!
THOOOOOM
I'M GONNA STOMP YOU!

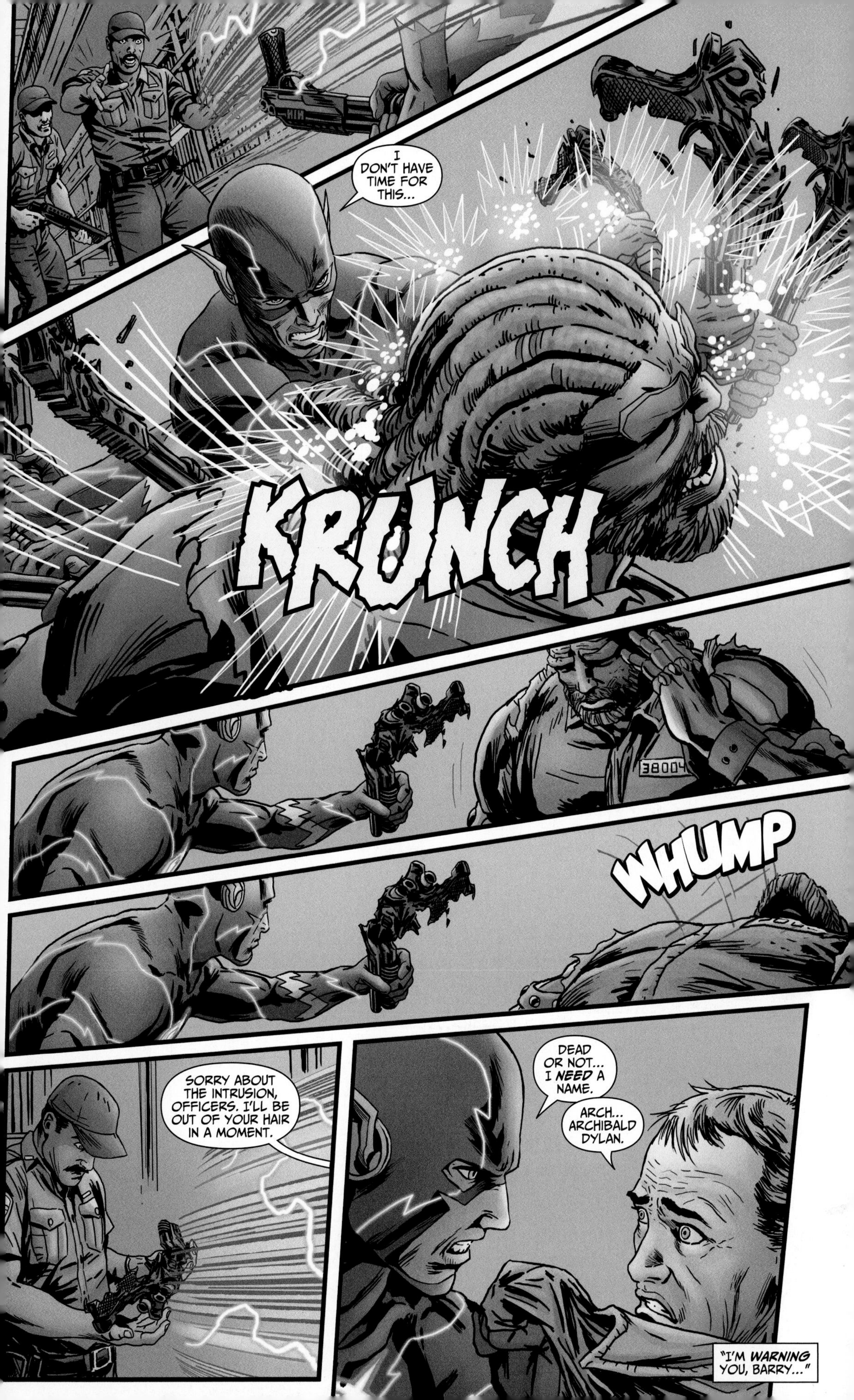

I DON'T HAVE TIME FOR THIS...
KRUNCH
38004
WHUMP
SORRY ABOUT THE INTRUSION, OFFICERS. I'LL BE OUT OF YOUR HAIR IN A MOMENT.
DEAD OR NOT... I *NEED* A NAME.
ARCH... ARCHIBALD DYLAN.
"I'M *WARNING* YOU, BARRY..."

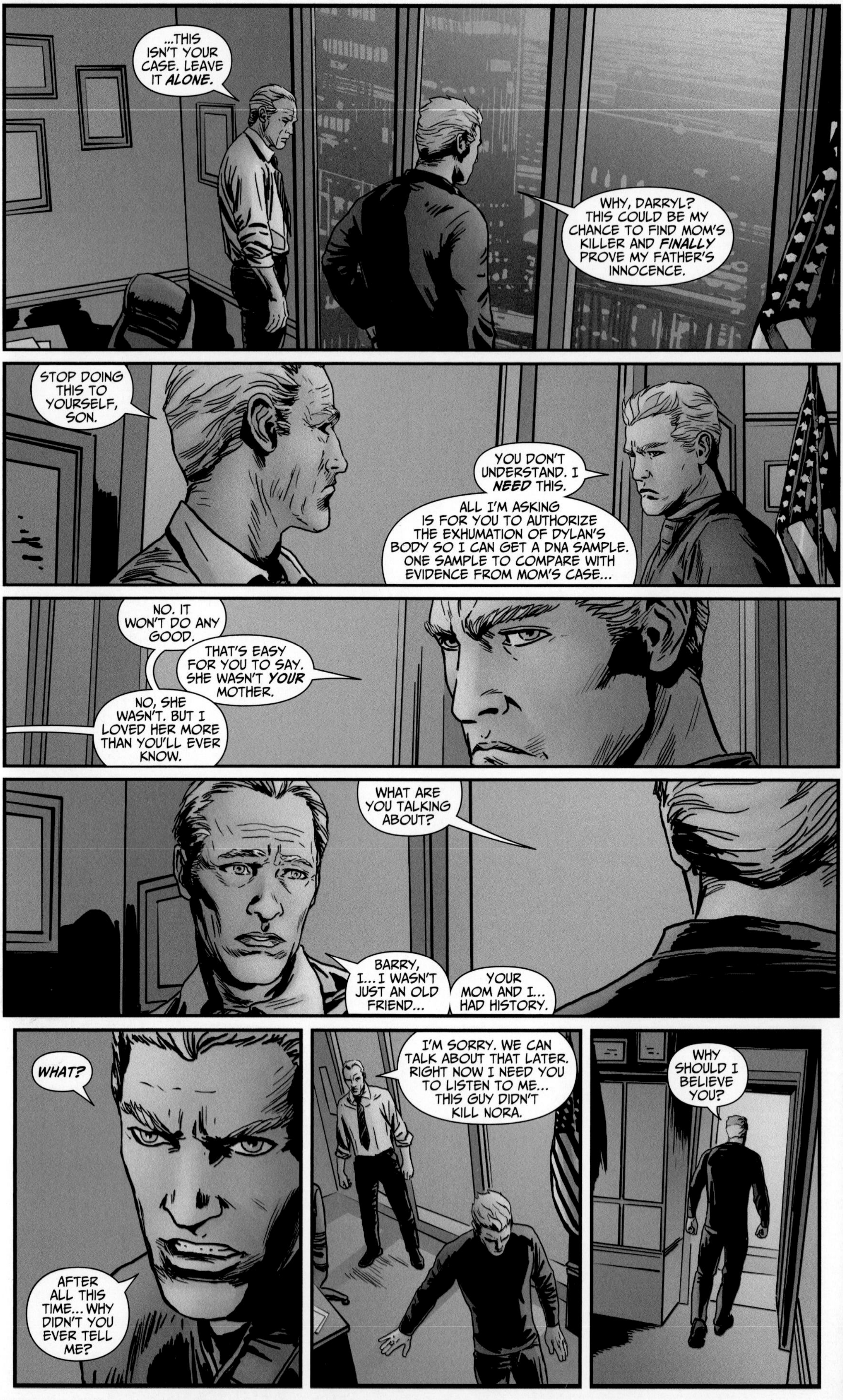
...THIS ISN'T YOUR CASE. LEAVE IT *ALONE.*
WHY, DARRYL? THIS COULD BE MY CHANCE TO FIND MOM'S KILLER AND *FINALLY* PROVE MY FATHER'S INNOCENCE.
STOP DOING THIS TO YOURSELF, SON.
YOU DON'T UNDERSTAND. I *NEED* THIS.
ALL I'M ASKING IS FOR YOU TO AUTHORIZE THE EXHUMATION OF DYLAN'S BODY SO I CAN GET A DNA SAMPLE. ONE SAMPLE TO COMPARE WITH EVIDENCE FROM MOM'S CASE...
NO. IT WON'T DO ANY GOOD.
THAT'S EASY FOR YOU TO SAY. SHE WASN'T *YOUR* MOTHER.
NO, SHE WASN'T. BUT I LOVED HER MORE THAN YOU'LL EVER KNOW.
WHAT ARE YOU TALKING ABOUT?
BARRY, I... I WASN'T JUST AN OLD FRIEND...
YOUR MOM AND I... HAD HISTORY.
WHAT?
AFTER ALL THIS TIME... WHY DIDN'T YOU EVER TELL ME?
I'M SORRY. WE CAN TALK ABOUT THAT LATER. RIGHT NOW I NEED YOU TO LISTEN TO ME... THIS GUY DIDN'T KILL NORA.
WHY SHOULD I BELIEVE YOU?

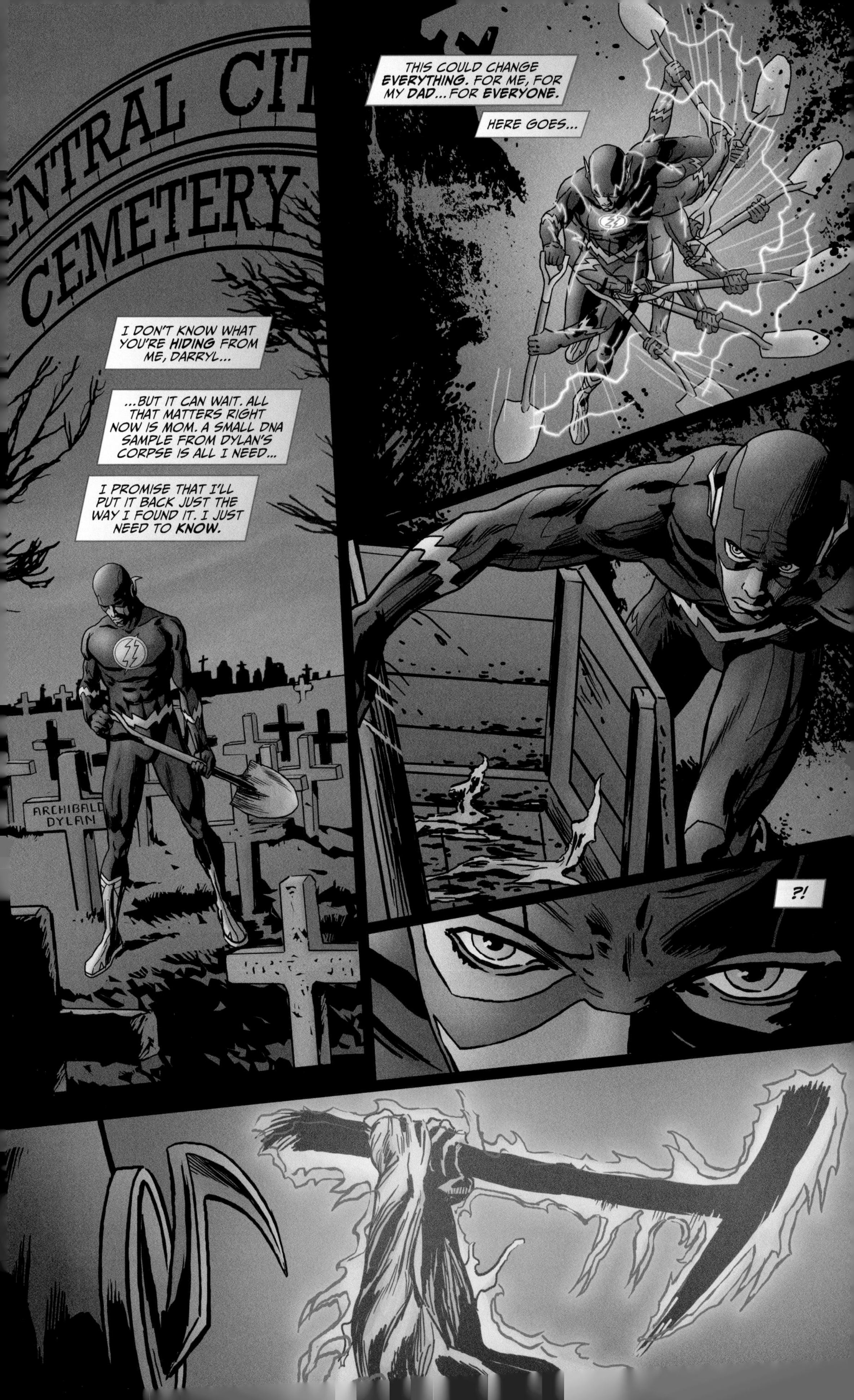

CENTRAL CIT
CEMETERY
I DON'T KNOW WHAT YOU'RE HIDING FROM ME, DARRYL...
...BUT IT CAN WAIT. ALL THAT MATTERS RIGHT NOW IS MOM. A SMALL DNA SAMPLE FROM DYLAN'S CORPSE IS ALL I NEED...
I PROMISE THAT I'LL PUT IT BACK JUST THE WAY I FOUND IT. I JUST NEED TO KNOW.
ARCHIBALD DYLAN
THIS COULD CHANGE EVERYTHING. FOR ME, FOR MY DAD... FOR EVERYONE.
HERE GOES...
?!

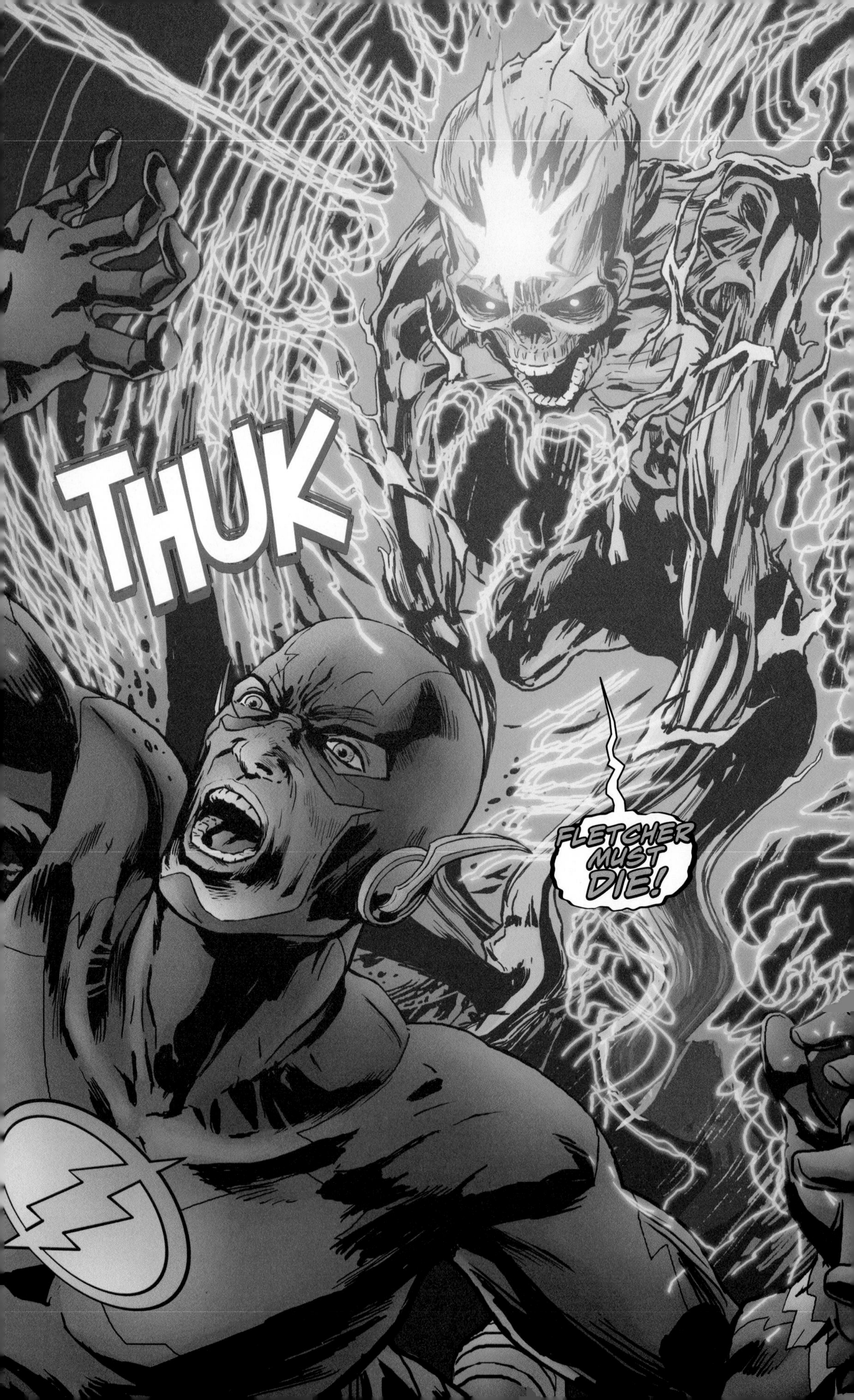
THUK
FLETCHER MUST DIE!

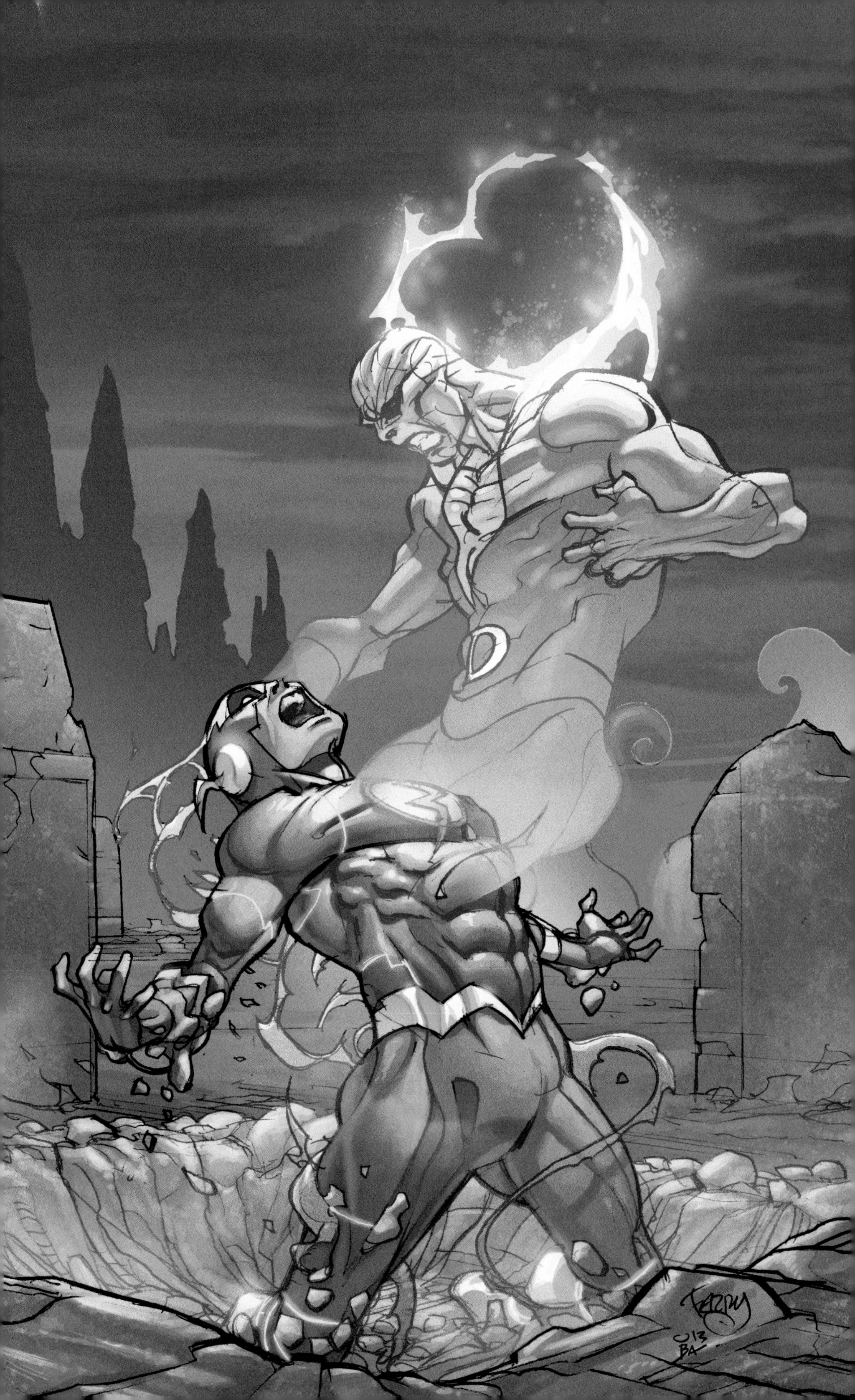

BRIAN BUCCELLATO writers PATRICK ZIRCHER artist cover art by PASQUAL FERRY & BRAD ANDERSON

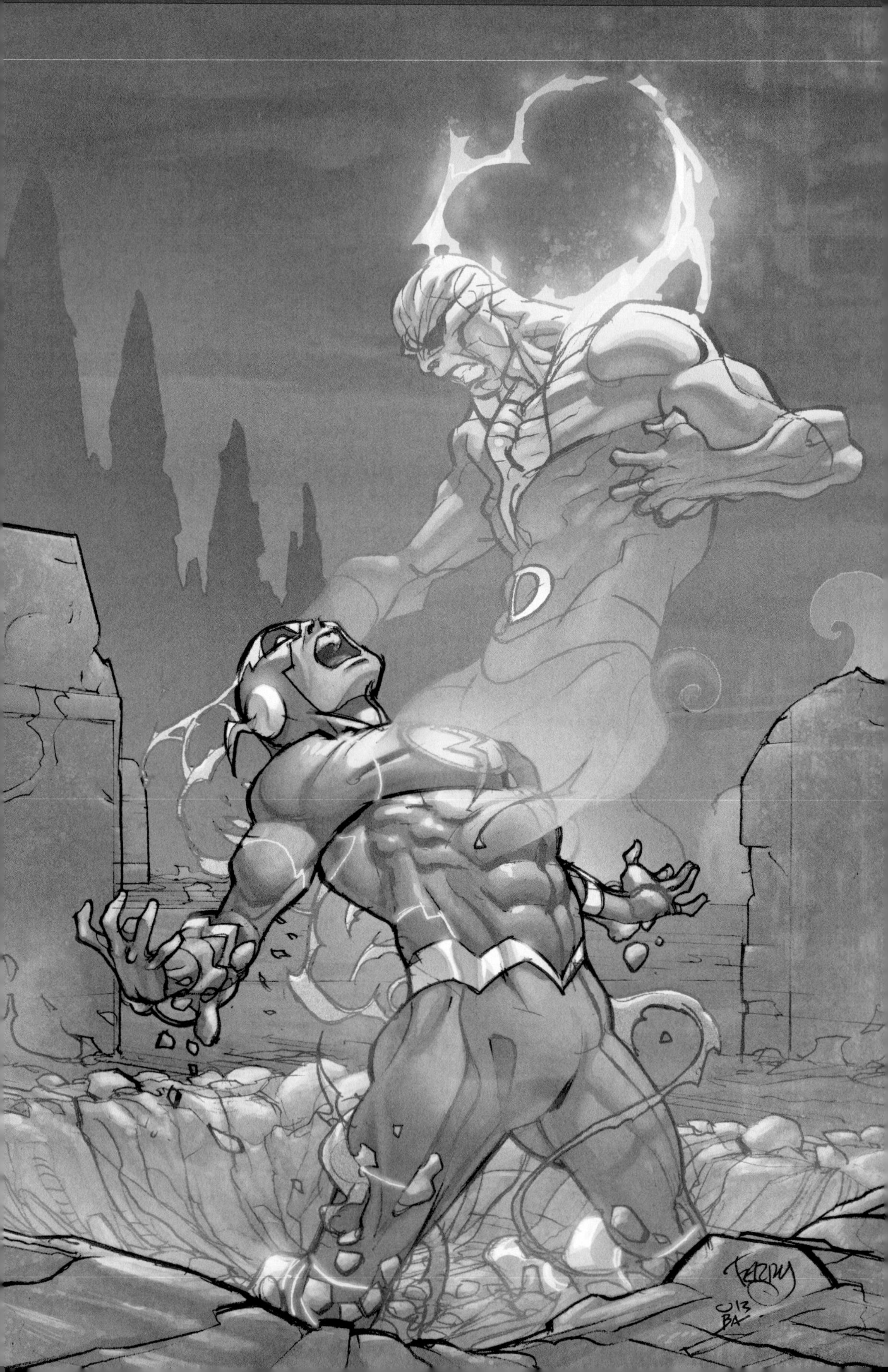

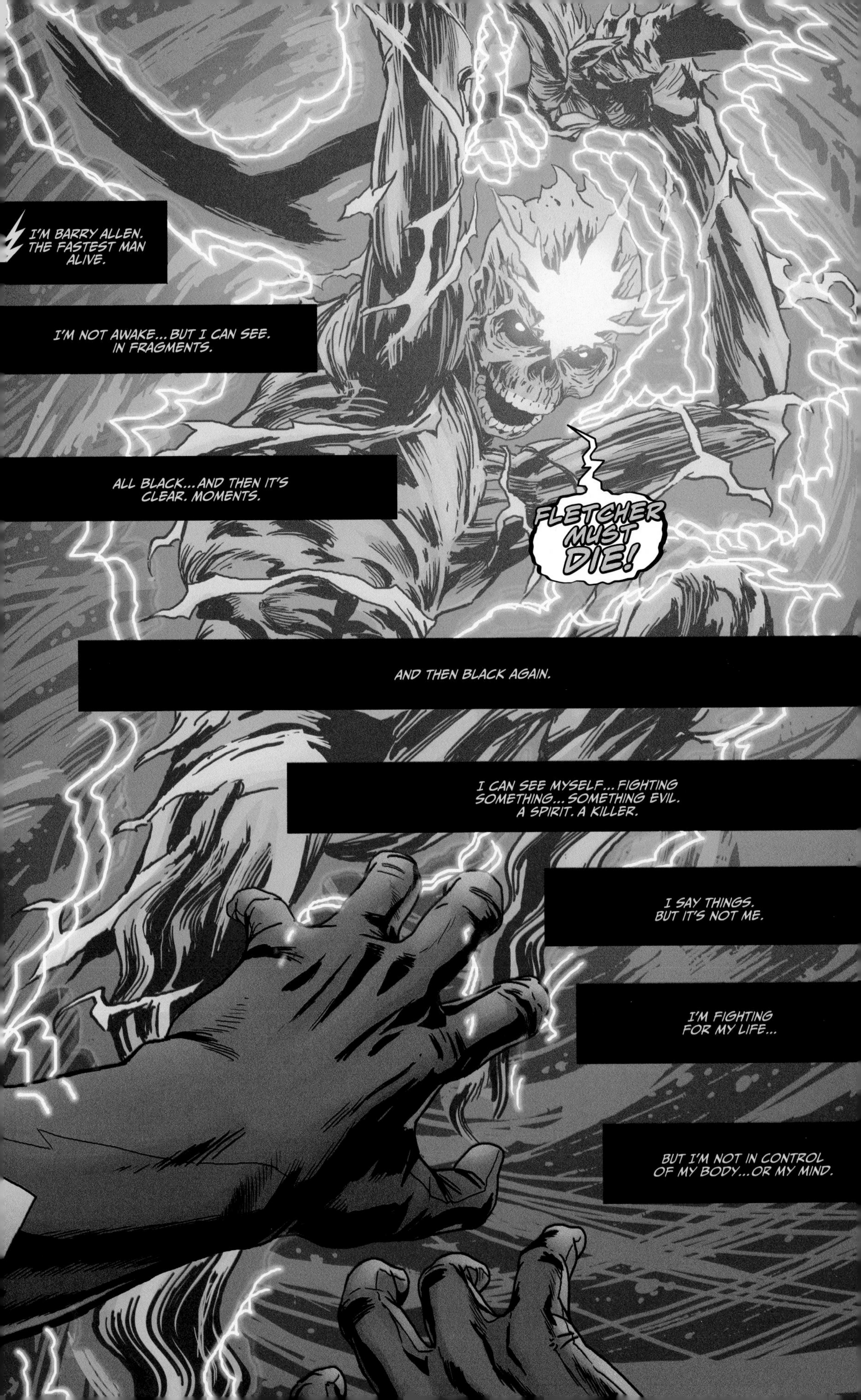
I'M BARRY ALLEN. THE FASTEST MAN ALIVE.
I'M NOT AWAKE... BUT I CAN SEE. IN FRAGMENTS.
ALL BLACK... AND THEN IT'S CLEAR. MOMENTS.
FLETCHER MUST DIE!
AND THEN BLACK AGAIN.
I CAN SEE MYSELF... FIGHTING SOMETHING... SOMETHING EVIL. A SPIRIT. A KILLER.
I SAY THINGS. BUT IT'S NOT ME.
I'M FIGHTING FOR MY LIFE...
BUT I'M NOT IN CONTROL OF MY BODY... OR MY MIND.

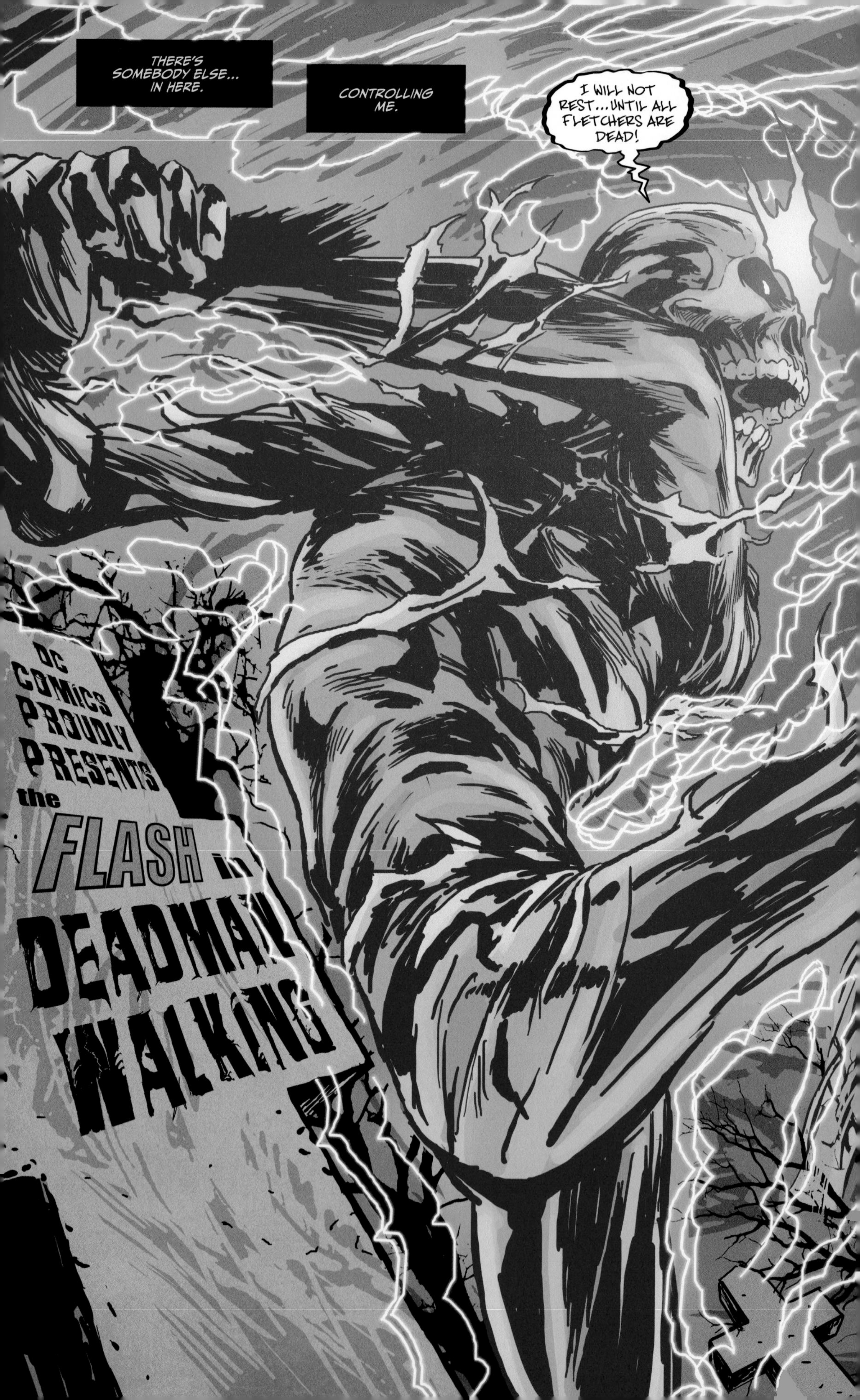
THERE'S SOMEBODY ELSE... IN HERE.
CONTROLLING ME.
I WILL NOT REST...UNTIL ALL FLETCHERS ARE DEAD!
DC COMICS PROUDLY PRESENTS
the FLASH in
DEADMAN WALKING

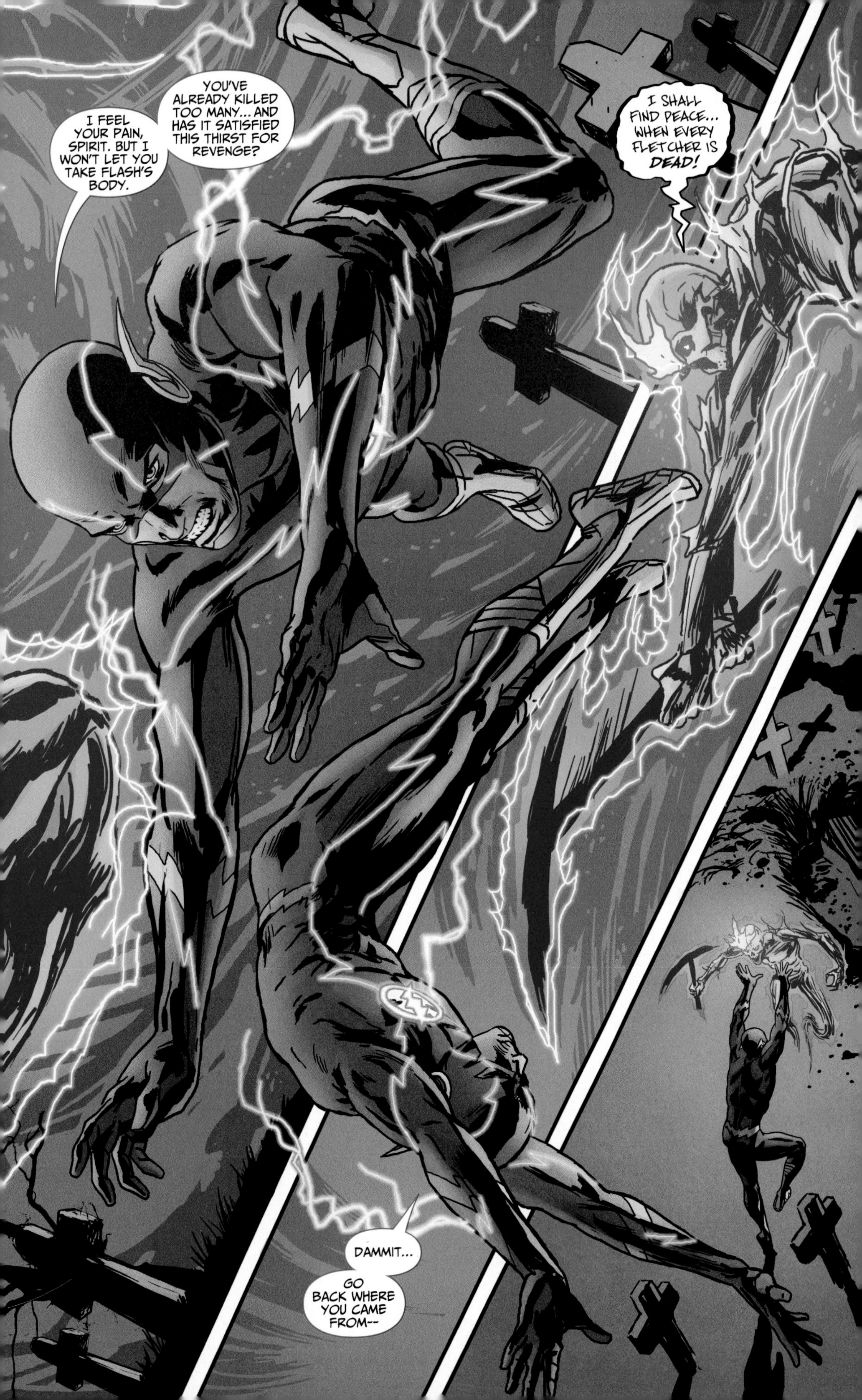
I FEEL YOUR PAIN, SPIRIT. BUT I WON'T LET YOU TAKE FLASH'S BODY.
YOU'VE ALREADY KILLED TOO MANY... AND HAS IT SATISFIED THIS THIRST FOR REVENGE?
I SHALL FIND PEACE... WHEN EVERY FLETCHER IS DEAD!
DAMMIT...
GO BACK WHERE YOU CAME FROM--

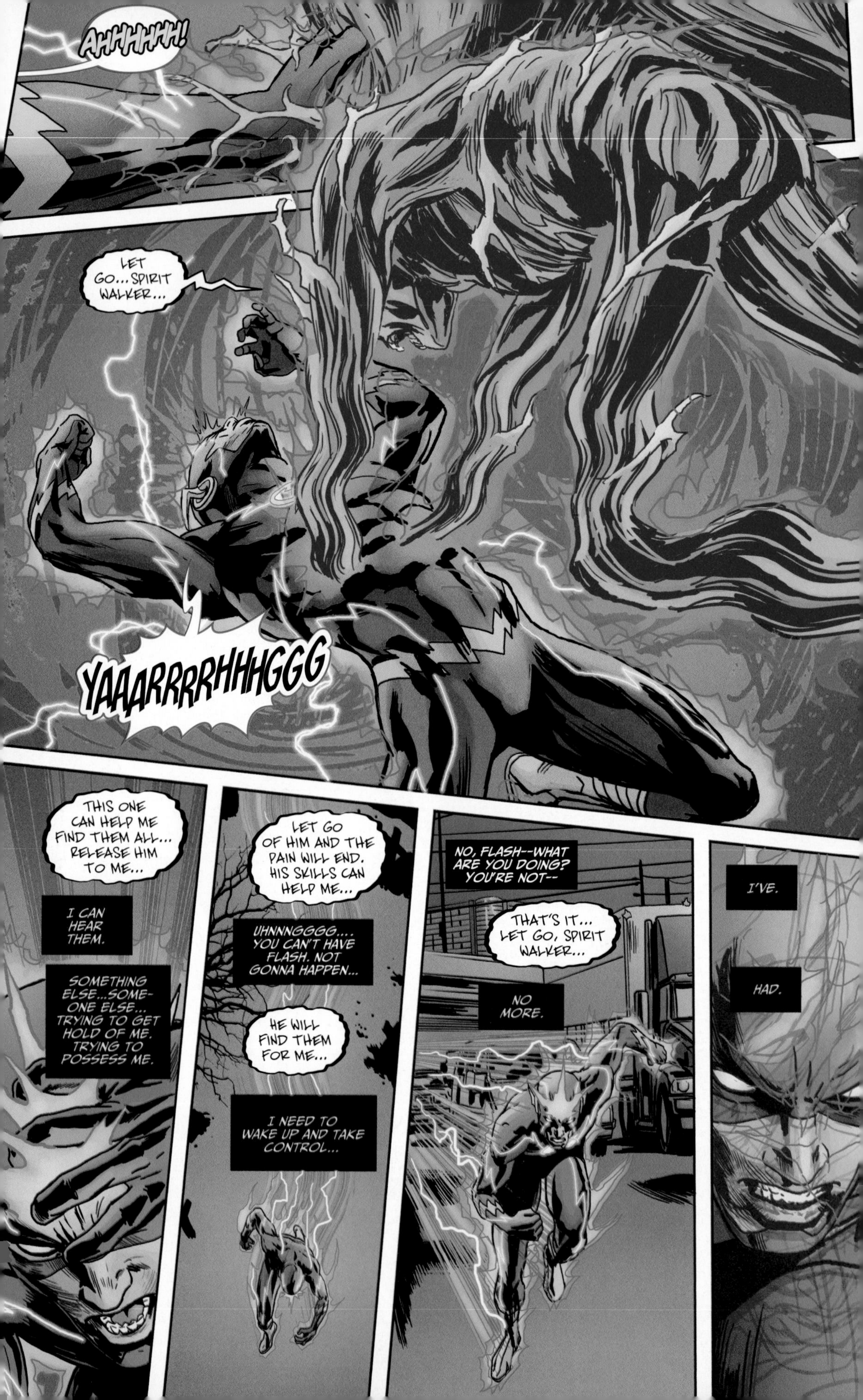
AHHHHHH!
LET GO... SPIRIT WALKER...
YAAARRRRHHHGGG
THIS ONE CAN HELP ME FIND THEM ALL... RELEASE HIM TO ME...
I CAN HEAR THEM.
SOMETHING ELSE...SOME-ONE ELSE... TRYING TO GET HOLD OF ME. TRYING TO POSSESS ME.
LET GO OF HIM AND THE PAIN WILL END. HIS SKILLS CAN HELP ME...
UHNNNGGGG.... YOU CAN'T HAVE FLASH. NOT GONNA HAPPEN...
HE WILL FIND THEM FOR ME...
I NEED TO WAKE UP AND TAKE CONTROL...
NO, FLASH--WHAT ARE YOU DOING? YOU'RE NOT--
THAT'S IT... LET GO, SPIRIT WALKER...
NO MORE.
I'VE.
HAD.

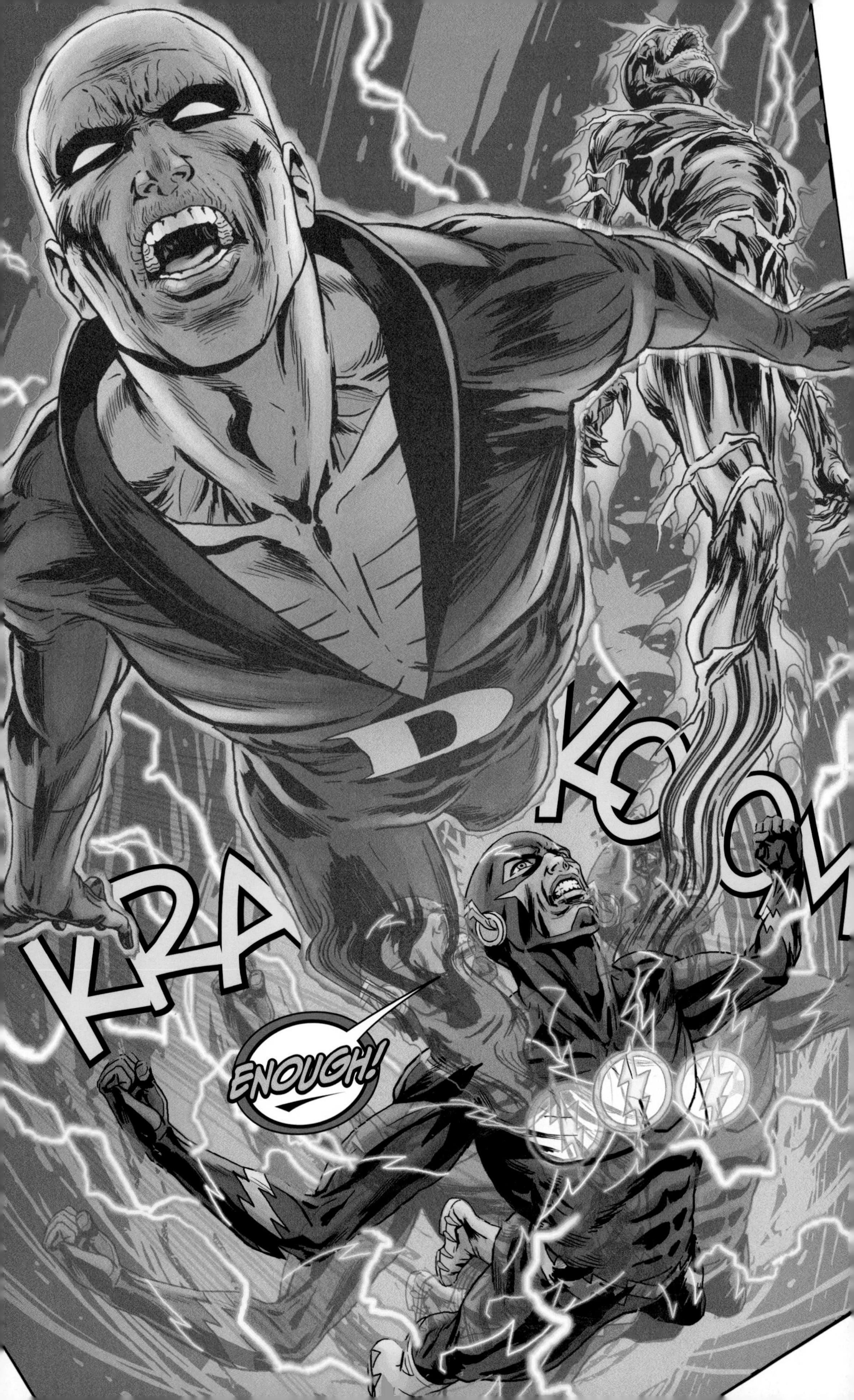

KRA KOOOM
ENOUGH!

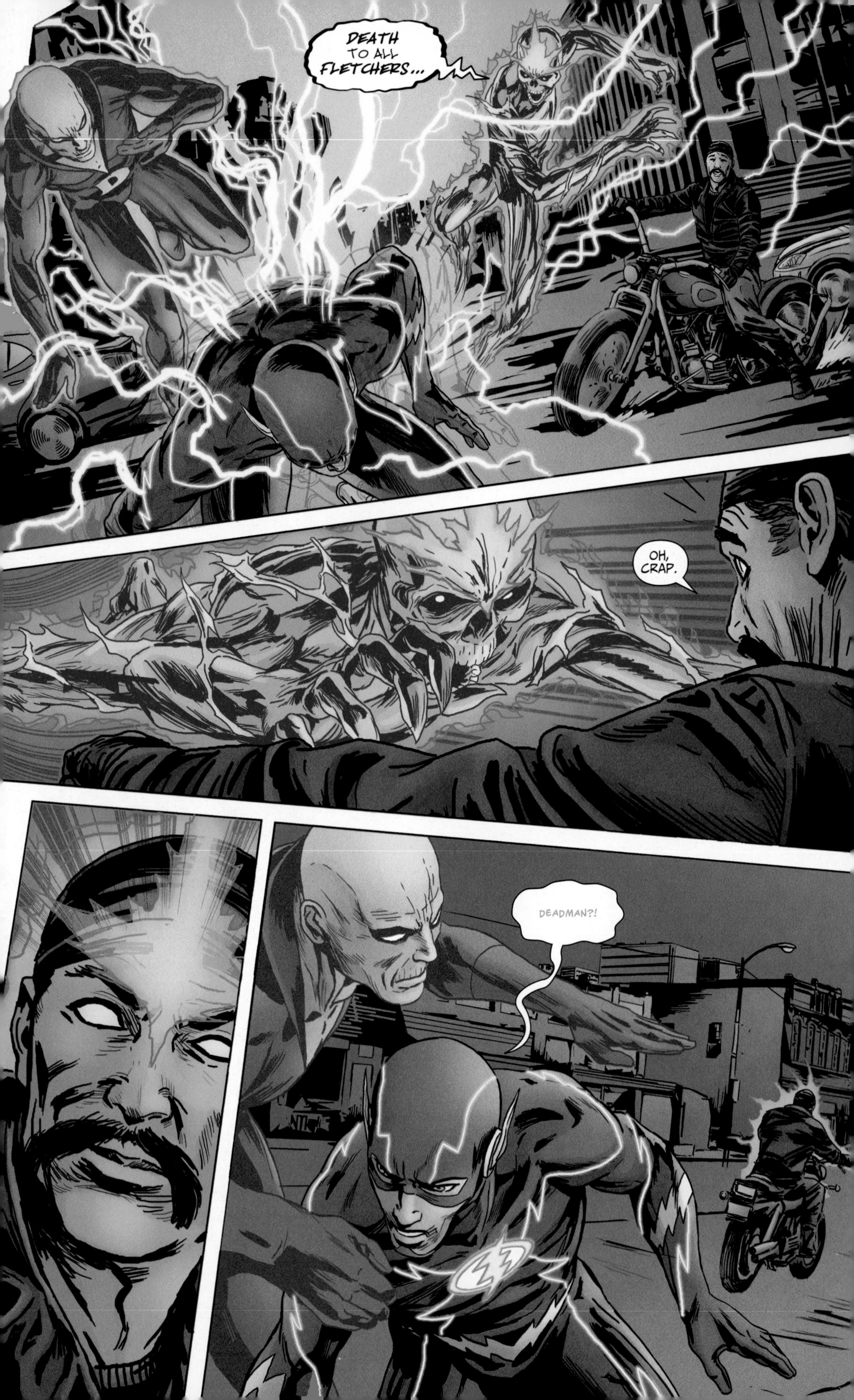
DEATH TO ALL FLETCHERS...
OH, CRAP.
DEADMAN?!

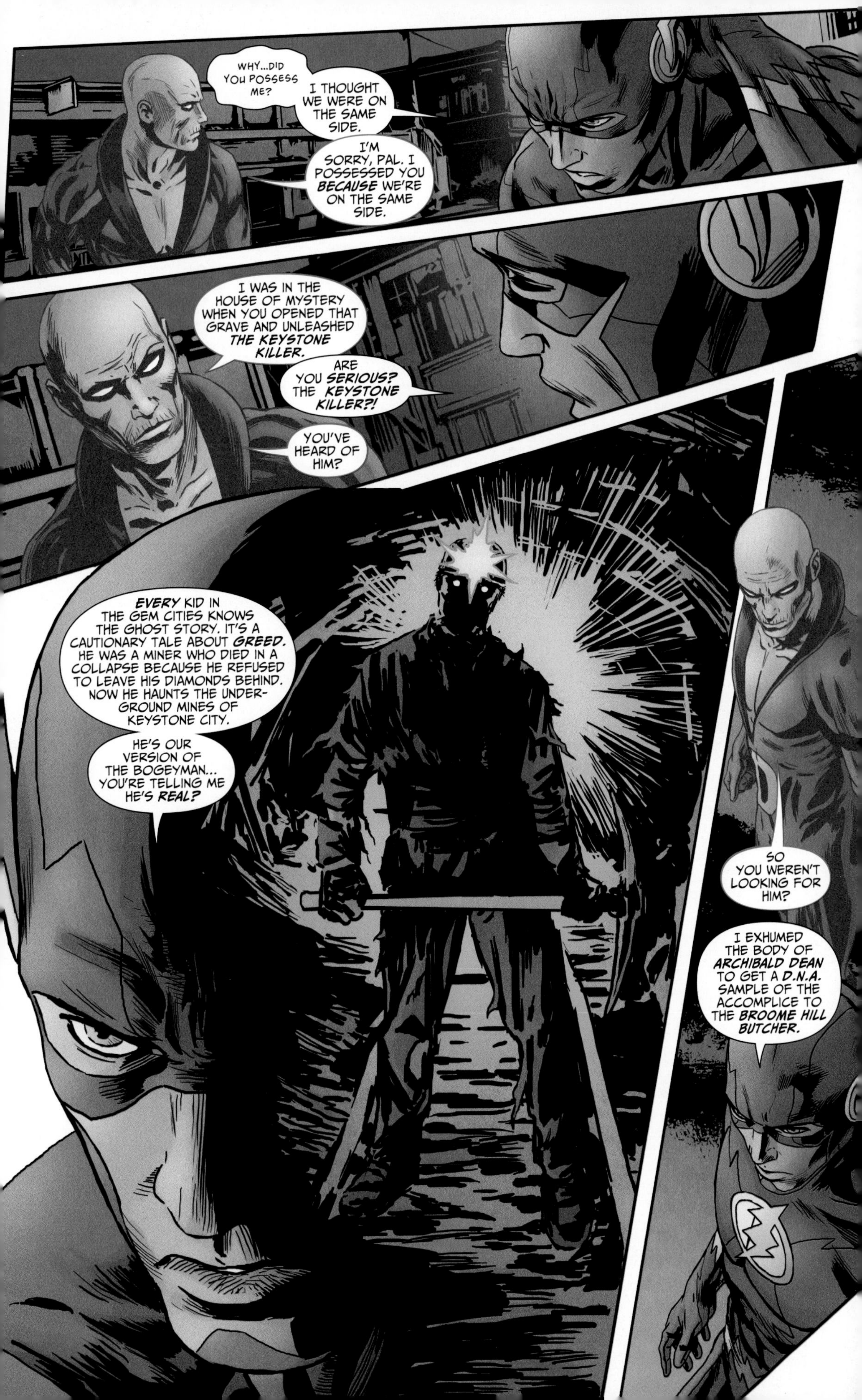
WHY...DID YOU POSSESS ME?
I THOUGHT WE WERE ON THE SAME SIDE.
I'M SORRY, PAL. I POSSESSED YOU *BECAUSE* WE'RE ON THE SAME SIDE.
I WAS IN THE HOUSE OF MYSTERY WHEN YOU OPENED THAT GRAVE AND UNLEASHED *THE KEYSTONE KILLER.*
ARE YOU *SERIOUS?* THE *KEYSTONE KILLER?!*
YOU'VE HEARD OF HIM?
EVERY KID IN THE GEM CITIES KNOWS THE GHOST STORY. IT'S A CAUTIONARY TALE ABOUT *GREED.* HE WAS A MINER WHO DIED IN A COLLAPSE BECAUSE HE REFUSED TO LEAVE HIS DIAMONDS BEHIND. NOW HE HAUNTS THE UNDER-GROUND MINES OF KEYSTONE CITY.
HE'S OUR VERSION OF THE BOGEYMAN... YOU'RE TELLING ME HE'S *REAL?*
SO YOU WEREN'T LOOKING FOR HIM?
I EXHUMED THE BODY OF *ARCHIBALD DEAN* TO GET A *D.N.A.* SAMPLE OF THE ACCOMPLICE TO THE *BROOME HILL BUTCHER.*

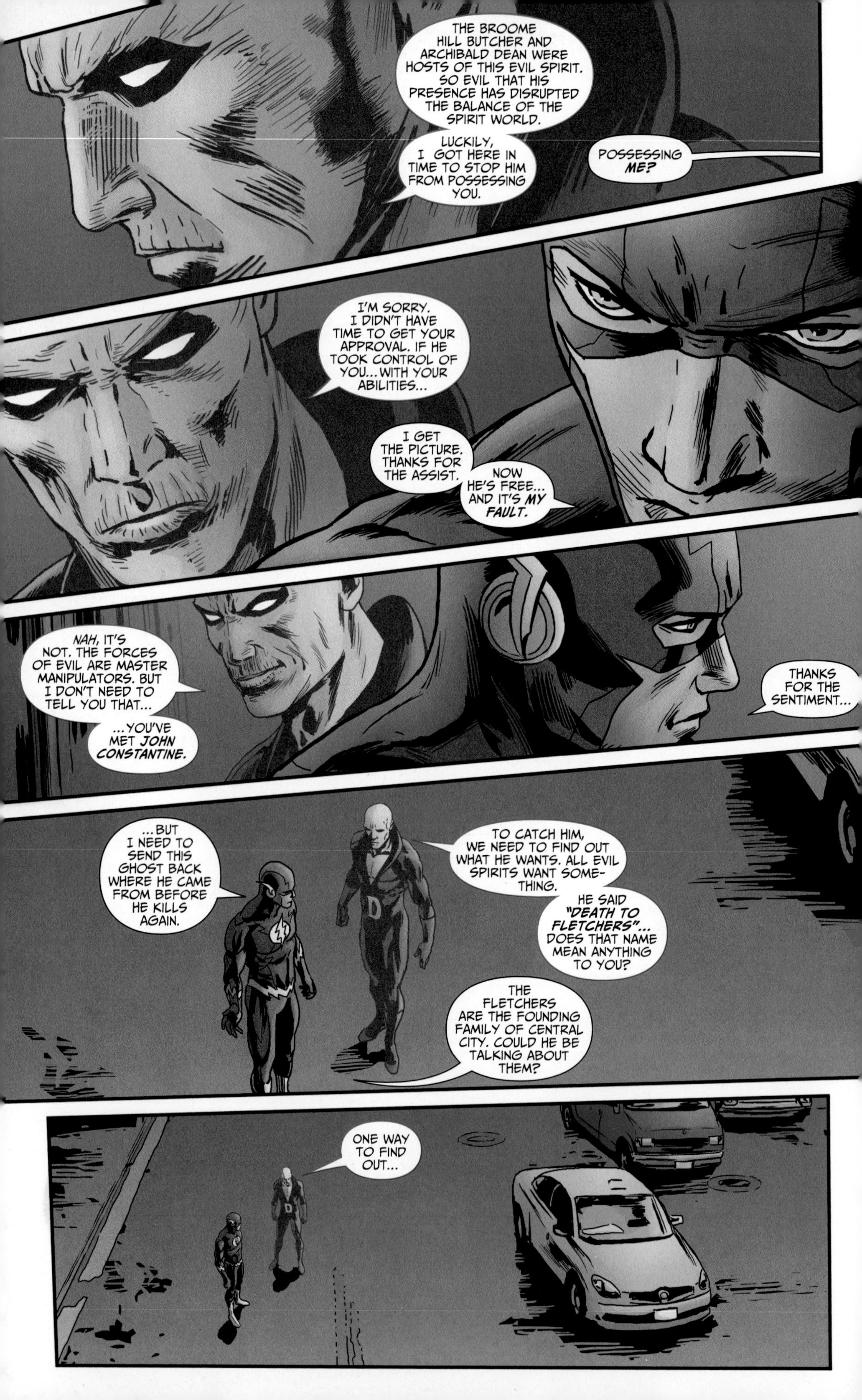
THE BROOME HILL BUTCHER AND ARCHIBALD DEAN WERE HOSTS OF THIS EVIL SPIRIT. SO EVIL THAT HIS PRESENCE HAS DISRUPTED THE BALANCE OF THE SPIRIT WORLD.
LUCKILY, I GOT HERE IN TIME TO STOP HIM FROM POSSESSING YOU.
POSSESSING *ME?*
I'M SORRY. I DIDN'T HAVE TIME TO GET YOUR APPROVAL. IF HE TOOK CONTROL OF YOU...WITH YOUR ABILITIES...
I GET THE PICTURE. THANKS FOR THE ASSIST.
NOW HE'S FREE... AND IT'S *MY FAULT.*
NAH, IT'S NOT. THE FORCES OF EVIL ARE MASTER MANIPULATORS. BUT I DON'T NEED TO TELL YOU THAT...
...YOU'VE MET *JOHN CONSTANTINE.*
THANKS FOR THE SENTIMENT...
...BUT I NEED TO SEND THIS GHOST BACK WHERE HE CAME FROM BEFORE HE KILLS AGAIN.
TO CATCH HIM, WE NEED TO FIND OUT WHAT HE WANTS. ALL EVIL SPIRITS WANT SOME-THING.
HE SAID *"DEATH TO FLETCHERS"*... DOES THAT NAME MEAN ANYTHING TO YOU?
THE FLETCHERS ARE THE FOUNDING FAMILY OF CENTRAL CITY. COULD HE BE TALKING ABOUT THEM?
ONE WAY TO FIND OUT...

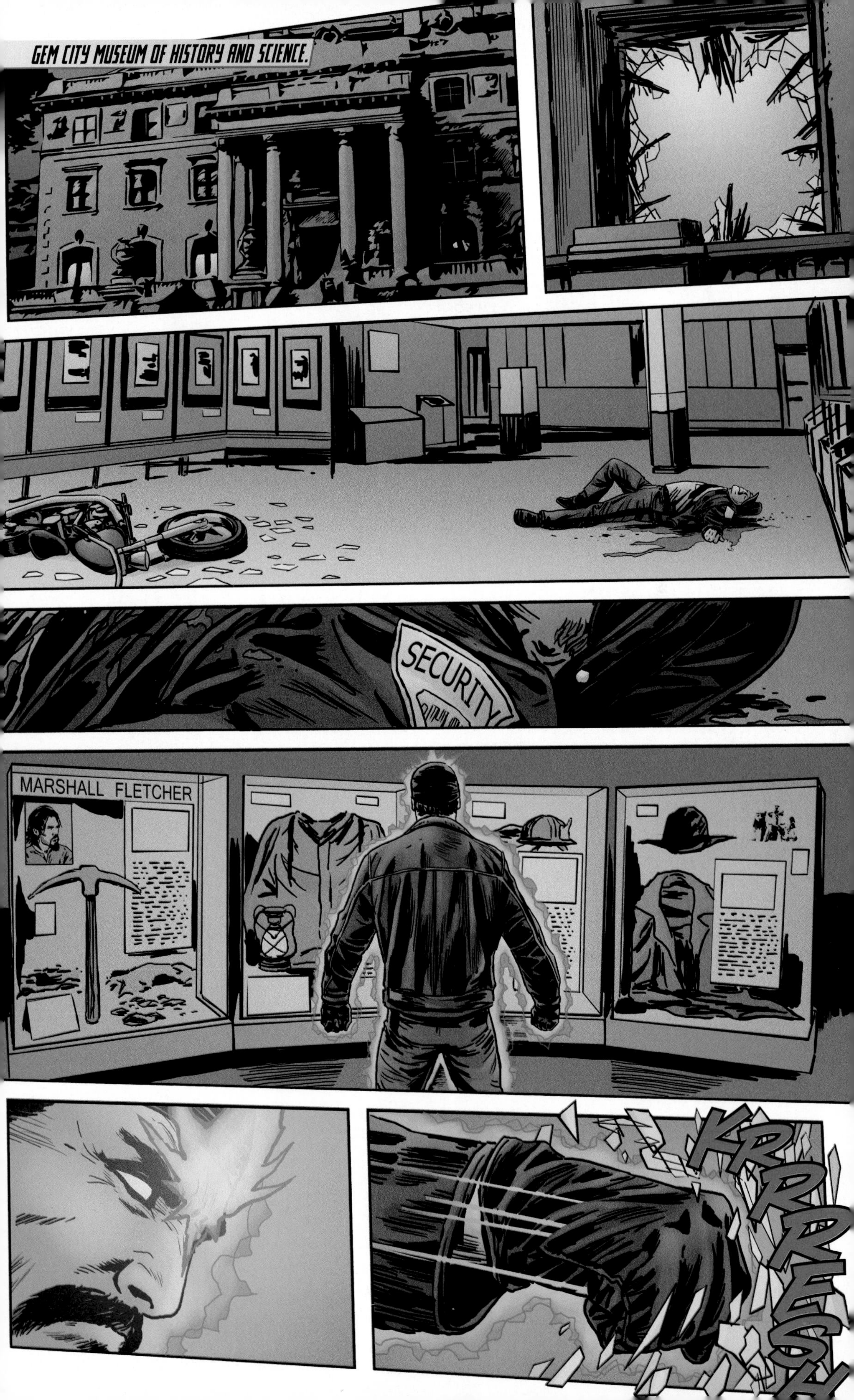
GEM CITY MUSEUM OF HISTORY AND SCIENCE.
SECURITY
MARSHALL FLETCHER
KRRRESH

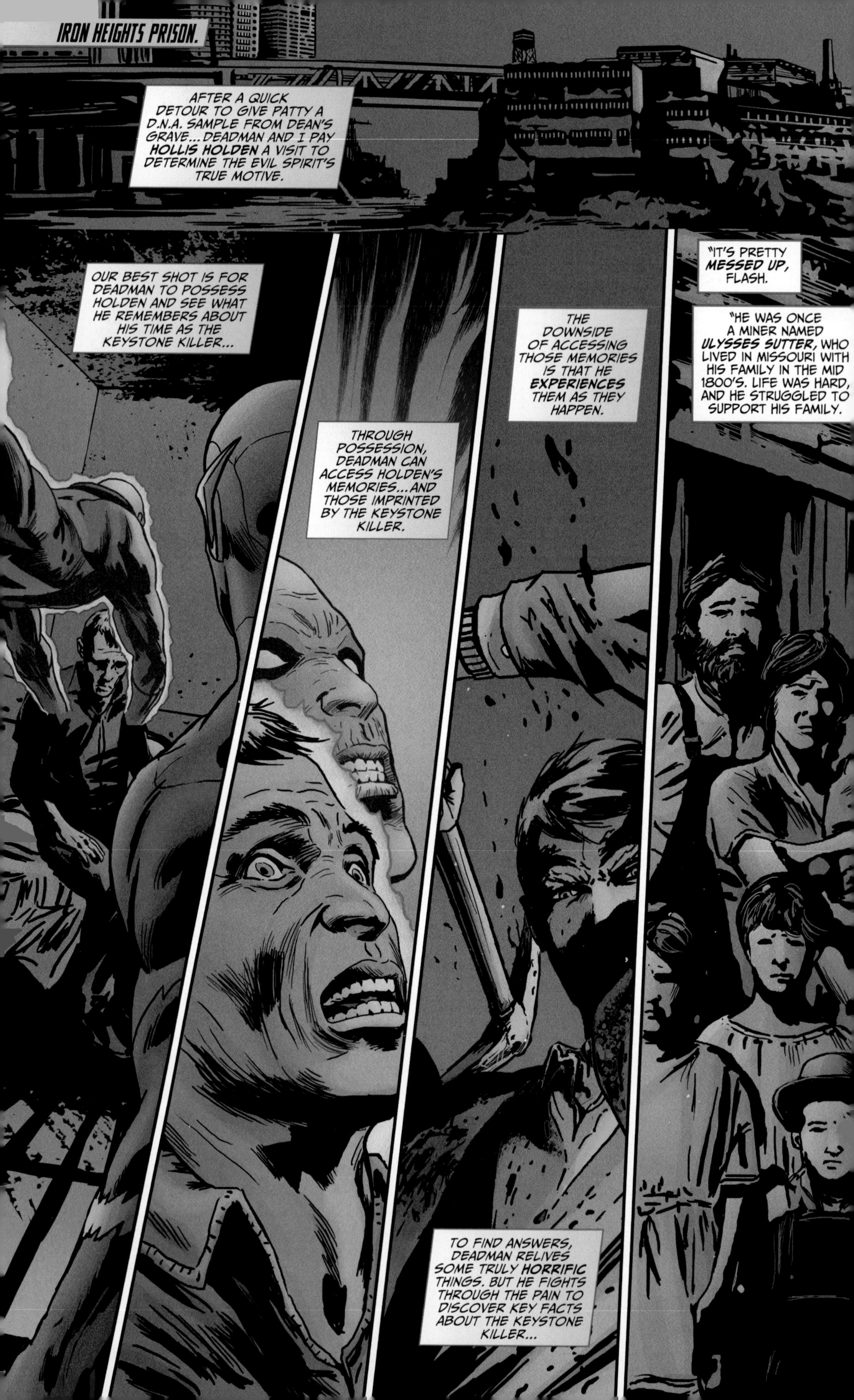
IRON HEIGHTS PRISON.
AFTER A QUICK DETOUR TO GIVE PATTY A D.N.A. SAMPLE FROM DEAN'S GRAVE... DEADMAN AND I PAY HOLLIS HOLDEN A VISIT TO DETERMINE THE EVIL SPIRIT'S TRUE MOTIVE.
OUR BEST SHOT IS FOR DEADMAN TO POSSESS HOLDEN AND SEE WHAT HE REMEMBERS ABOUT HIS TIME AS THE KEYSTONE KILLER...
THROUGH POSSESSION, DEADMAN CAN ACCESS HOLDEN'S MEMORIES... AND THOSE IMPRINTED BY THE KEYSTONE KILLER.
THE DOWNSIDE OF ACCESSING THOSE MEMORIES IS THAT HE EXPERIENCES THEM AS THEY HAPPEN.
TO FIND ANSWERS, DEADMAN RELIVES SOME TRULY HORRIFIC THINGS. BUT HE FIGHTS THROUGH THE PAIN TO DISCOVER KEY FACTS ABOUT THE KEYSTONE KILLER...
"IT'S PRETTY MESSED UP, FLASH.
"HE WAS ONCE A MINER NAMED ULYSSES SUTTER, WHO LIVED IN MISSOURI WITH HIS FAMILY IN THE MID 1800'S. LIFE WAS HARD, AND HE STRUGGLED TO SUPPORT HIS FAMILY.

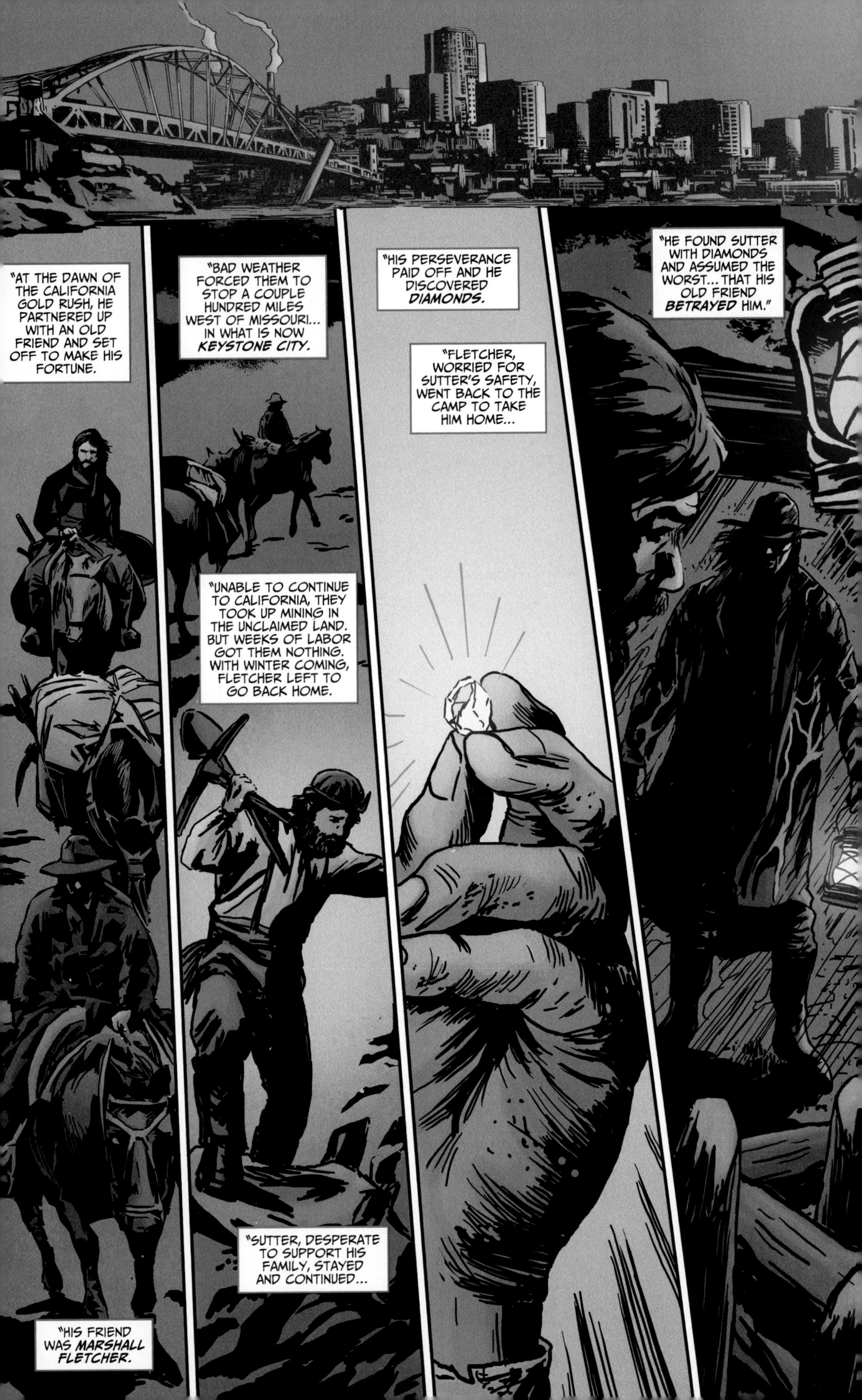
"AT THE DAWN OF THE CALIFORNIA GOLD RUSH, HE PARTNERED UP WITH AN OLD FRIEND AND SET OFF TO MAKE HIS FORTUNE.
"HIS FRIEND WAS MARSHALL FLETCHER.
"BAD WEATHER FORCED THEM TO STOP A COUPLE HUNDRED MILES WEST OF MISSOURI... IN WHAT IS NOW KEYSTONE CITY.
"UNABLE TO CONTINUE TO CALIFORNIA, THEY TOOK UP MINING IN THE UNCLAIMED LAND. BUT WEEKS OF LABOR GOT THEM NOTHING. WITH WINTER COMING, FLETCHER LEFT TO GO BACK HOME.
"SUTTER, DESPERATE TO SUPPORT HIS FAMILY, STAYED AND CONTINUED...
"HIS PERSEVERANCE PAID OFF AND HE DISCOVERED DIAMONDS.
"FLETCHER, WORRIED FOR SUTTER'S SAFETY, WENT BACK TO THE CAMP TO TAKE HIM HOME...
"HE FOUND SUTTER WITH DIAMONDS AND ASSUMED THE WORST... THAT HIS OLD FRIEND BETRAYED HIM."

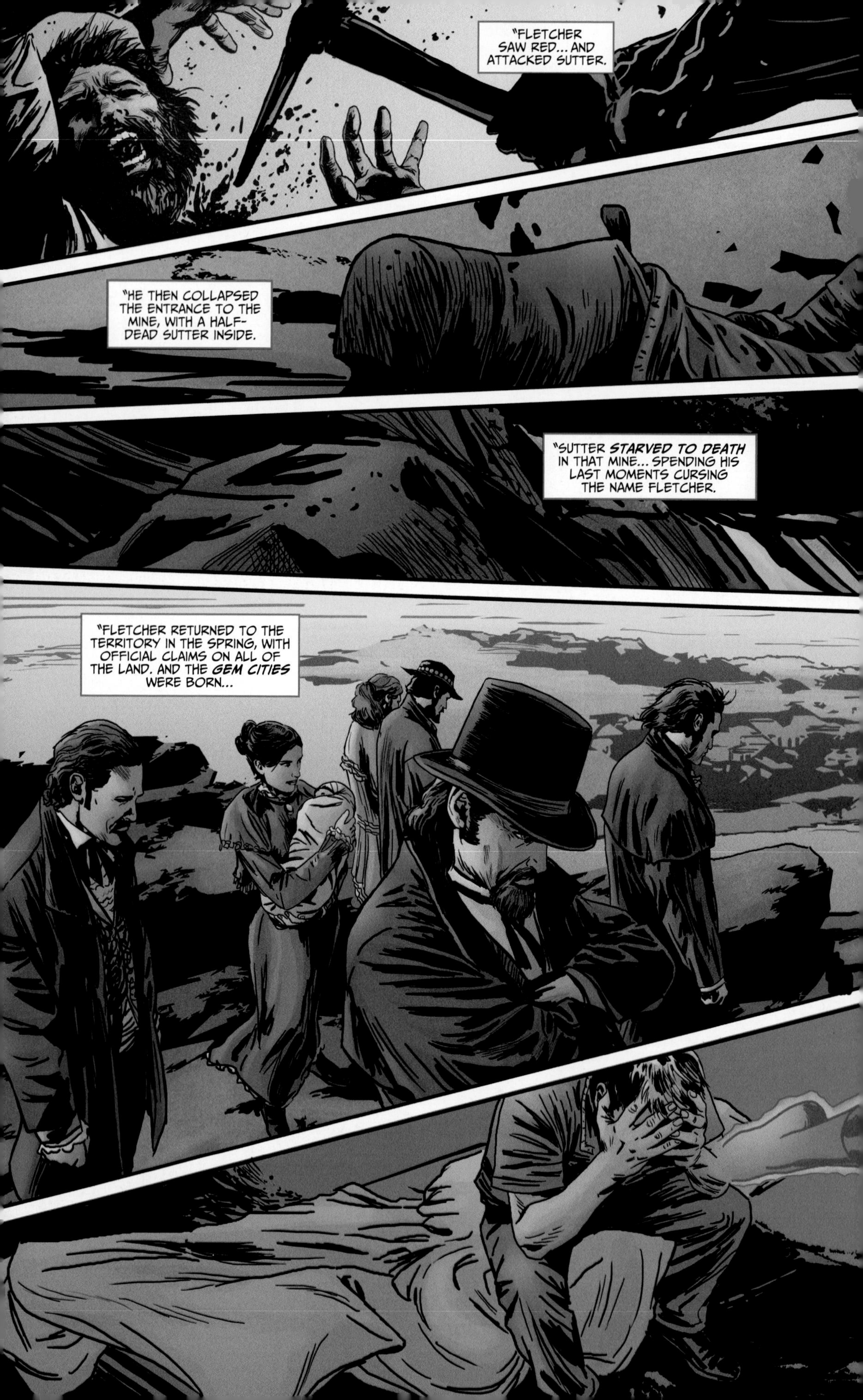
"FLETCHER SAW RED... AND ATTACKED SUTTER.
"HE THEN COLLAPSED THE ENTRANCE TO THE MINE, WITH A HALF-DEAD SUTTER INSIDE.
"SUTTER STARVED TO DEATH IN THAT MINE... SPENDING HIS LAST MOMENTS CURSING THE NAME FLETCHER.
"FLETCHER RETURNED TO THE TERRITORY IN THE SPRING, WITH OFFICIAL CLAIMS ON ALL OF THE LAND. AND THE GEM CITIES WERE BORN...

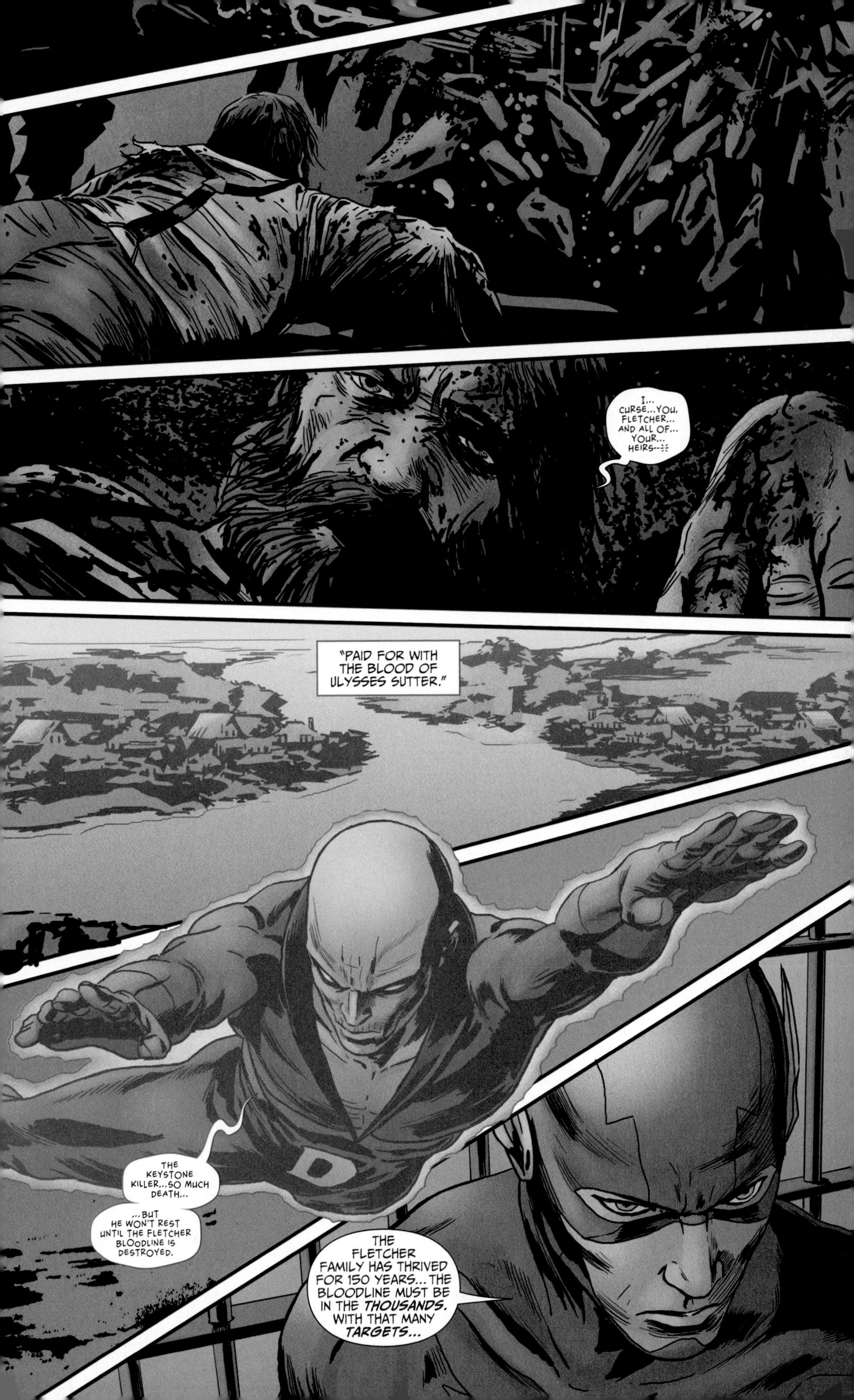
I... CURSE...YOU, FLETCHER... AND ALL OF... YOUR... HEIRS--
"PAID FOR WITH THE BLOOD OF ULYSSES SUTTER."
THE KEYSTONE KILLER...SO MUCH DEATH...
...BUT HE WON'T REST UNTIL THE FLETCHER BLOODLINE IS DESTROYED.
THE FLETCHER FAMILY HAS THRIVED FOR 150 YEARS... THE BLOODLINE MUST BE IN THE *THOUSANDS.* WITH THAT MANY *TARGETS...*

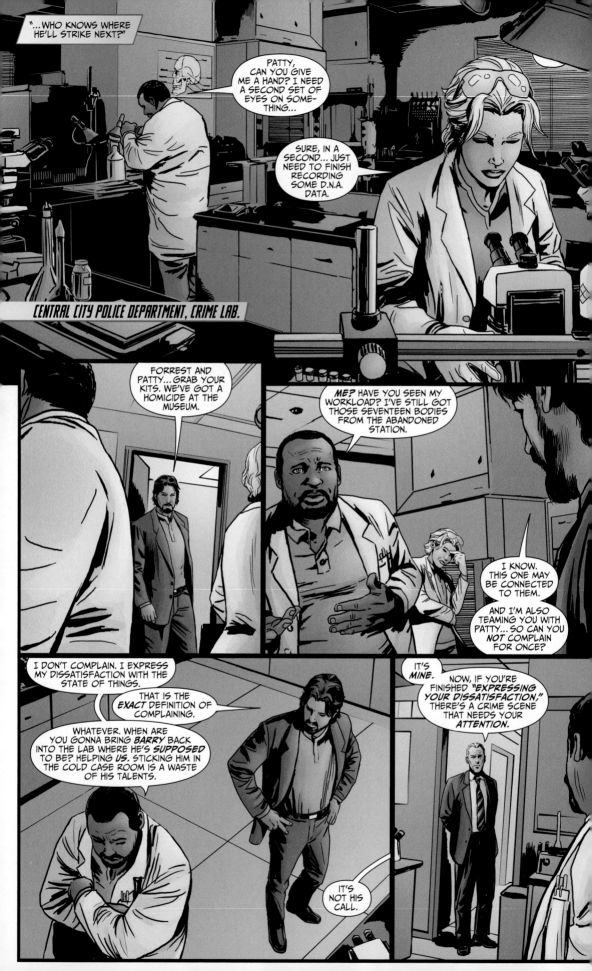

"...WHO KNOWS WHERE HE'LL STRIKE NEXT?"

PATTY, CAN YOU GIVE ME A HAND? I NEED A SECOND SET OF EYES ON SOMETHING...

SURE, IN A SECOND... JUST NEED TO FINISH RECORDING SOME D.N.A. DATA.

CENTRAL CITY POLICE DEPARTMENT, CRIME LAB.

FORREST AND PATTY... GRAB YOUR KITS. WE'VE GOT A HOMICIDE AT THE MUSEUM.

ME? HAVE YOU SEEN MY WORKLOAD? I'VE STILL GOT THOSE SEVENTEEN BODIES FROM THE ABANDONED STATION.

I KNOW. THIS ONE MAY BE CONNECTED TO THEM.

AND I'M ALSO TEAMING YOU WITH PATTY... SO CAN YOU NOT COMPLAIN FOR ONCE?

I DON'T COMPLAIN. I EXPRESS MY DISSATISFACTION WITH THE STATE OF THINGS.

THAT IS THE EXACT DEFINITION OF COMPLAINING.

WHATEVER. WHEN ARE YOU GONNA BRING BARRY BACK INTO THE LAB WHERE HE'S SUPPOSED TO BE? HELPING US. STICKING HIM IN THE COLD CASE ROOM IS A WASTE OF HIS TALENTS.

IT'S NOT HIS CALL.

IT'S MINE.

NOW, IF YOU'RE FINISHED "EXPRESSING YOUR DISSATISFACTION," THERE'S A CRIME SCENE THAT NEEDS YOUR ATTENTION.

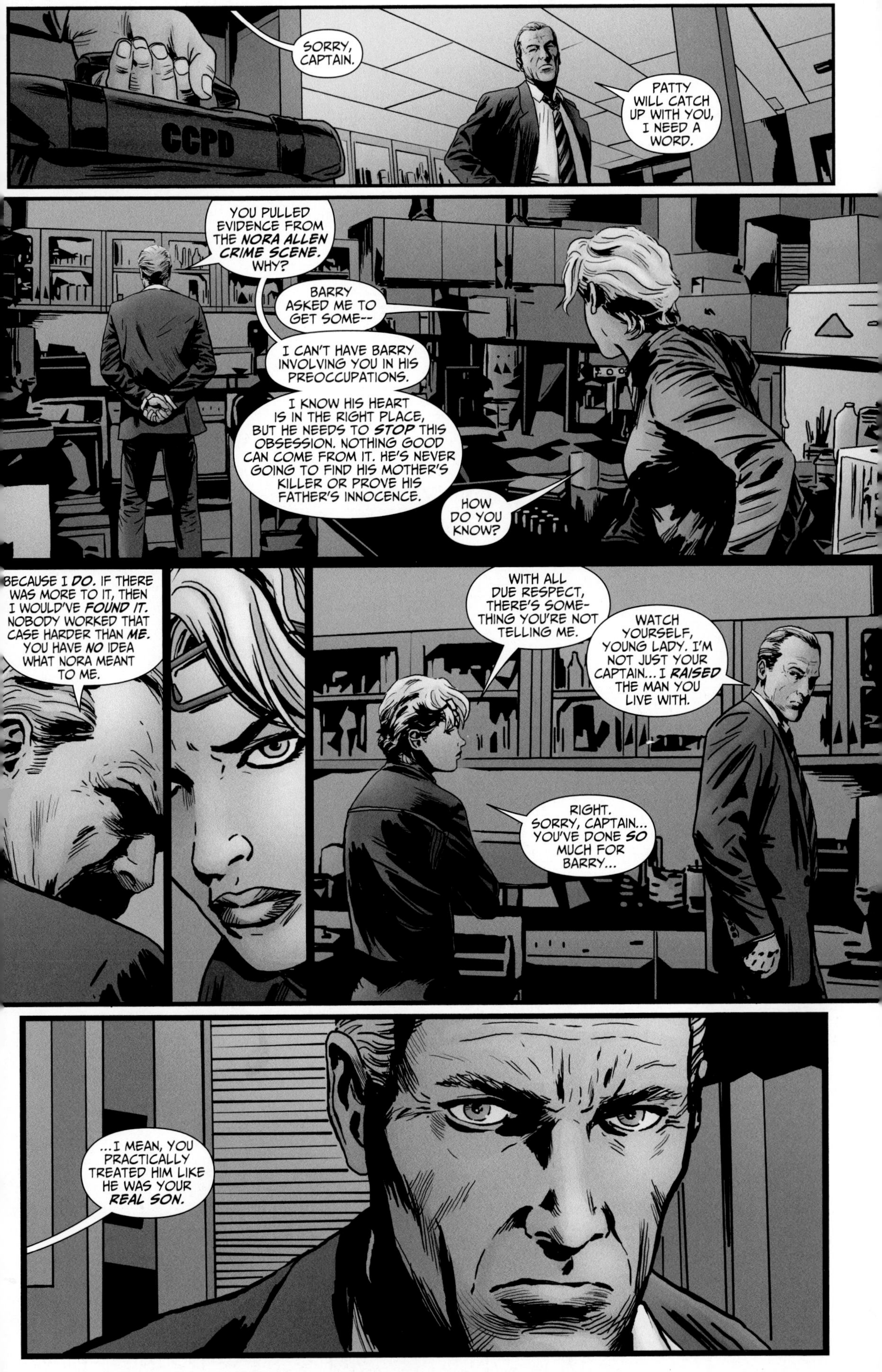

CCPD
SORRY, CAPTAIN.
PATTY WILL CATCH UP WITH YOU, I NEED A WORD.
YOU PULLED EVIDENCE FROM THE NORA ALLEN CRIME SCENE. WHY?
BARRY ASKED ME TO GET SOME--
I CAN'T HAVE BARRY INVOLVING YOU IN HIS PREOCCUPATIONS.
I KNOW HIS HEART IS IN THE RIGHT PLACE, BUT HE NEEDS TO STOP THIS OBSESSION. NOTHING GOOD CAN COME FROM IT. HE'S NEVER GOING TO FIND HIS MOTHER'S KILLER OR PROVE HIS FATHER'S INNOCENCE.
HOW DO YOU KNOW?
BECAUSE I DO. IF THERE WAS MORE TO IT, THEN I WOULD'VE FOUND IT. NOBODY WORKED THAT CASE HARDER THAN ME. YOU HAVE NO IDEA WHAT NORA MEANT TO ME.
WITH ALL DUE RESPECT, THERE'S SOME-THING YOU'RE NOT TELLING ME.
WATCH YOURSELF, YOUNG LADY. I'M NOT JUST YOUR CAPTAIN... I RAISED THE MAN YOU LIVE WITH.
RIGHT. SORRY, CAPTAIN... YOU'VE DONE SO MUCH FOR BARRY...
...I MEAN, YOU PRACTICALLY TREATED HIM LIKE HE WAS YOUR REAL SON.

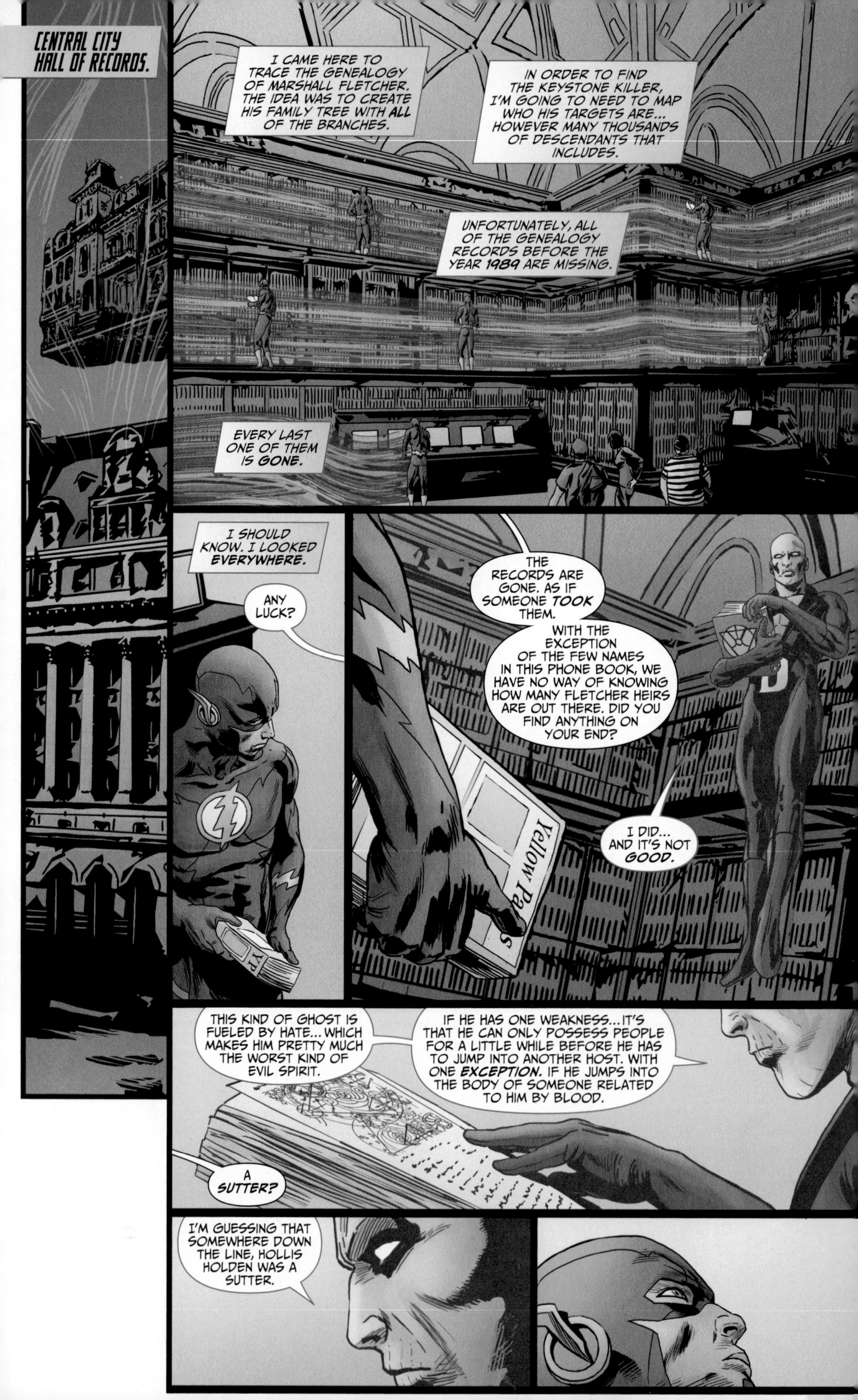
CENTRAL CITY HALL OF RECORDS.
I CAME HERE TO TRACE THE GENEALOGY OF MARSHALL FLETCHER. THE IDEA WAS TO CREATE HIS FAMILY TREE WITH ALL OF THE BRANCHES.
IN ORDER TO FIND THE KEYSTONE KILLER, I'M GOING TO NEED TO MAP WHO HIS TARGETS ARE... HOWEVER MANY THOUSANDS OF DESCENDANTS THAT INCLUDES.
UNFORTUNATELY, ALL OF THE GENEALOGY RECORDS BEFORE THE YEAR 1989 ARE MISSING.
EVERY LAST ONE OF THEM IS GONE.
I SHOULD KNOW. I LOOKED EVERYWHERE.
ANY LUCK?
THE RECORDS ARE GONE. AS IF SOMEONE TOOK THEM.
WITH THE EXCEPTION OF THE FEW NAMES IN THIS PHONE BOOK, WE HAVE NO WAY OF KNOWING HOW MANY FLETCHER HEIRS ARE OUT THERE. DID YOU FIND ANYTHING ON YOUR END?
Yellow Pages
I DID... AND IT'S NOT GOOD.
THIS KIND OF GHOST IS FUELED BY HATE... WHICH MAKES HIM PRETTY MUCH THE WORST KIND OF EVIL SPIRIT.
IF HE HAS ONE WEAKNESS... IT'S THAT HE CAN ONLY POSSESS PEOPLE FOR A LITTLE WHILE BEFORE HE HAS TO JUMP INTO ANOTHER HOST. WITH ONE EXCEPTION. IF HE JUMPS INTO THE BODY OF SOMEONE RELATED TO HIM BY BLOOD.
A SUTTER?
I'M GUESSING THAT SOMEWHERE DOWN THE LINE, HOLLIS HOLDEN WAS A SUTTER.

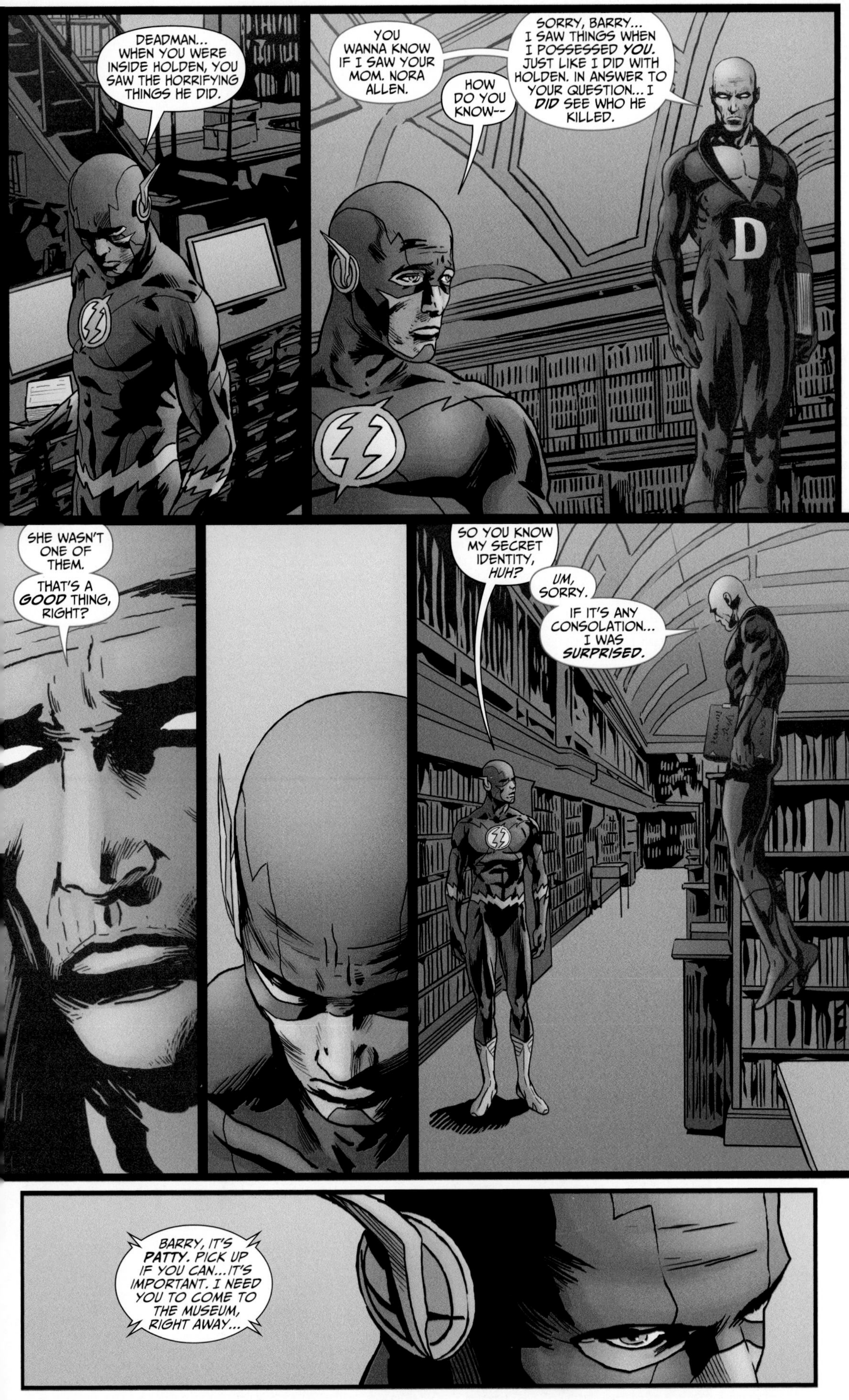
DEADMAN... WHEN YOU WERE INSIDE HOLDEN, YOU SAW THE HORRIFYING THINGS HE DID.
YOU WANNA KNOW IF I SAW YOUR MOM. NORA ALLEN.
HOW DO YOU KNOW--
SORRY, BARRY... I SAW THINGS WHEN I POSSESSED YOU. JUST LIKE I DID WITH HOLDEN. IN ANSWER TO YOUR QUESTION... I DID SEE WHO HE KILLED.
SHE WASN'T ONE OF THEM.
THAT'S A GOOD THING, RIGHT?
SO YOU KNOW MY SECRET IDENTITY, HUH?
UM, SORRY.
IF IT'S ANY CONSOLATION... I WAS SURPRISED.
BARRY, IT'S PATTY. PICK UP IF YOU CAN...IT'S IMPORTANT. I NEED YOU TO COME TO THE MUSEUM, RIGHT AWAY...

GEM CITY MUSEUM OF HISTORY AND SCIENCE.

"THE BROOME HILL BUTCHER HAS KILLED AGAIN..."

HOW IS THIS EVEN *POSSIBLE*, BARRY? COPYCAT?

I'LL TELL YOU ALL ABOUT IT LATER. RIGHT NOW, I'M TRYING TO FIGURE OUT WHERE HE WILL STRIKE NEXT...

MARSHALL FLETCHER

AND WHY THE HELMET AND AXE WERE STOLEN.

NOSTALGIA, MAYBE?

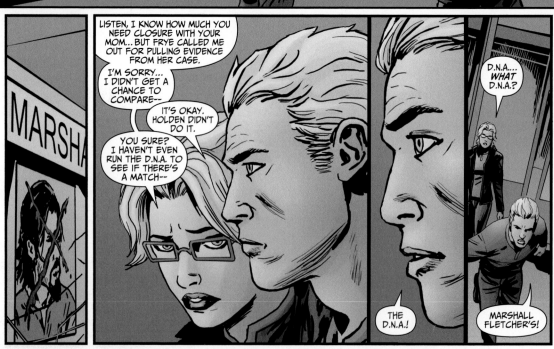

LISTEN, I KNOW HOW MUCH YOU NEED CLOSURE WITH YOUR MOM... BUT FRYE CALLED ME OUT FOR PULLING EVIDENCE FROM HER CASE.

I'M SORRY... I DIDN'T GET A CHANCE TO COMPARE--

IT'S OKAY. HOLDEN DIDN'T DO IT.

YOU SURE? I HAVEN'T EVEN RUN THE D.N.A. TO SEE IF THERE'S A MATCH--

MARSHA

D.N.A.... *WHAT* D.N.A.?

THE D.N.A.!

MARSHALL FLETCHER'S!

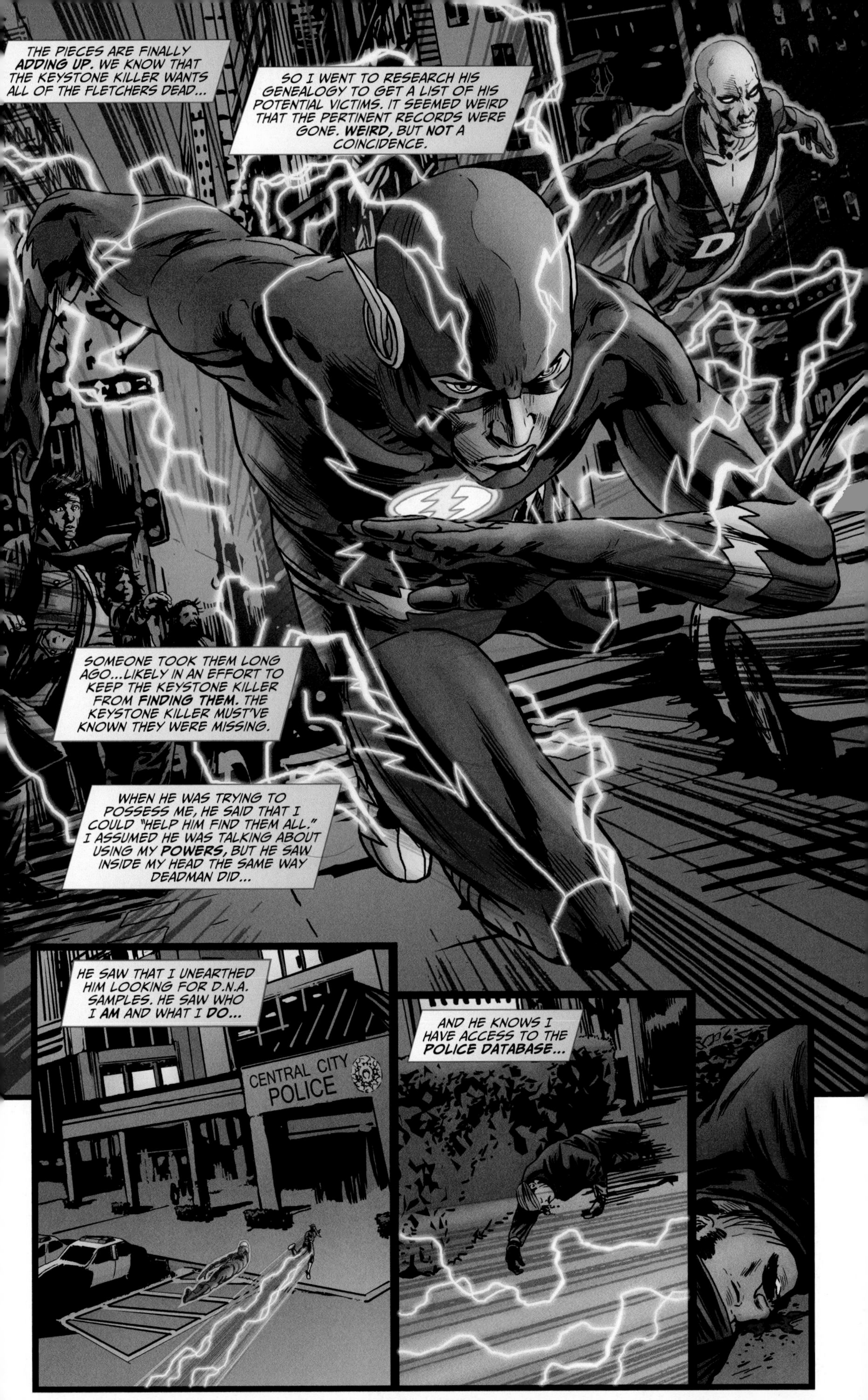
THE PIECES ARE FINALLY ADDING UP. WE KNOW THAT THE KEYSTONE KILLER WANTS ALL OF THE FLETCHERS DEAD...
SO I WENT TO RESEARCH HIS GENEALOGY TO GET A LIST OF HIS POTENTIAL VICTIMS. IT SEEMED WEIRD THAT THE PERTINENT RECORDS WERE GONE. WEIRD, BUT NOT A COINCIDENCE.
SOMEONE TOOK THEM LONG AGO...LIKELY IN AN EFFORT TO KEEP THE KEYSTONE KILLER FROM FINDING THEM. THE KEYSTONE KILLER MUST'VE KNOWN THEY WERE MISSING.
WHEN HE WAS TRYING TO POSSESS ME, HE SAID THAT I COULD "HELP HIM FIND THEM ALL." I ASSUMED HE WAS TALKING ABOUT USING MY POWERS, BUT HE SAW INSIDE MY HEAD THE SAME WAY DEADMAN DID...
HE SAW THAT I UNEARTHED HIM LOOKING FOR D.N.A. SAMPLES. HE SAW WHO I AM AND WHAT I DO...
CENTRAL CITY POLICE
AND HE KNOWS I HAVE ACCESS TO THE POLICE DATABASE...

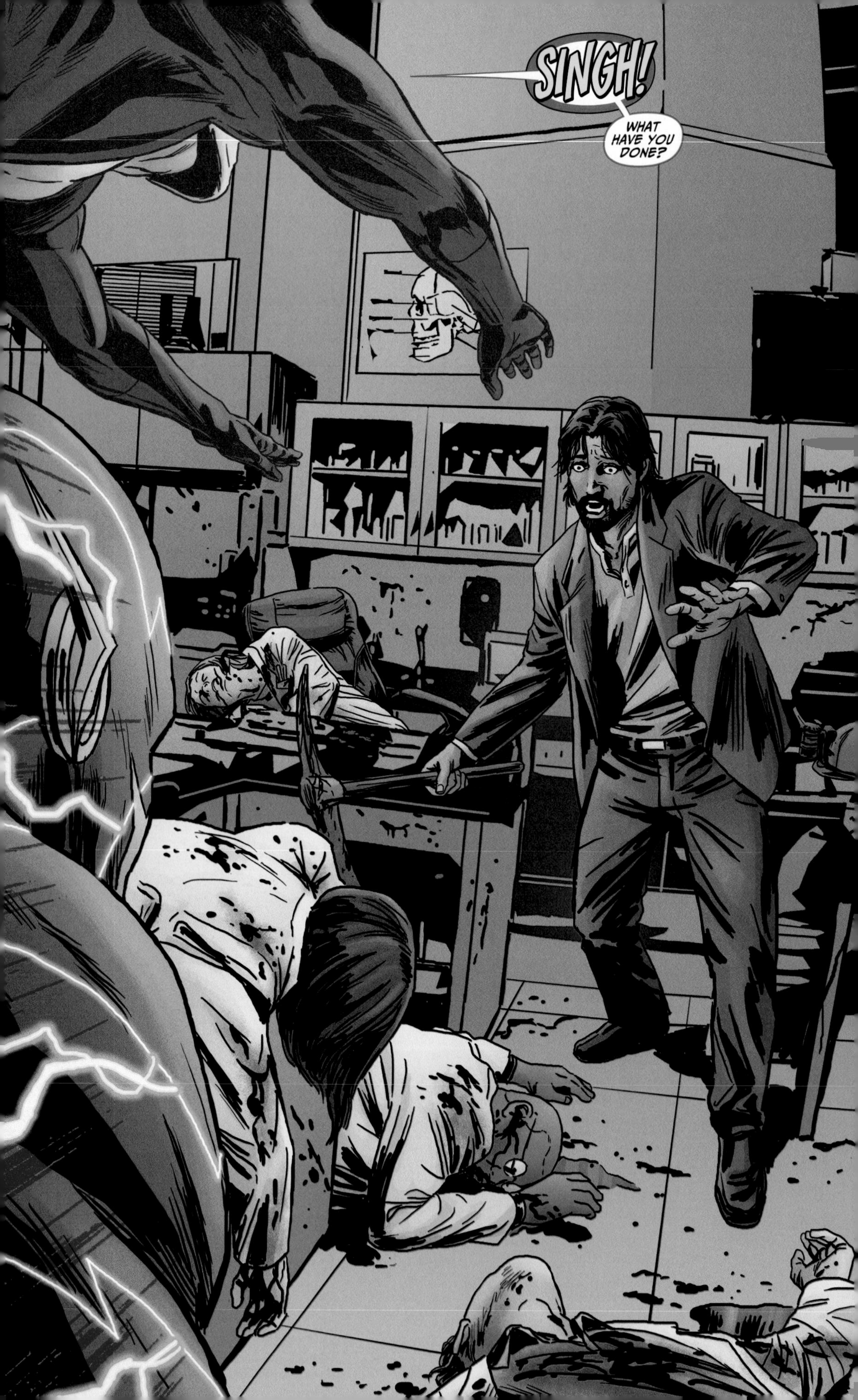
SINGH!
WHAT HAVE YOU DONE?

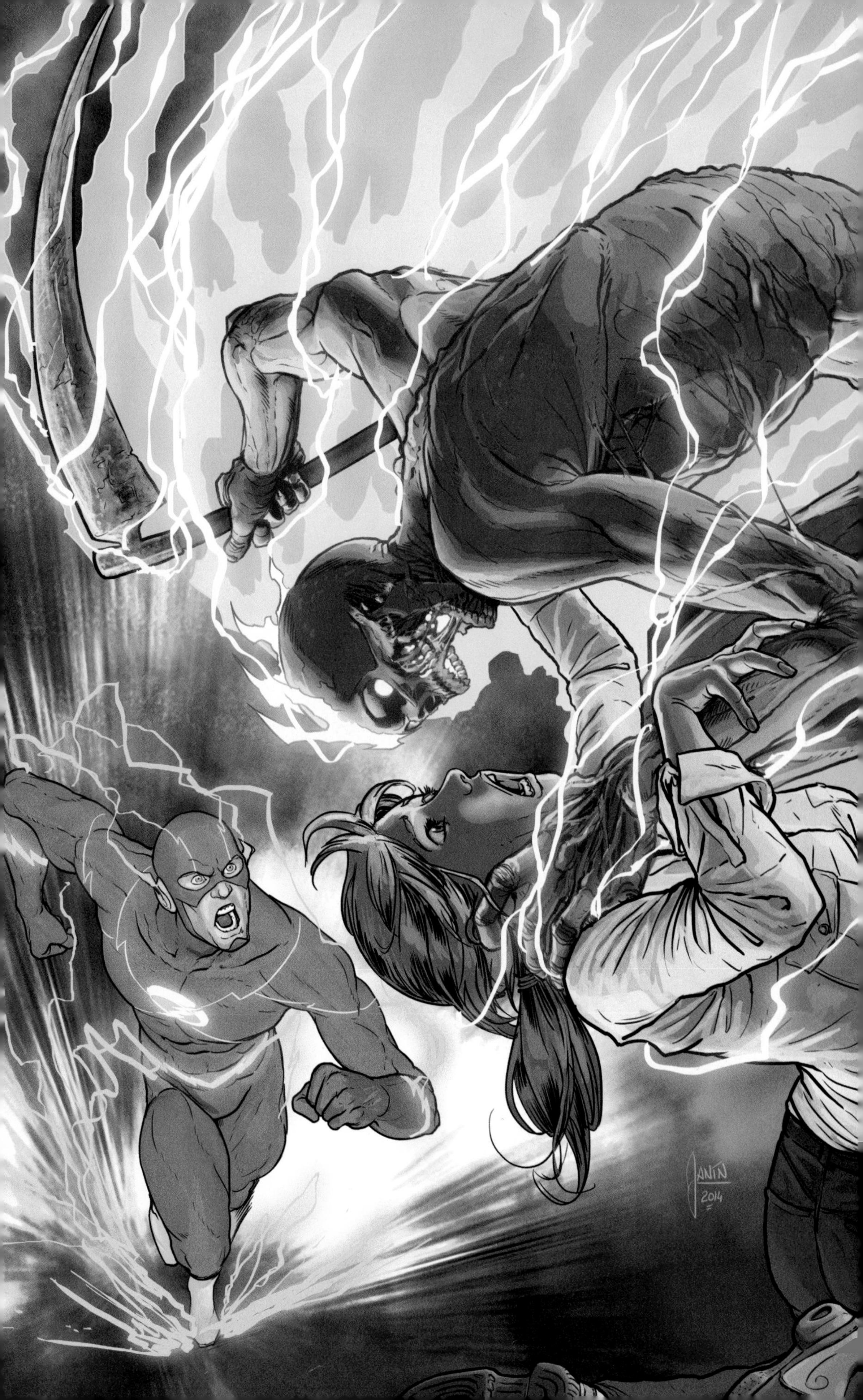
JANIN
2014

BRIAN BUCCELLATO writer **AGUSTIN PADILLA** artist cover art **MIKEL JANIN**

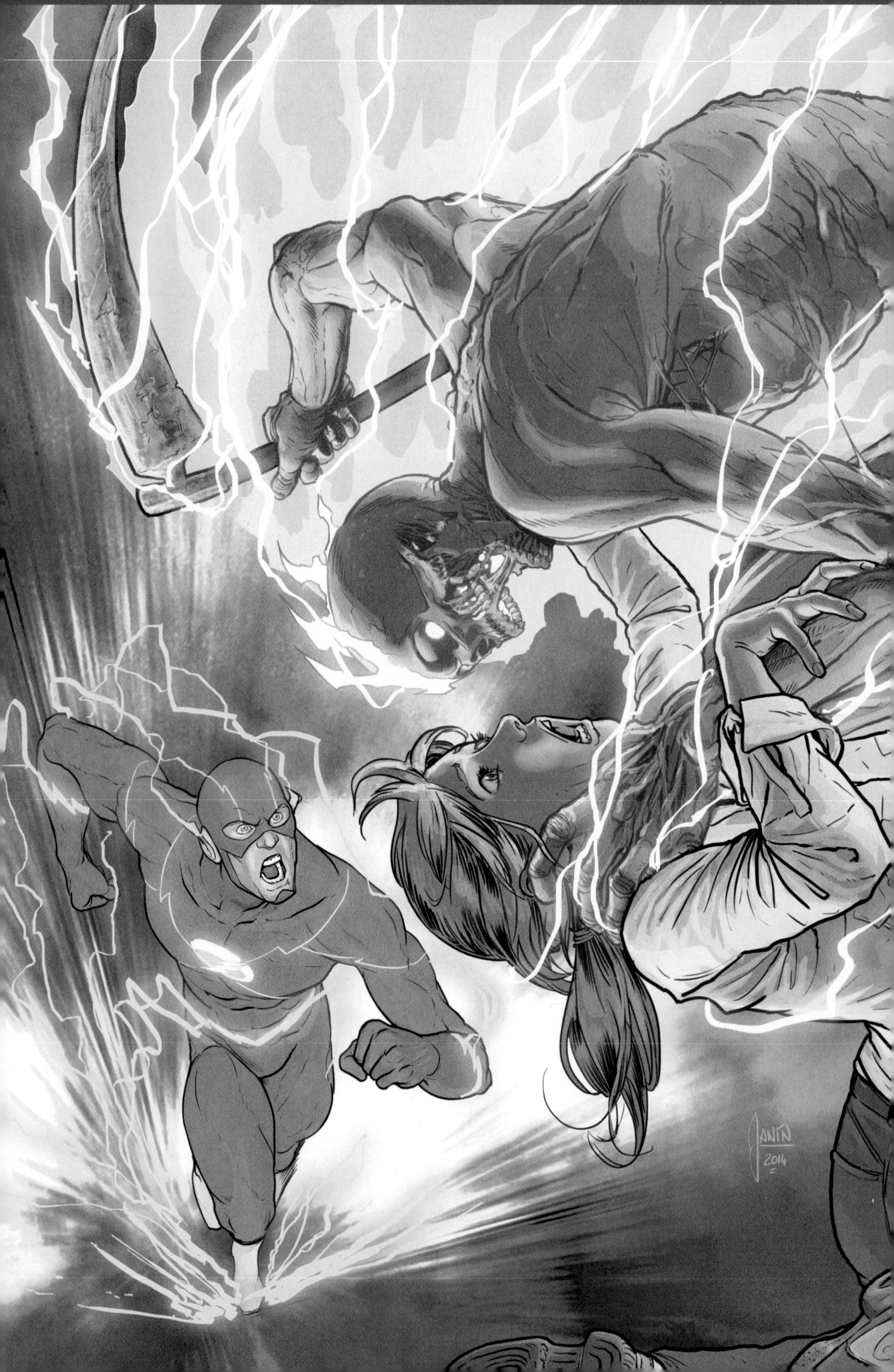
JANÍN
2014

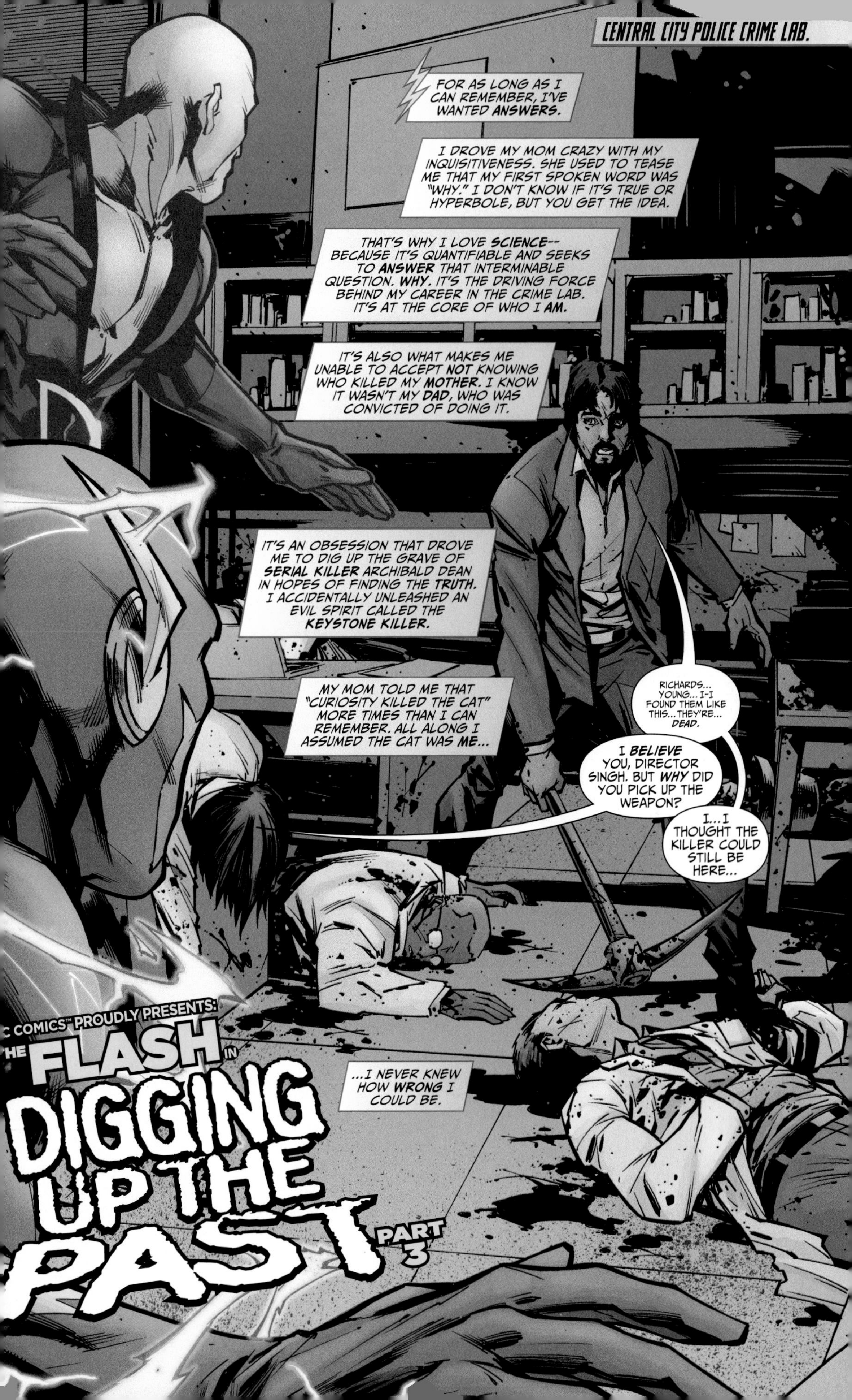
CENTRAL CITY POLICE CRIME LAB.
FOR AS LONG AS I CAN REMEMBER, I'VE WANTED ANSWERS.
I DROVE MY MOM CRAZY WITH MY INQUISITIVENESS. SHE USED TO TEASE ME THAT MY FIRST SPOKEN WORD WAS "WHY." I DON'T KNOW IF IT'S TRUE OR HYPERBOLE, BUT YOU GET THE IDEA.
THAT'S WHY I LOVE SCIENCE-- BECAUSE IT'S QUANTIFIABLE AND SEEKS TO ANSWER THAT INTERMINABLE QUESTION. WHY. IT'S THE DRIVING FORCE BEHIND MY CAREER IN THE CRIME LAB. IT'S AT THE CORE OF WHO I AM.
IT'S ALSO WHAT MAKES ME UNABLE TO ACCEPT NOT KNOWING WHO KILLED MY MOTHER. I KNOW IT WASN'T MY DAD, WHO WAS CONVICTED OF DOING IT.
IT'S AN OBSESSION THAT DROVE ME TO DIG UP THE GRAVE OF SERIAL KILLER ARCHIBALD DEAN IN HOPES OF FINDING THE TRUTH. I ACCIDENTALLY UNLEASHED AN EVIL SPIRIT CALLED THE KEYSTONE KILLER.
MY MOM TOLD ME THAT "CURIOSITY KILLED THE CAT" MORE TIMES THAN I CAN REMEMBER. ALL ALONG I ASSUMED THE CAT WAS ME...
RICHARDS... YOUNG... I-I FOUND THEM LIKE THIS... THEY'RE... DEAD.
I BELIEVE YOU, DIRECTOR SINGH. BUT WHY DID YOU PICK UP THE WEAPON?
I... I THOUGHT THE KILLER COULD STILL BE HERE...
C COMICS™ PROUDLY PRESENTS:
HE FLASH IN
DIGGING UP THE PAST PART 3
...I NEVER KNEW HOW WRONG I COULD BE.

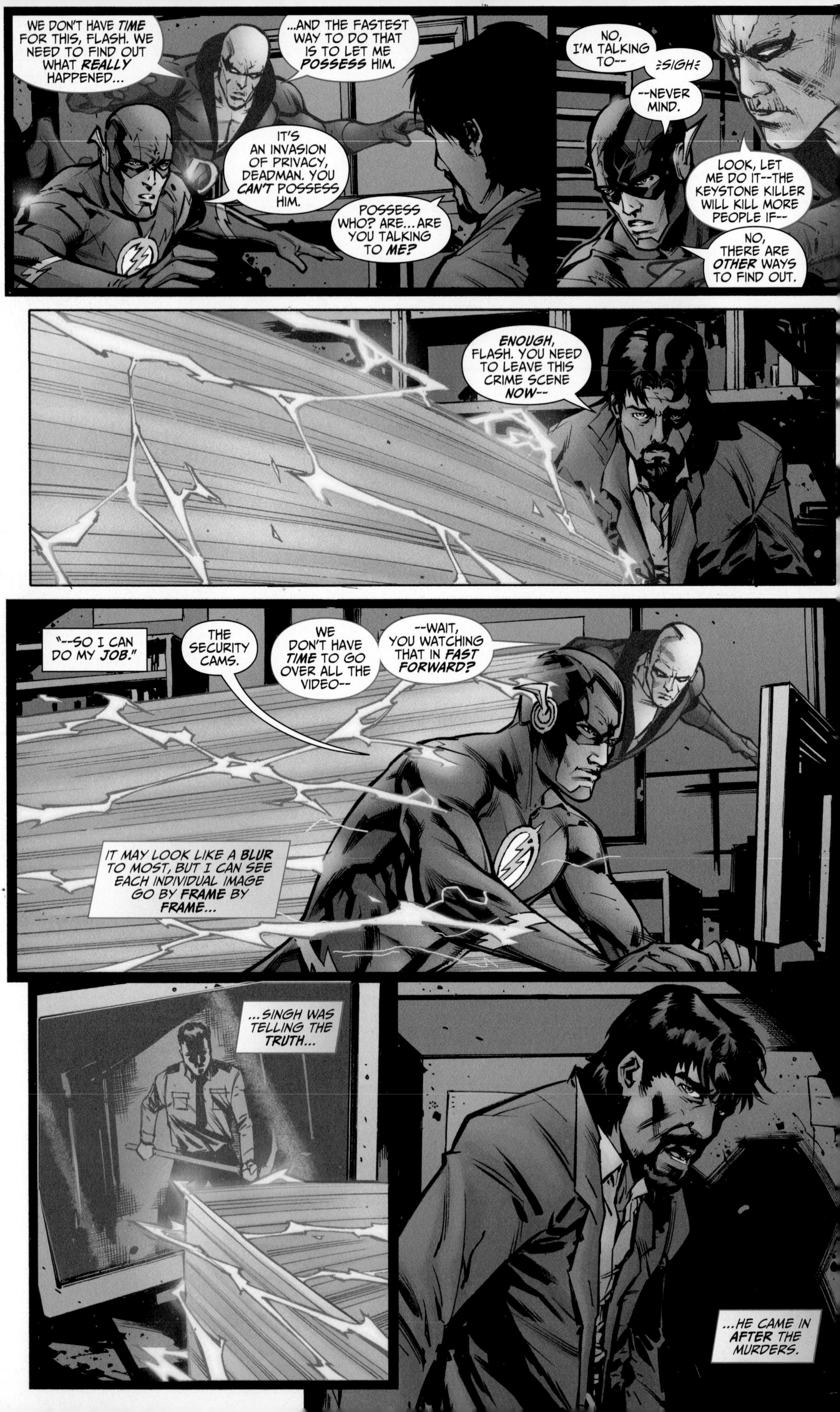
WE DON'T HAVE TIME FOR THIS, FLASH. WE NEED TO FIND OUT WHAT REALLY HAPPENED...
...AND THE FASTEST WAY TO DO THAT IS TO LET ME POSSESS HIM.
IT'S AN INVASION OF PRIVACY, DEADMAN. YOU CAN'T POSSESS HIM.
POSSESS WHO? ARE...ARE YOU TALKING TO ME?
NO, I'M TALKING TO--
SIGH
--NEVER MIND.
LOOK, LET ME DO IT--THE KEYSTONE KILLER WILL KILL MORE PEOPLE IF--
NO, THERE ARE OTHER WAYS TO FIND OUT.
ENOUGH, FLASH. YOU NEED TO LEAVE THIS CRIME SCENE NOW--
"--SO I CAN DO MY JOB."
THE SECURITY CAMS.
WE DON'T HAVE TIME TO GO OVER ALL THE VIDEO--
--WAIT, YOU WATCHING THAT IN FAST FORWARD?
IT MAY LOOK LIKE A BLUR TO MOST, BUT I CAN SEE EACH INDIVIDUAL IMAGE GO BY FRAME BY FRAME...
...SINGH WAS TELLING THE TRUTH...
...HE CAME IN AFTER THE MURDERS.

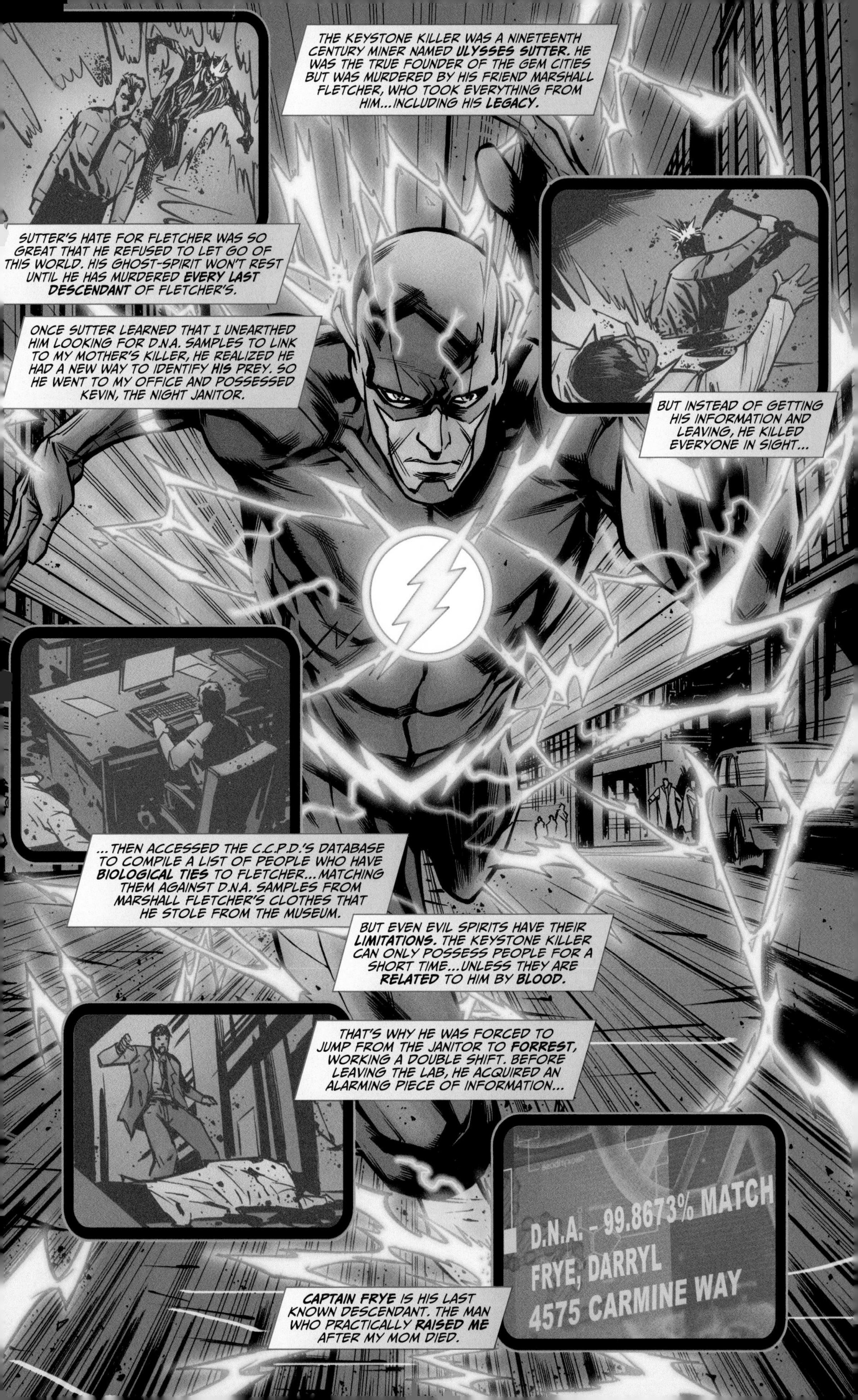
THE KEYSTONE KILLER WAS A NINETEENTH CENTURY MINER NAMED ULYSSES SUTTER. HE WAS THE TRUE FOUNDER OF THE GEM CITIES BUT WAS MURDERED BY HIS FRIEND MARSHALL FLETCHER, WHO TOOK EVERYTHING FROM HIM...INCLUDING HIS LEGACY.
SUTTER'S HATE FOR FLETCHER WAS SO GREAT THAT HE REFUSED TO LET GO OF THIS WORLD. HIS GHOST-SPIRIT WON'T REST UNTIL HE HAS MURDERED EVERY LAST DESCENDANT OF FLETCHER'S.
ONCE SUTTER LEARNED THAT I UNEARTHED HIM LOOKING FOR D.N.A. SAMPLES TO LINK TO MY MOTHER'S KILLER, HE REALIZED HE HAD A NEW WAY TO IDENTIFY HIS PREY. SO HE WENT TO MY OFFICE AND POSSESSED KEVIN, THE NIGHT JANITOR.
BUT INSTEAD OF GETTING HIS INFORMATION AND LEAVING, HE KILLED EVERYONE IN SIGHT...
...THEN ACCESSED THE C.C.P.D.'S DATABASE TO COMPILE A LIST OF PEOPLE WHO HAVE BIOLOGICAL TIES TO FLETCHER...MATCHING THEM AGAINST D.N.A. SAMPLES FROM MARSHALL FLETCHER'S CLOTHES THAT HE STOLE FROM THE MUSEUM.
BUT EVEN EVIL SPIRITS HAVE THEIR LIMITATIONS. THE KEYSTONE KILLER CAN ONLY POSSESS PEOPLE FOR A SHORT TIME...UNLESS THEY ARE RELATED TO HIM BY BLOOD.
THAT'S WHY HE WAS FORCED TO JUMP FROM THE JANITOR TO FORREST, WORKING A DOUBLE SHIFT. BEFORE LEAVING THE LAB, HE ACQUIRED AN ALARMING PIECE OF INFORMATION...
D.N.A. - 99.8673% MATCH
FRYE, DARRYL
4575 CARMINE WAY
CAPTAIN FRYE IS HIS LAST KNOWN DESCENDANT. THE MAN WHO PRACTICALLY RAISED ME AFTER MY MOM DIED.

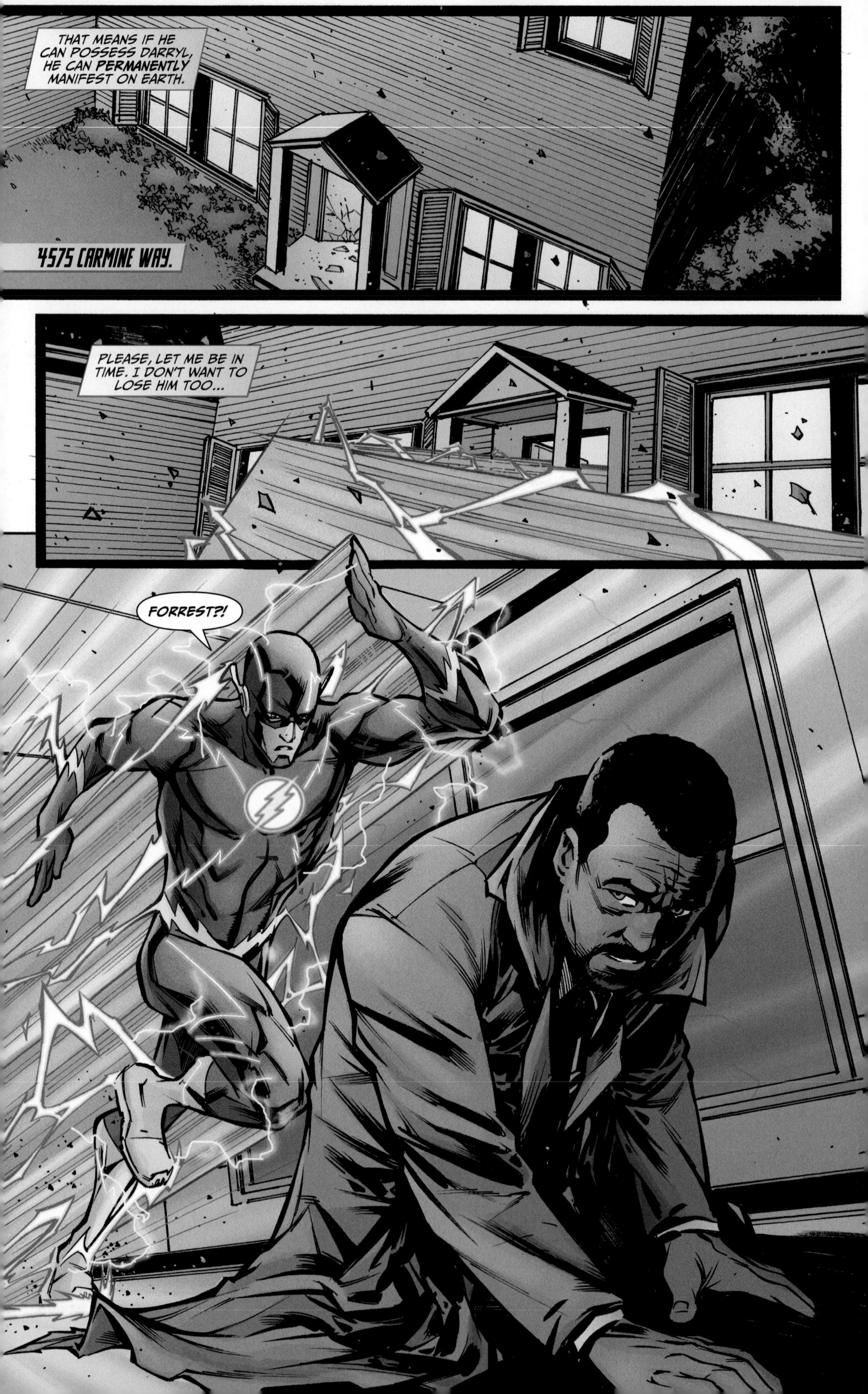
THAT MEANS IF HE CAN POSSESS DARRYL, HE CAN PERMANENTLY MANIFEST ON EARTH.
4575 CARMINE WAY.
PLEASE, LET ME BE IN TIME. I DON'T WANT TO LOSE HIM TOO...
FORREST?!

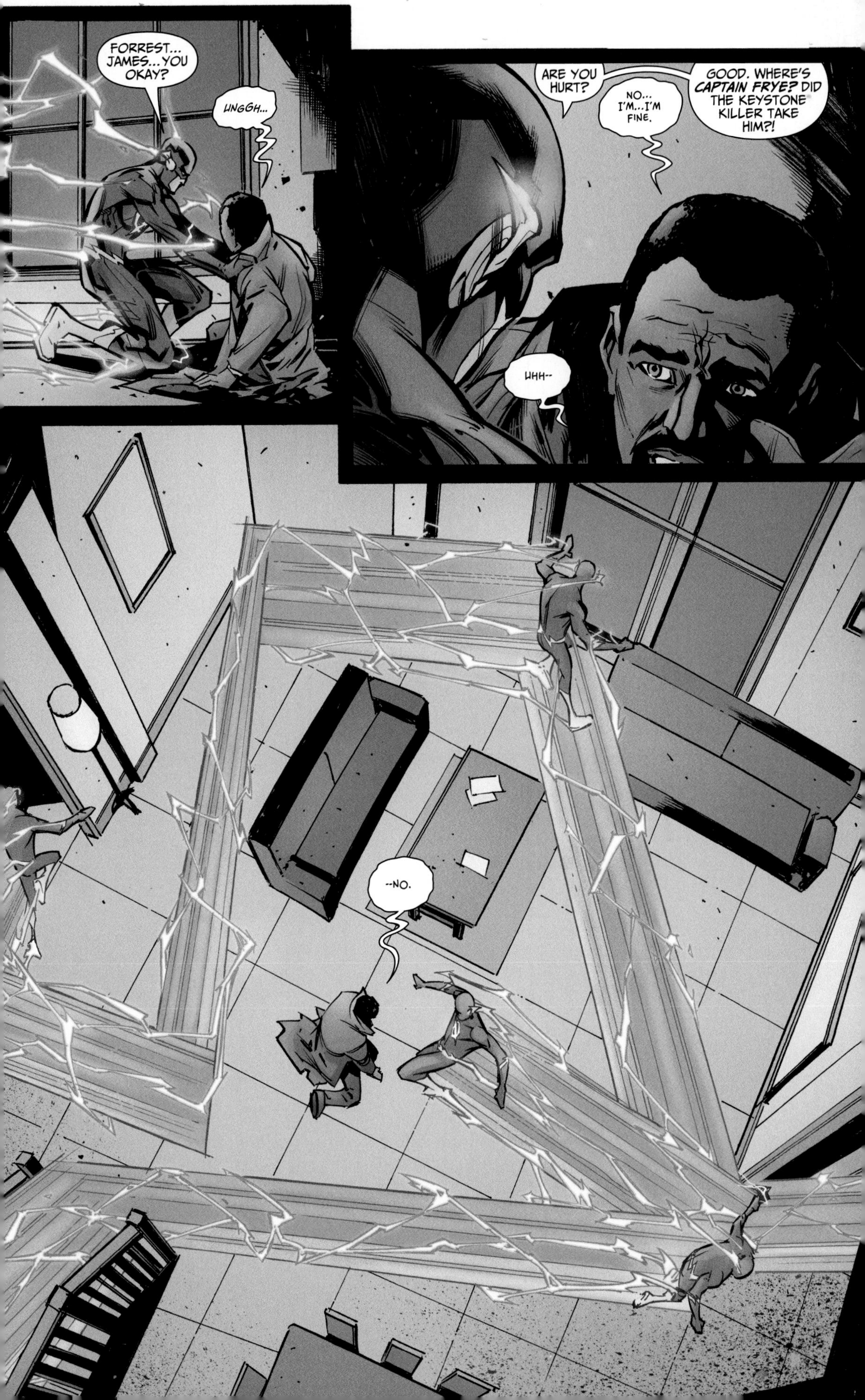
FORREST... JAMES... YOU OKAY?
UNGGH...
ARE YOU HURT?
NO... I'M...I'M FINE.
GOOD. WHERE'S CAPTAIN FRYE? DID THE KEYSTONE KILLER TAKE HIM?!
UHH--
--NO.

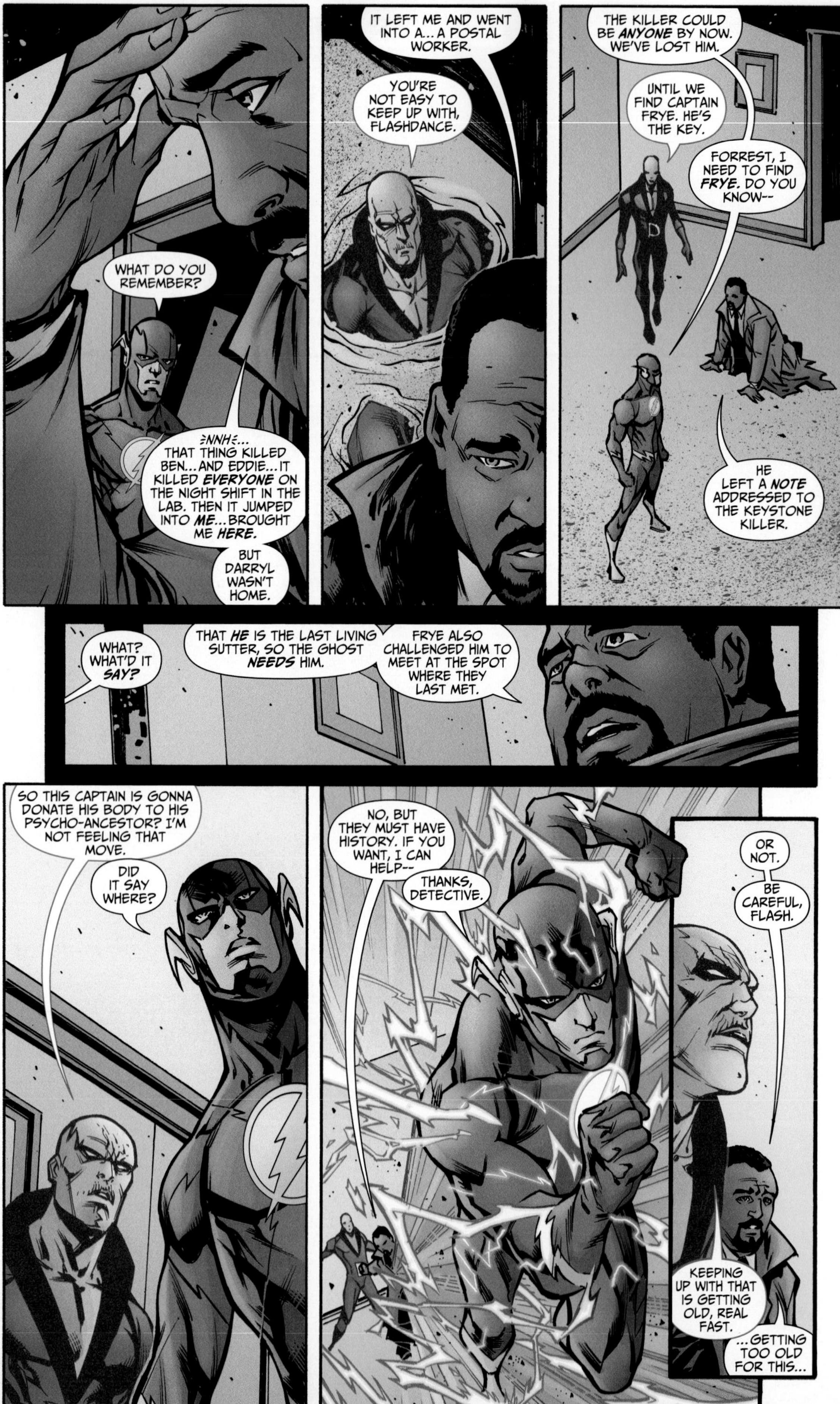
WHAT DO YOU REMEMBER?
ƎNNH... THAT THING KILLED BEN...AND EDDIE...IT KILLED EVERYONE ON THE NIGHT SHIFT IN THE LAB. THEN IT JUMPED INTO ME...BROUGHT ME HERE.
BUT DARRYL WASN'T HOME.
IT LEFT ME AND WENT INTO A...A POSTAL WORKER.
YOU'RE NOT EASY TO KEEP UP WITH, FLASHDANCE.
THE KILLER COULD BE ANYONE BY NOW. WE'VE LOST HIM.
UNTIL WE FIND CAPTAIN FRYE. HE'S THE KEY.
FORREST, I NEED TO FIND FRYE. DO YOU KNOW--
HE LEFT A NOTE ADDRESSED TO THE KEYSTONE KILLER.
WHAT? WHAT'D IT SAY?
THAT HE IS THE LAST LIVING SUTTER, SO THE GHOST NEEDS HIM.
FRYE ALSO CHALLENGED HIM TO MEET AT THE SPOT WHERE THEY LAST MET.
SO THIS CAPTAIN IS GONNA DONATE HIS BODY TO HIS PSYCHO-ANCESTOR? I'M NOT FEELING THAT MOVE.
DID IT SAY WHERE?
NO, BUT THEY MUST HAVE HISTORY. IF YOU WANT, I CAN HELP--
THANKS, DETECTIVE.
OR NOT.
BE CAREFUL, FLASH.
KEEPING UP WITH THAT IS GETTING OLD, REAL FAST.
...GETTING TOO OLD FOR THIS...

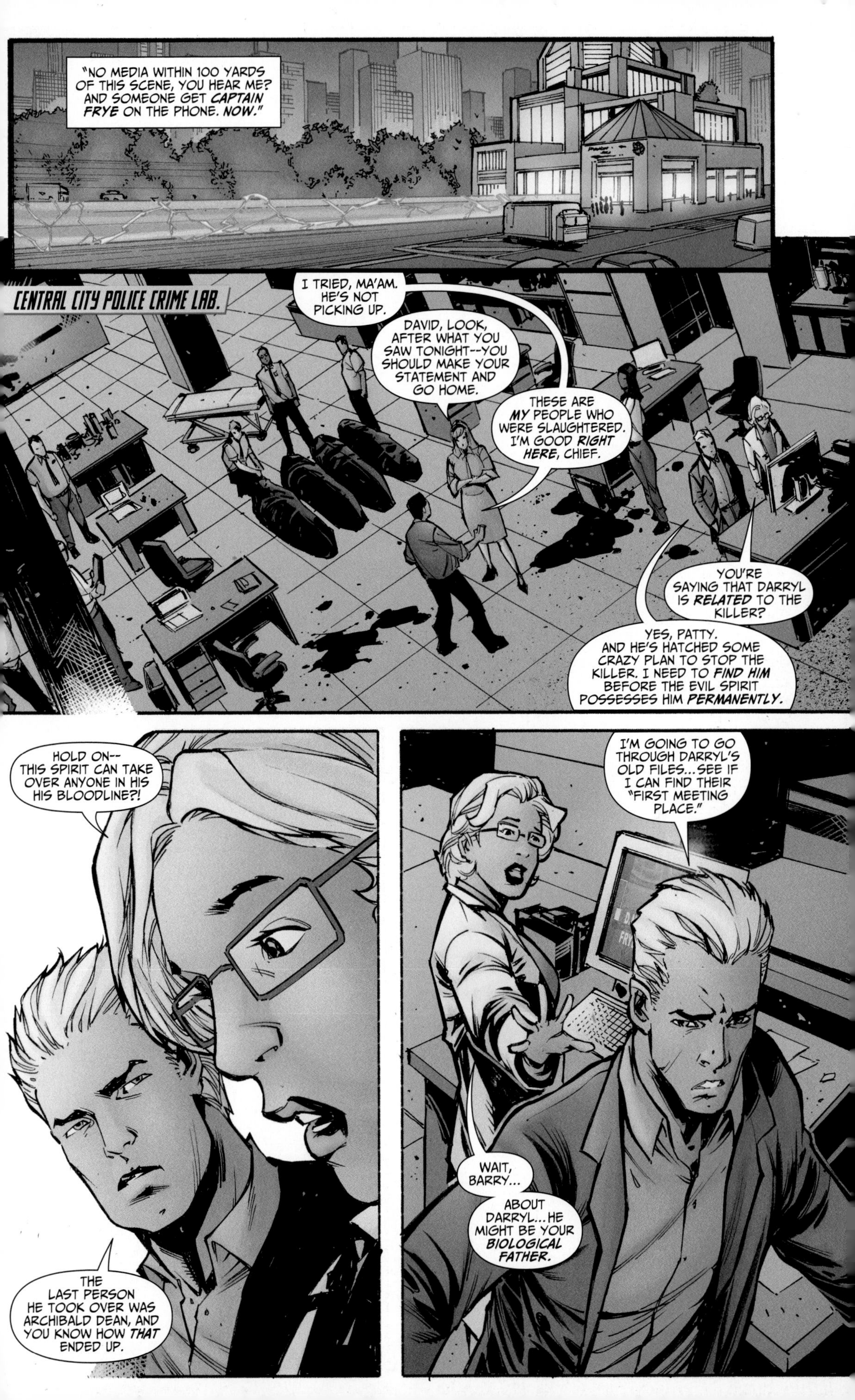
"NO MEDIA WITHIN 100 YARDS OF THIS SCENE, YOU HEAR ME? AND SOMEONE GET CAPTAIN FRYE ON THE PHONE. NOW."
CENTRAL CITY POLICE CRIME LAB.
I TRIED, MA'AM. HE'S NOT PICKING UP.
DAVID, LOOK, AFTER WHAT YOU SAW TONIGHT--YOU SHOULD MAKE YOUR STATEMENT AND GO HOME.
THESE ARE MY PEOPLE WHO WERE SLAUGHTERED. I'M GOOD RIGHT HERE, CHIEF.
YOU'RE SAYING THAT DARRYL IS RELATED TO THE KILLER?
YES, PATTY. AND HE'S HATCHED SOME CRAZY PLAN TO STOP THE KILLER. I NEED TO FIND HIM BEFORE THE EVIL SPIRIT POSSESSES HIM PERMANENTLY.
HOLD ON-- THIS SPIRIT CAN TAKE OVER ANYONE IN HIS HIS BLOODLINE?!
THE LAST PERSON HE TOOK OVER WAS ARCHIBALD DEAN, AND YOU KNOW HOW THAT ENDED UP.
I'M GOING TO GO THROUGH DARRYL'S OLD FILES...SEE IF I CAN FIND THEIR "FIRST MEETING PLACE."
WAIT, BARRY...
ABOUT DARRYL...HE MIGHT BE YOUR BIOLOGICAL FATHER.

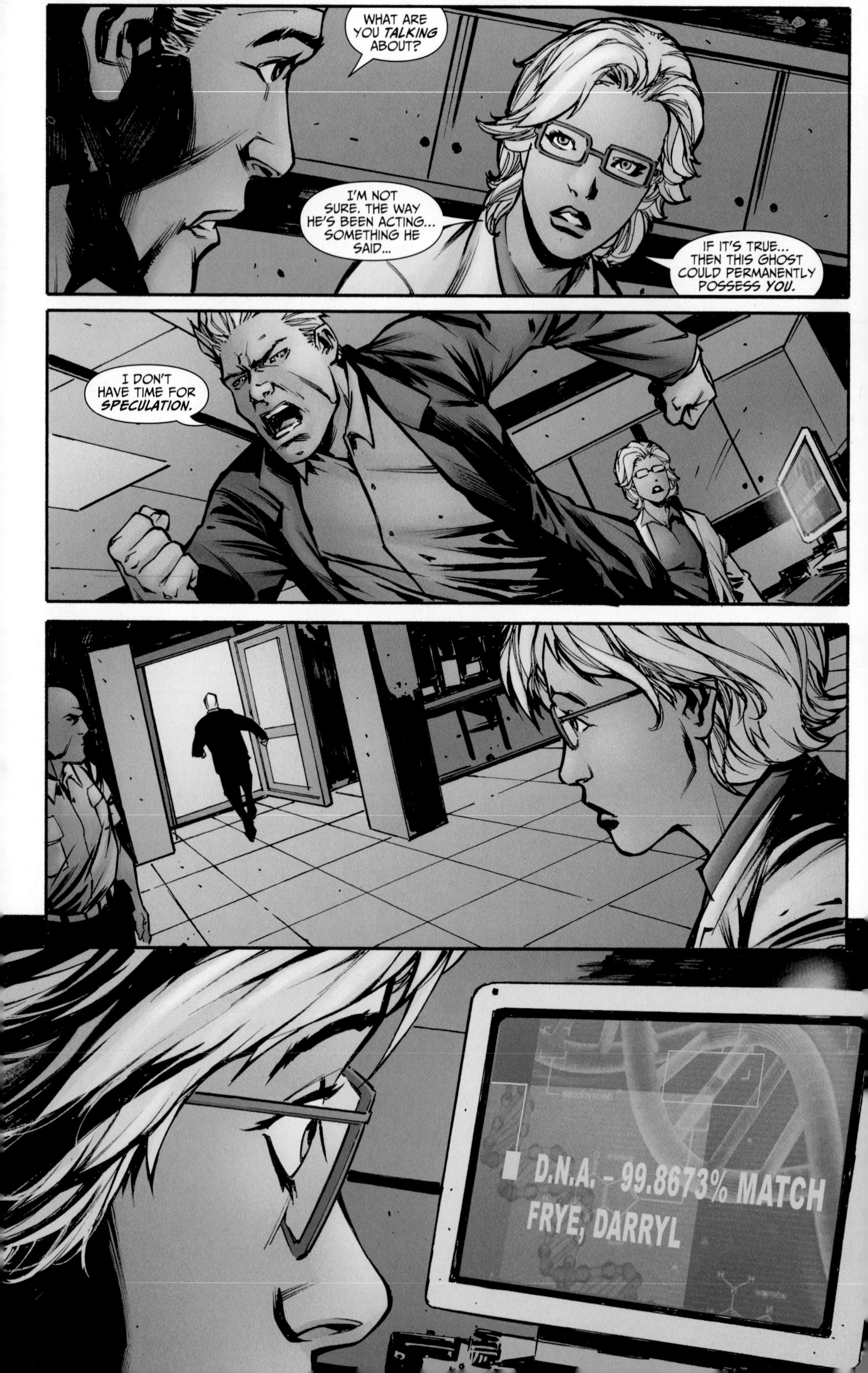
WHAT ARE YOU TALKING ABOUT?
I'M NOT SURE. THE WAY HE'S BEEN ACTING... SOMETHING HE SAID...
IF IT'S TRUE... THEN THIS GHOST COULD PERMANENTLY POSSESS YOU.
I DON'T HAVE TIME FOR SPECULATION.
D.N.A. - 99.8673% MATCH
FRYE, DARRYL

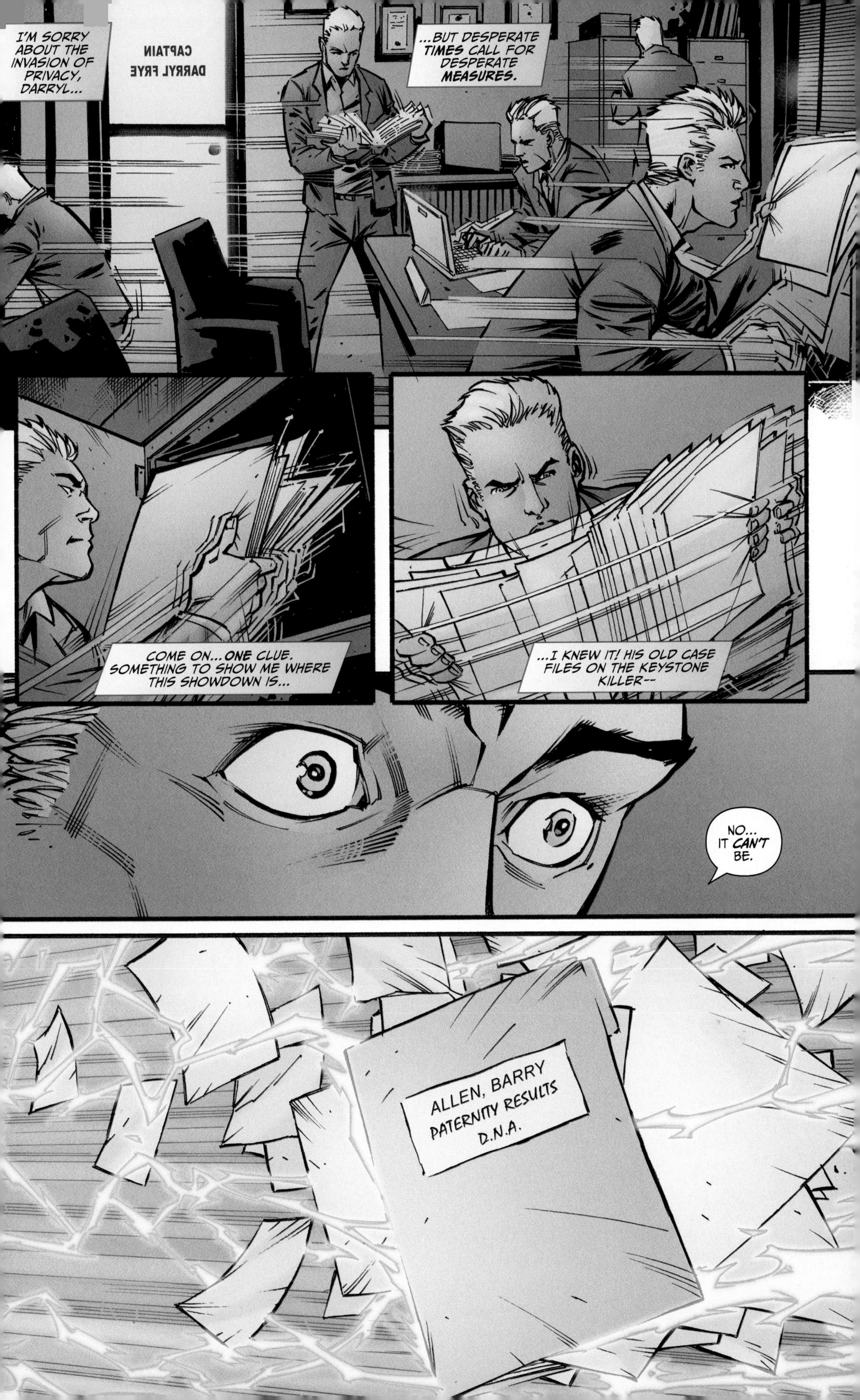
I'M SORRY ABOUT THE INVASION OF PRIVACY, DARRYL...
CAPTAIN DARRYL FRYE
...BUT DESPERATE TIMES CALL FOR DESPERATE MEASURES.
COME ON...ONE CLUE. SOMETHING TO SHOW ME WHERE THIS SHOWDOWN IS...
...I KNEW IT! HIS OLD CASE FILES ON THE KEYSTONE KILLER--
NO... IT CAN'T BE.
ALLEN, BARRY
PATERNITY RESULTS
D.N.A.

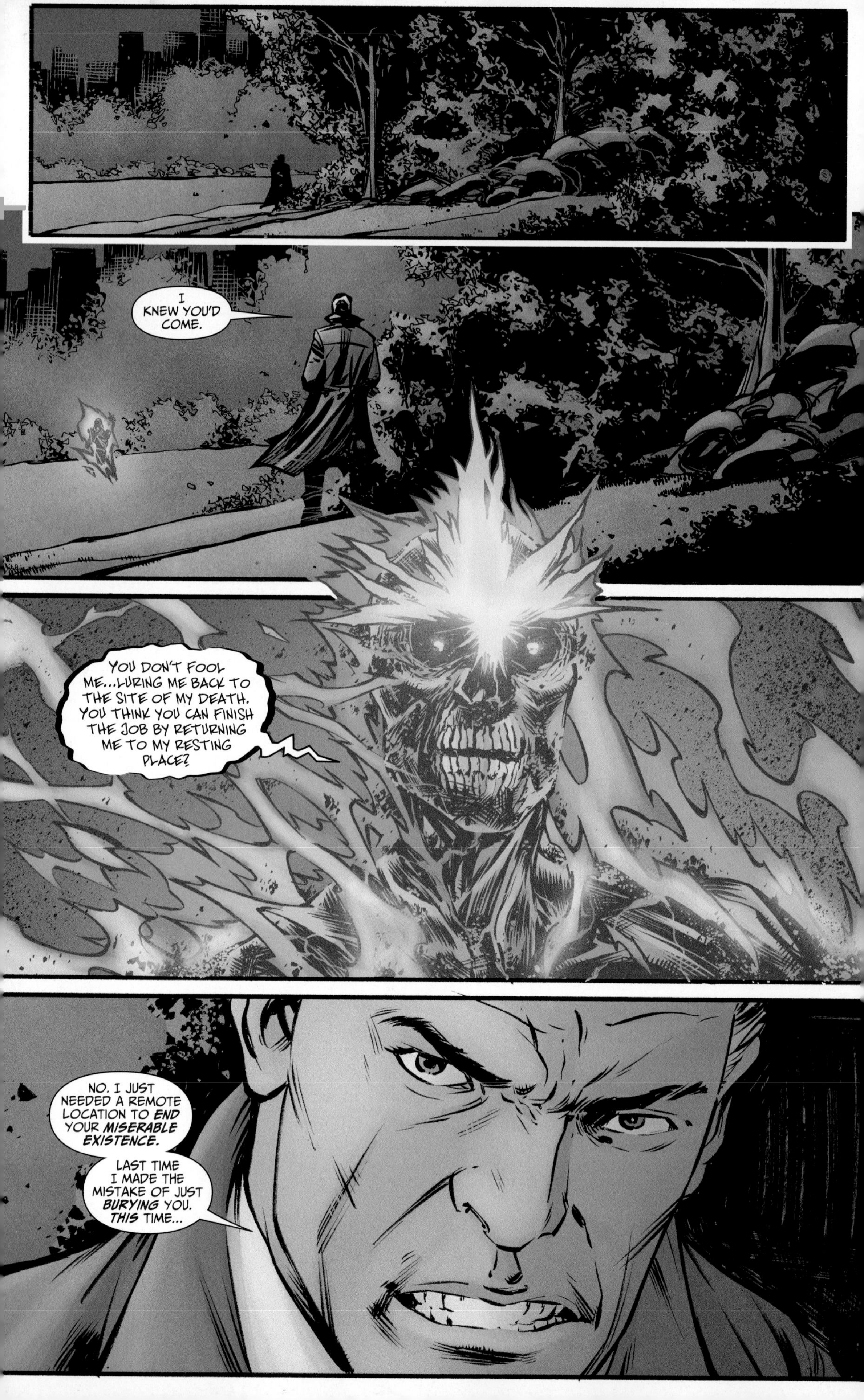
I KNEW YOU'D COME.
YOU DON'T FOOL ME...LURING ME BACK TO THE SITE OF MY DEATH. YOU THINK YOU CAN FINISH THE JOB BY RETURNING ME TO MY RESTING PLACE?
NO. I JUST NEEDED A REMOTE LOCATION TO END YOUR MISERABLE EXISTENCE.
LAST TIME I MADE THE MISTAKE OF JUST BURYING YOU. THIS TIME...

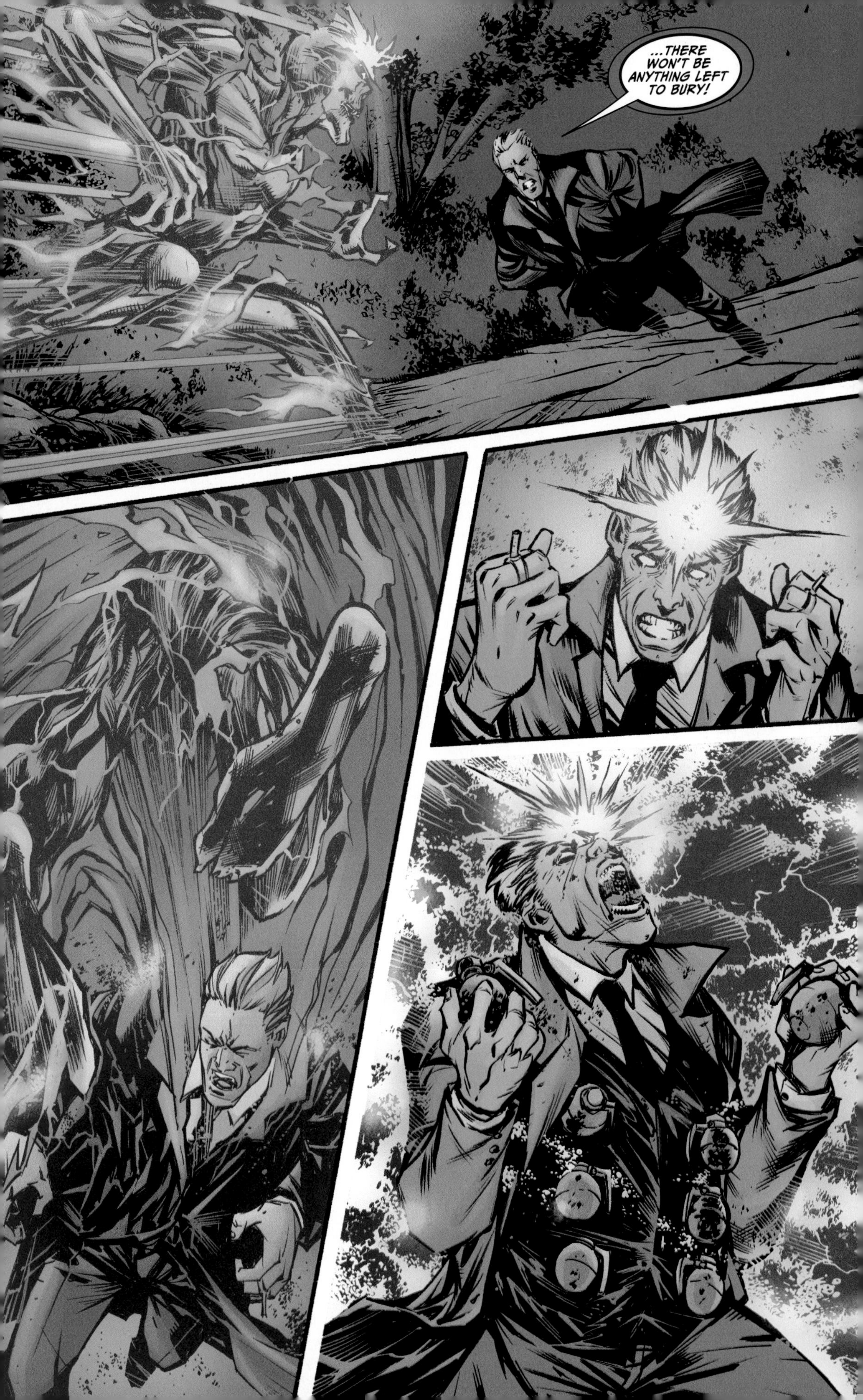
...THERE WON'T BE ANYTHING LEFT TO BURY!

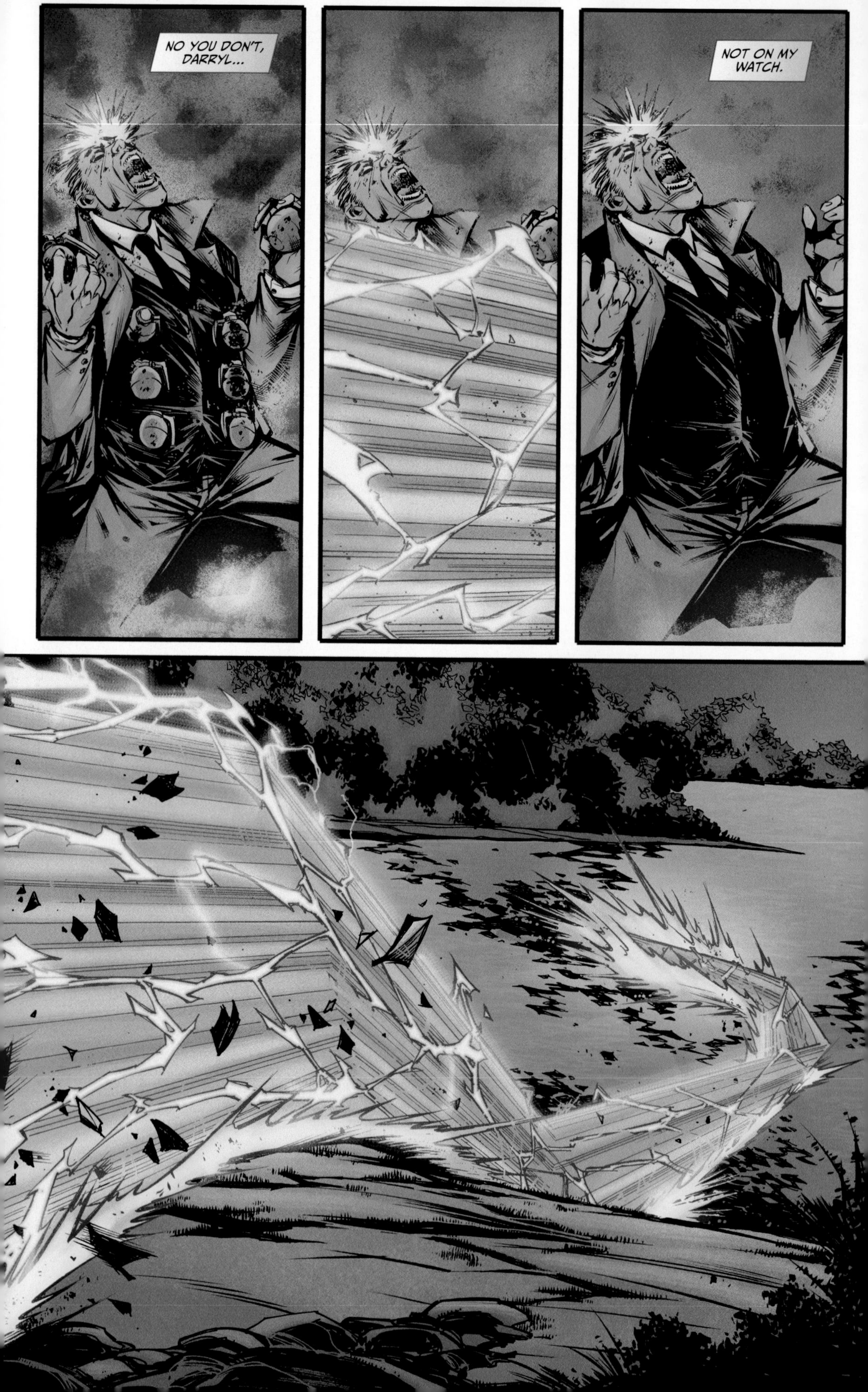
NO YOU DON'T, DARRYL...
NOT ON MY WATCH.

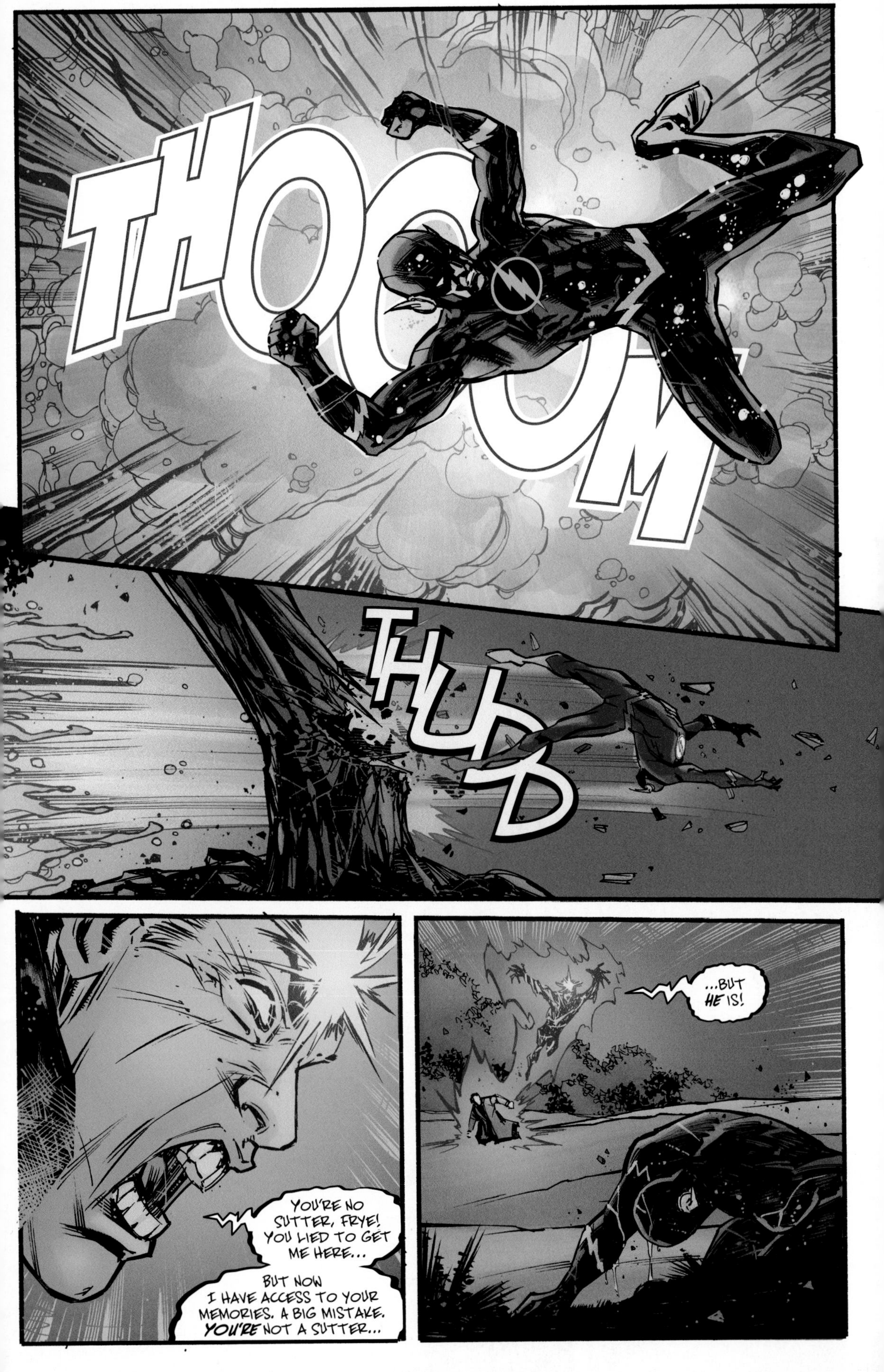
THOOOM
THUDD
YOU'RE NO SUTTER, FRYE! YOU LIED TO GET ME HERE...
BUT NOW I HAVE ACCESS TO YOUR MEMORIES. A BIG MISTAKE. YOU'RE NOT A SUTTER...
...BUT HE IS!

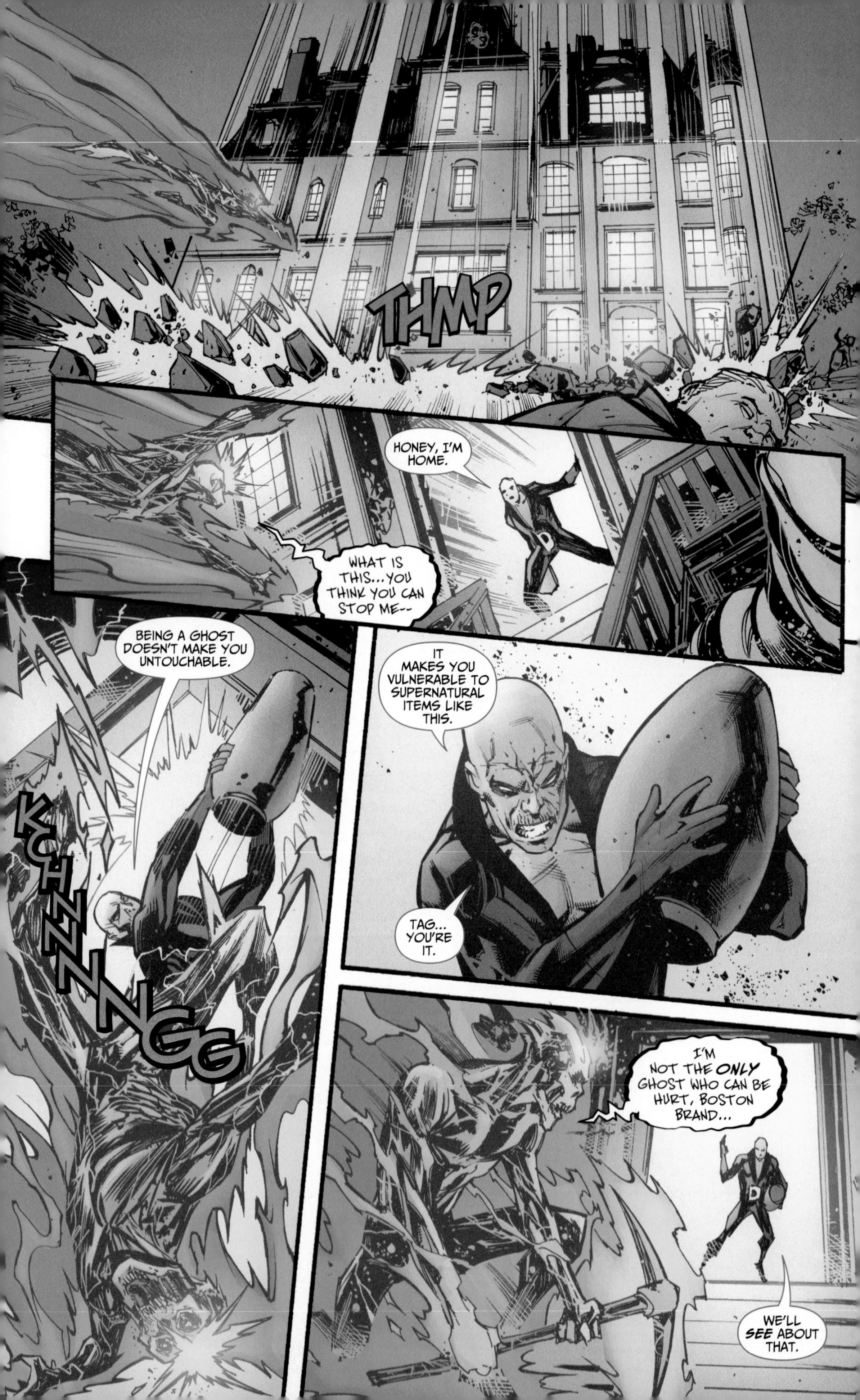
THMP
HONEY, I'M HOME.
WHAT IS THIS...YOU THINK YOU CAN STOP ME--
BEING A GHOST DOESN'T MAKE YOU UNTOUCHABLE.
KCHNNNNGG
IT MAKES YOU VULNERABLE TO SUPERNATURAL ITEMS LIKE THIS.
TAG... YOU'RE IT.
I'M NOT THE ONLY GHOST WHO CAN BE HURT, BOSTON BRAND...
WE'LL SEE ABOUT THAT.

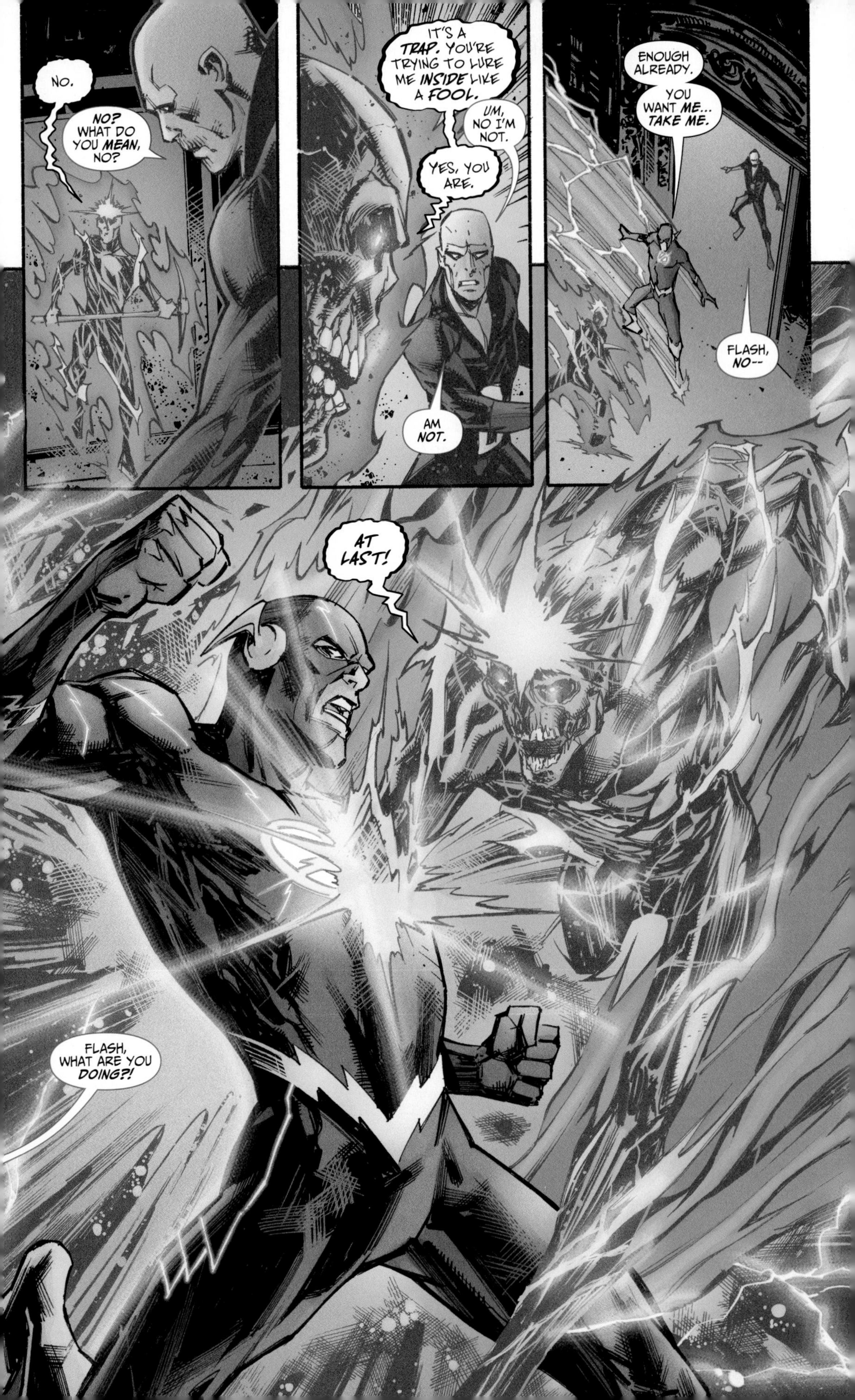
NO.
NO? WHAT DO YOU MEAN, NO?
IT'S A TRAP. YOU'RE TRYING TO LURE ME INSIDE LIKE A FOOL.
UM, NO I'M NOT.
YES, YOU ARE.
AM NOT.
ENOUGH ALREADY.
YOU WANT ME... TAKE ME.
FLASH, NO--
AT LAST!
FLASH, WHAT ARE YOU DOING?!

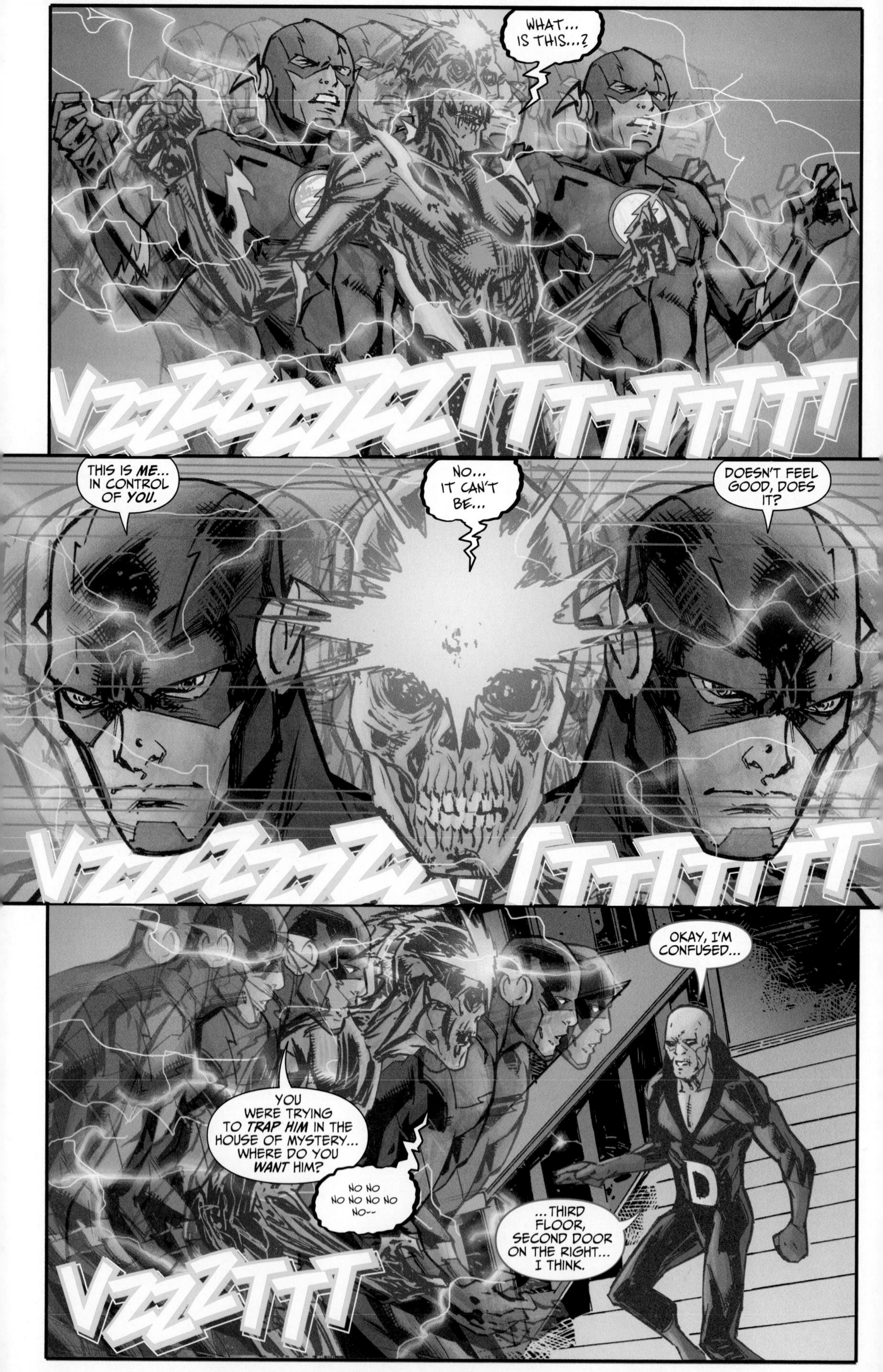
WHAT... IS THIS...?
VZZZZZZZZTTTTTTTTT
THIS IS ME... IN CONTROL OF YOU.
NO... IT CAN'T BE...
DOESN'T FEEL GOOD, DOES IT?
VZZZZZZZZTTTTTTT
OKAY, I'M CONFUSED...
YOU WERE TRYING TO TRAP HIM IN THE HOUSE OF MYSTERY... WHERE DO YOU WANT HIM?
NO NO NO NO NO NO NO--
...THIRD FLOOR, SECOND DOOR ON THE RIGHT... I THINK.
VZZZTTT

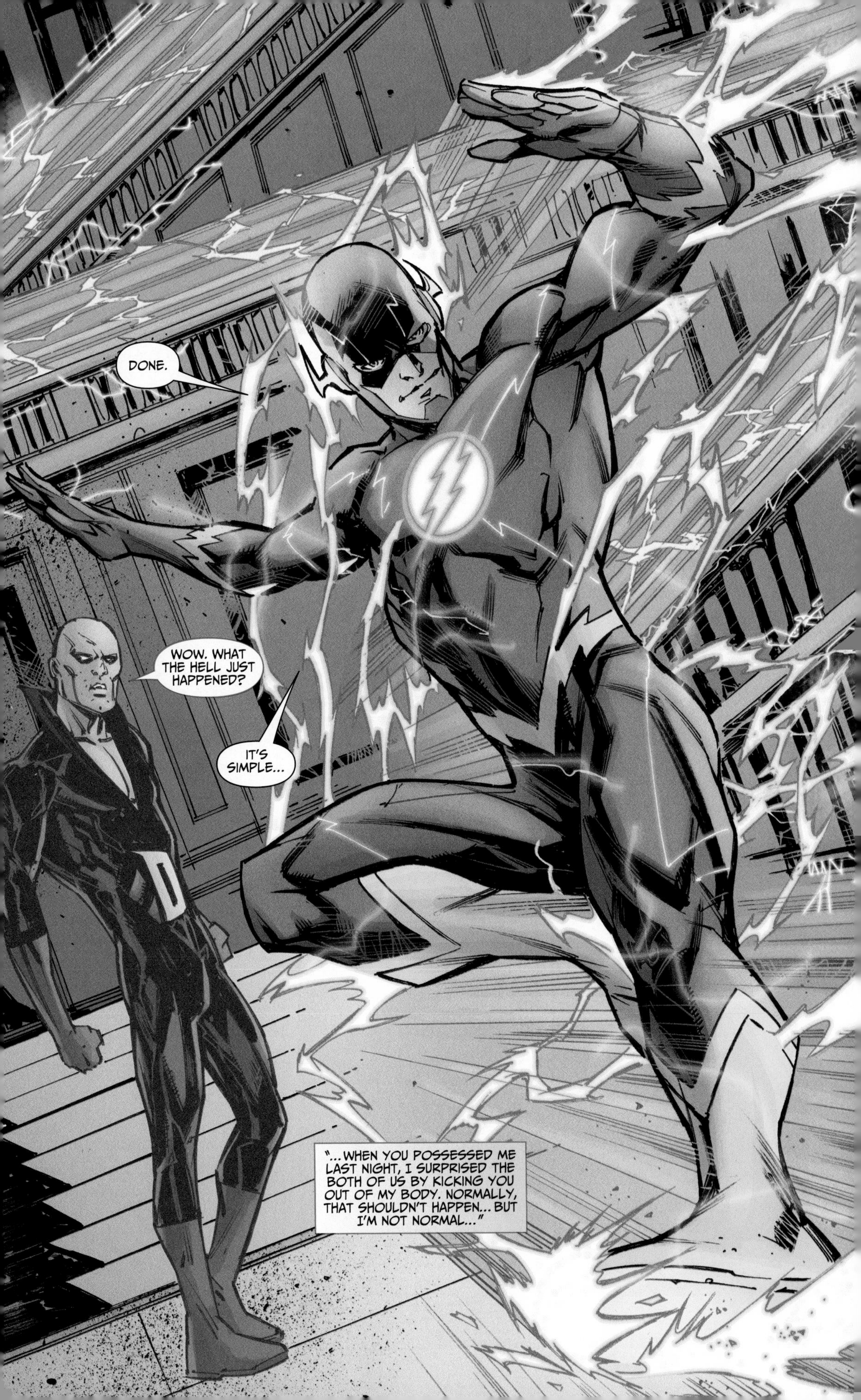
DONE.
WOW. WHAT THE HELL JUST HAPPENED?
IT'S SIMPLE...
"...WHEN YOU POSSESSED ME LAST NIGHT, I SURPRISED THE BOTH OF US BY KICKING YOU OUT OF MY BODY. NORMALLY, THAT SHOULDN'T HAPPEN... BUT I'M NOT NORMAL..."

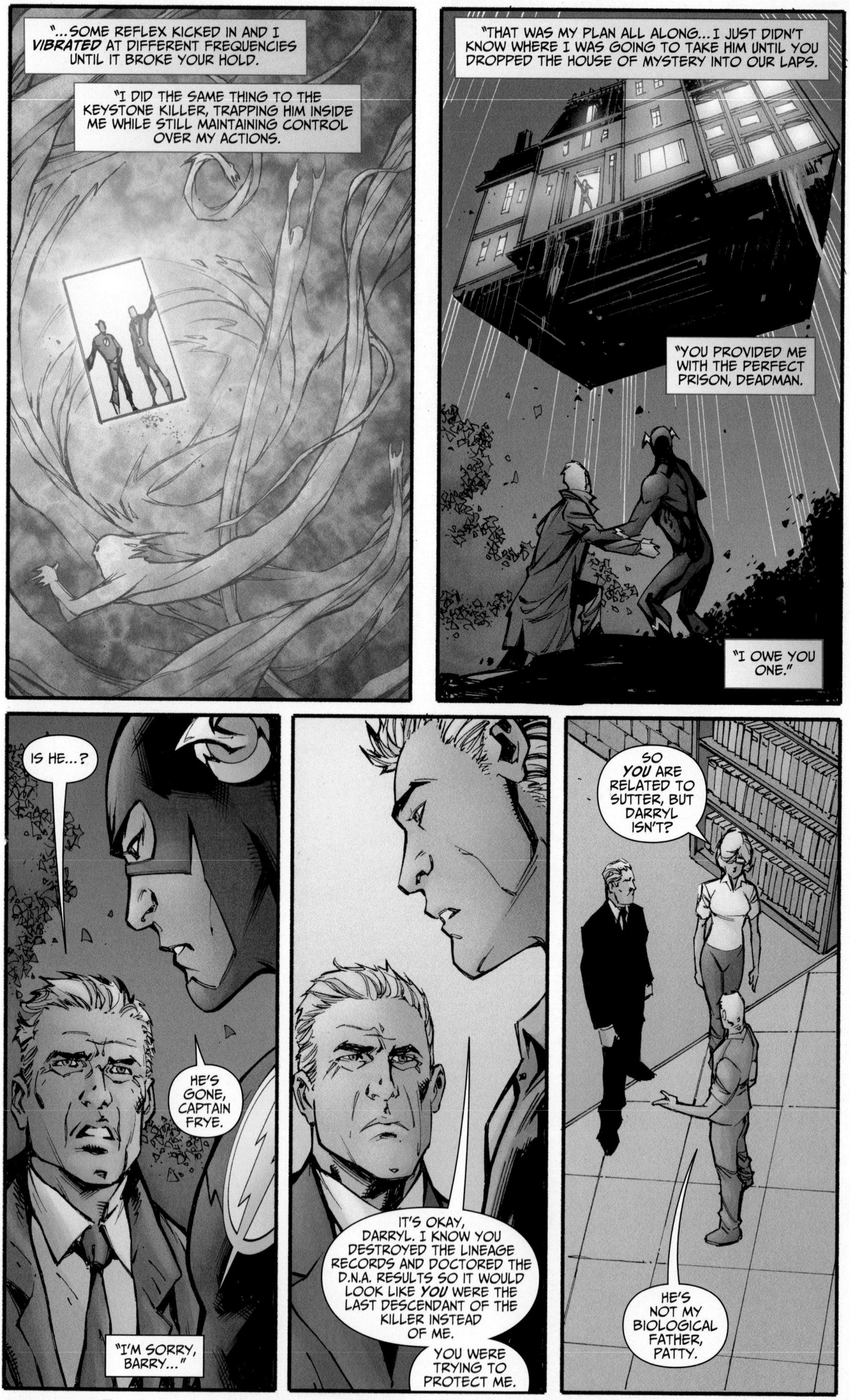
"...SOME REFLEX KICKED IN AND I *VIBRATED* AT DIFFERENT FREQUENCIES UNTIL IT BROKE YOUR HOLD.
"I DID THE SAME THING TO THE KEYSTONE KILLER, TRAPPING HIM INSIDE ME WHILE STILL MAINTAINING CONTROL OVER MY ACTIONS.
"THAT WAS MY PLAN ALL ALONG... I JUST DIDN'T KNOW WHERE I WAS GOING TO TAKE HIM UNTIL YOU DROPPED THE HOUSE OF MYSTERY INTO OUR LAPS.
"YOU PROVIDED ME WITH THE PERFECT PRISON, DEADMAN.
"I OWE YOU ONE."
IS HE...?
HE'S GONE, CAPTAIN FRYE.
"I'M SORRY, BARRY..."
IT'S OKAY, DARRYL. I KNOW YOU DESTROYED THE LINEAGE RECORDS AND DOCTORED THE D.N.A. RESULTS SO IT WOULD LOOK LIKE *YOU* WERE THE LAST DESCENDANT OF THE KILLER INSTEAD OF ME.
YOU WERE TRYING TO PROTECT ME.
SO *YOU* ARE RELATED TO SUTTER, BUT DARRYL ISN'T?
HE'S NOT MY BIOLOGICAL FATHER, PATTY.

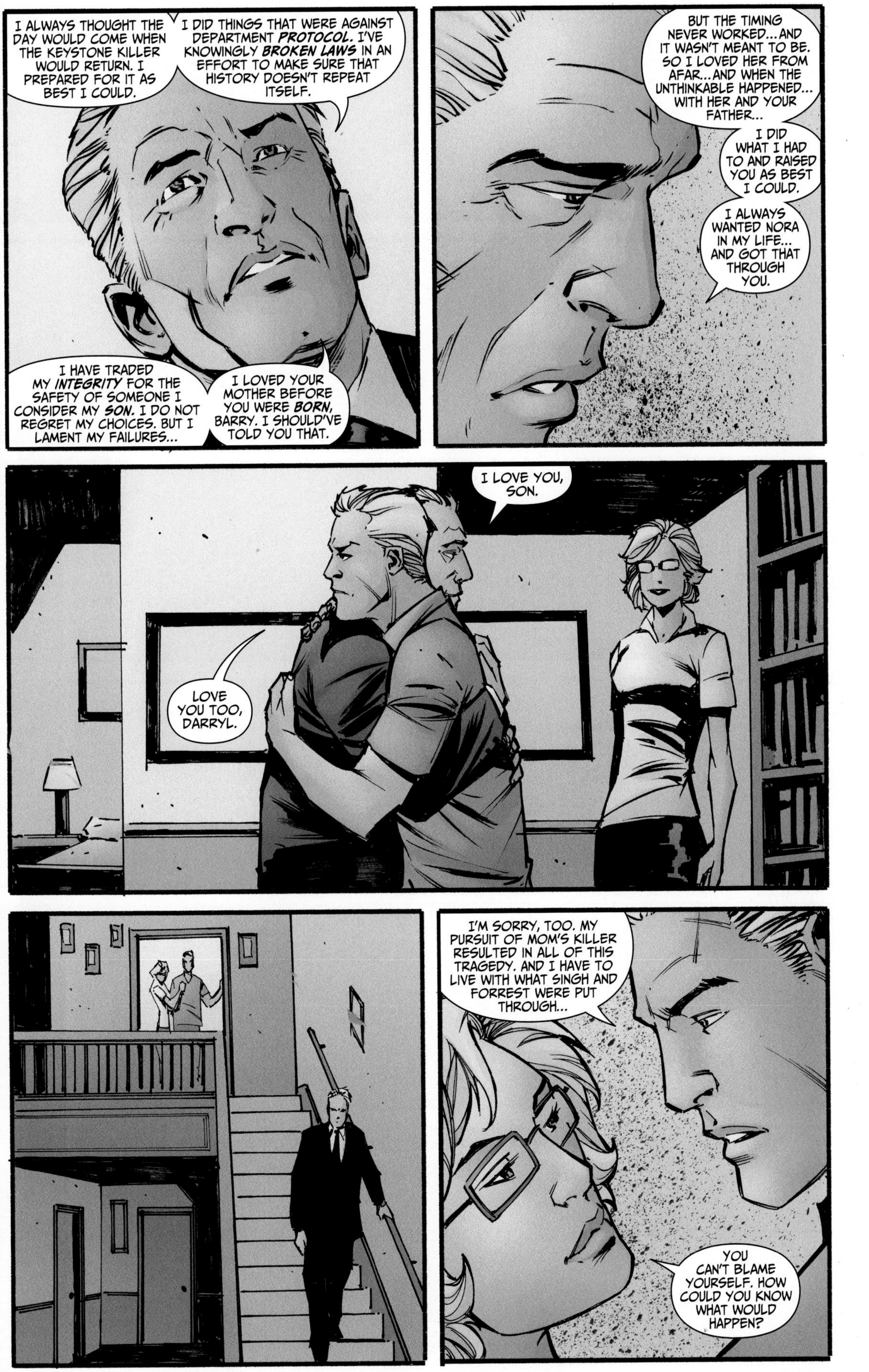
I ALWAYS THOUGHT THE DAY WOULD COME WHEN THE KEYSTONE KILLER WOULD RETURN. I PREPARED FOR IT AS BEST I COULD.
I DID THINGS THAT WERE AGAINST DEPARTMENT *PROTOCOL.* I'VE KNOWINGLY *BROKEN LAWS* IN AN EFFORT TO MAKE SURE THAT HISTORY DOESN'T REPEAT ITSELF.
I HAVE TRADED MY *INTEGRITY* FOR THE SAFETY OF SOMEONE I CONSIDER MY *SON.* I DO NOT REGRET MY CHOICES. BUT I LAMENT MY FAILURES...
I LOVED YOUR MOTHER BEFORE YOU WERE *BORN,* BARRY. I SHOULD'VE TOLD YOU THAT.
BUT THE TIMING NEVER WORKED...AND IT WASN'T MEANT TO BE. SO I LOVED HER FROM AFAR...AND WHEN THE UNTHINKABLE HAPPENED... WITH HER AND YOUR FATHER...
I DID WHAT I HAD TO AND RAISED YOU AS BEST I COULD.
I ALWAYS WANTED NORA IN MY LIFE... AND GOT THAT THROUGH YOU.
I LOVE YOU, SON.
LOVE YOU TOO, DARRYL.
I'M SORRY, TOO. MY PURSUIT OF MOM'S KILLER RESULTED IN ALL OF THIS TRAGEDY. AND I HAVE TO LIVE WITH WHAT SINGH AND FORREST WERE PUT THROUGH...
YOU CAN'T BLAME YOURSELF. HOW COULD YOU KNOW WHAT WOULD HAPPEN?

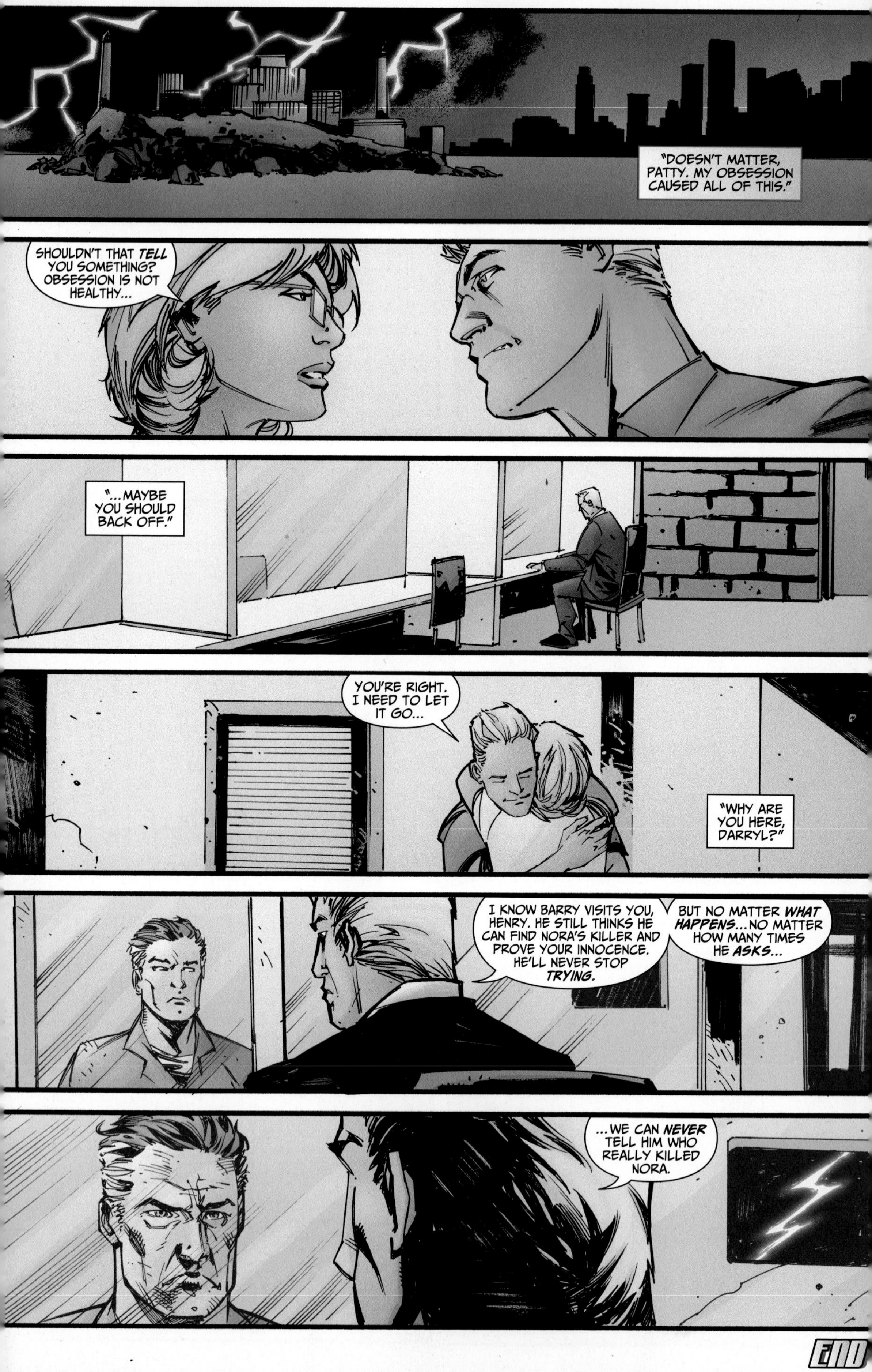
"DOESN'T MATTER, PATTY. MY OBSESSION CAUSED ALL OF THIS."
SHOULDN'T THAT TELL YOU SOMETHING? OBSESSION IS NOT HEALTHY...
"...MAYBE YOU SHOULD BACK OFF."
YOU'RE RIGHT. I NEED TO LET IT GO...
"WHY ARE YOU HERE, DARRYL?"
I KNOW BARRY VISITS YOU, HENRY. HE STILL THINKS HE CAN FIND NORA'S KILLER AND PROVE YOUR INNOCENCE. HE'LL NEVER STOP TRYING.
BUT NO MATTER WHAT HAPPENS...NO MATTER HOW MANY TIMES HE ASKS...
...WE CAN NEVER TELL HIM WHO REALLY KILLED NORA.
END

VARIANT COVER GALLERY

THE FLASH #27
Scribblenauts variant cover by John Katz after Carmine Infantino

THE FLASH #28
Variant cover by Howard Chaykin & Jesus Aburto

THE FLASH #29
Robot Chicken variant cover by RC Stoodios

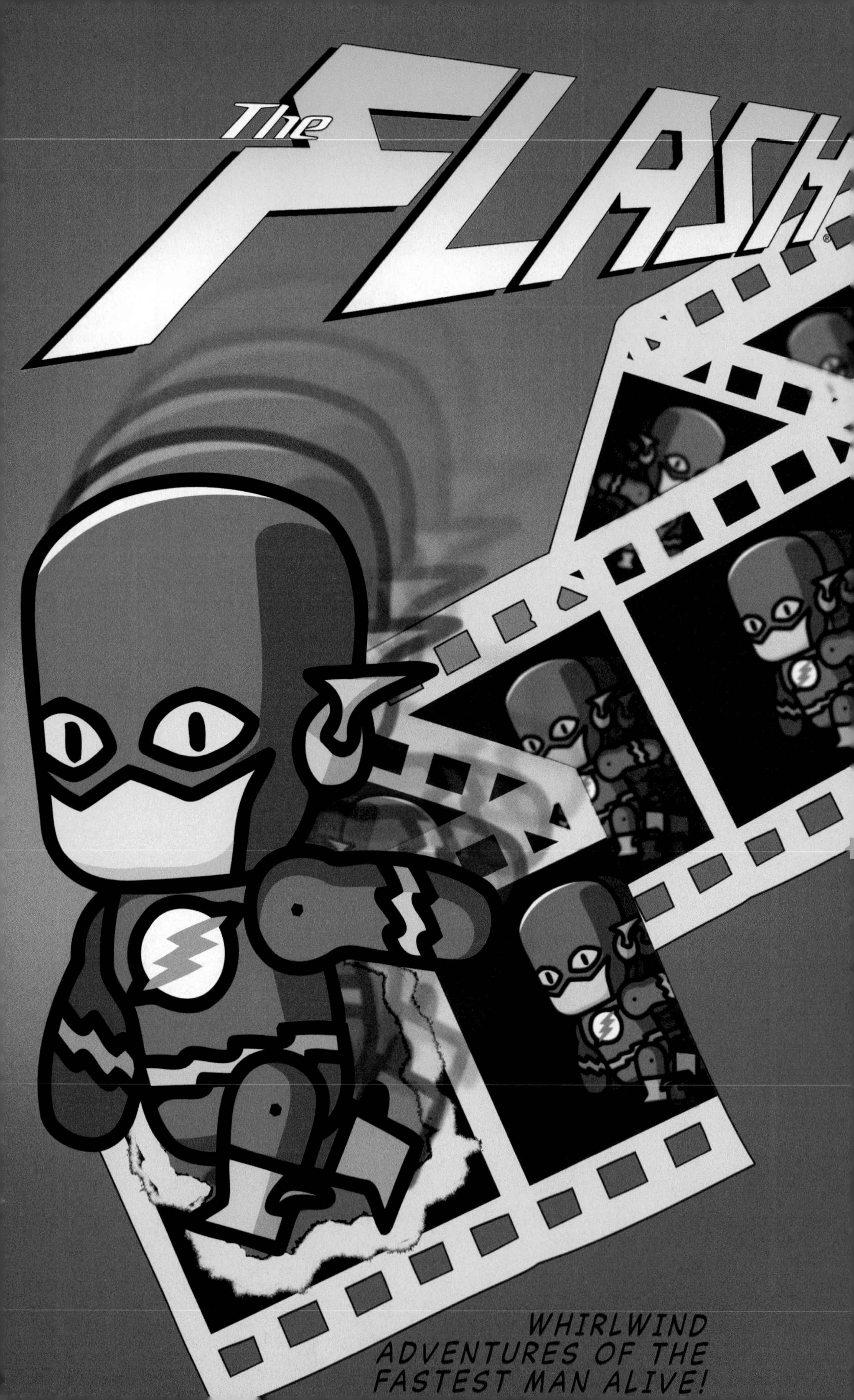
The FLASH®
WHIRLWIND
ADVENTURES OF THE
FASTEST MAN ALIVE!

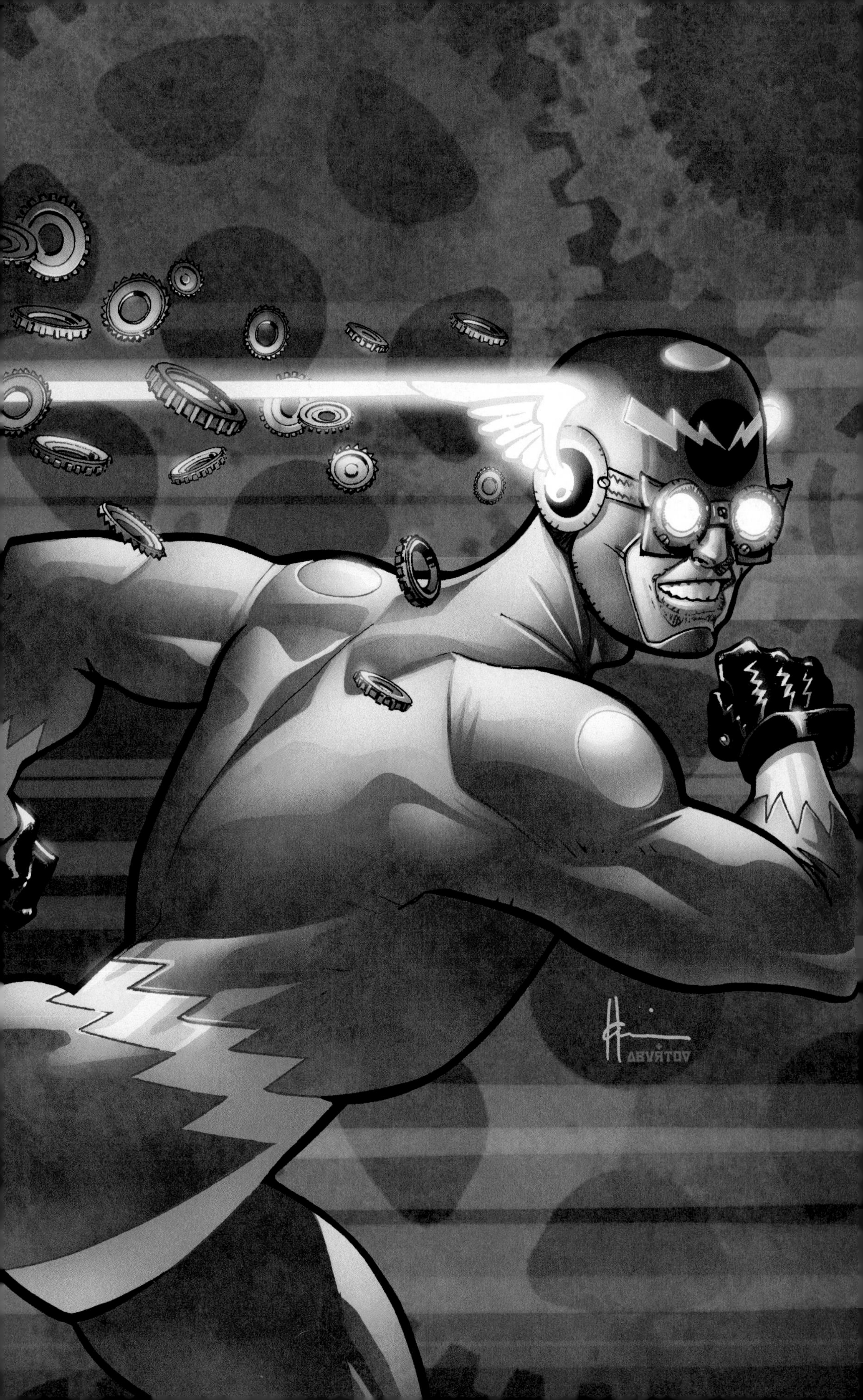

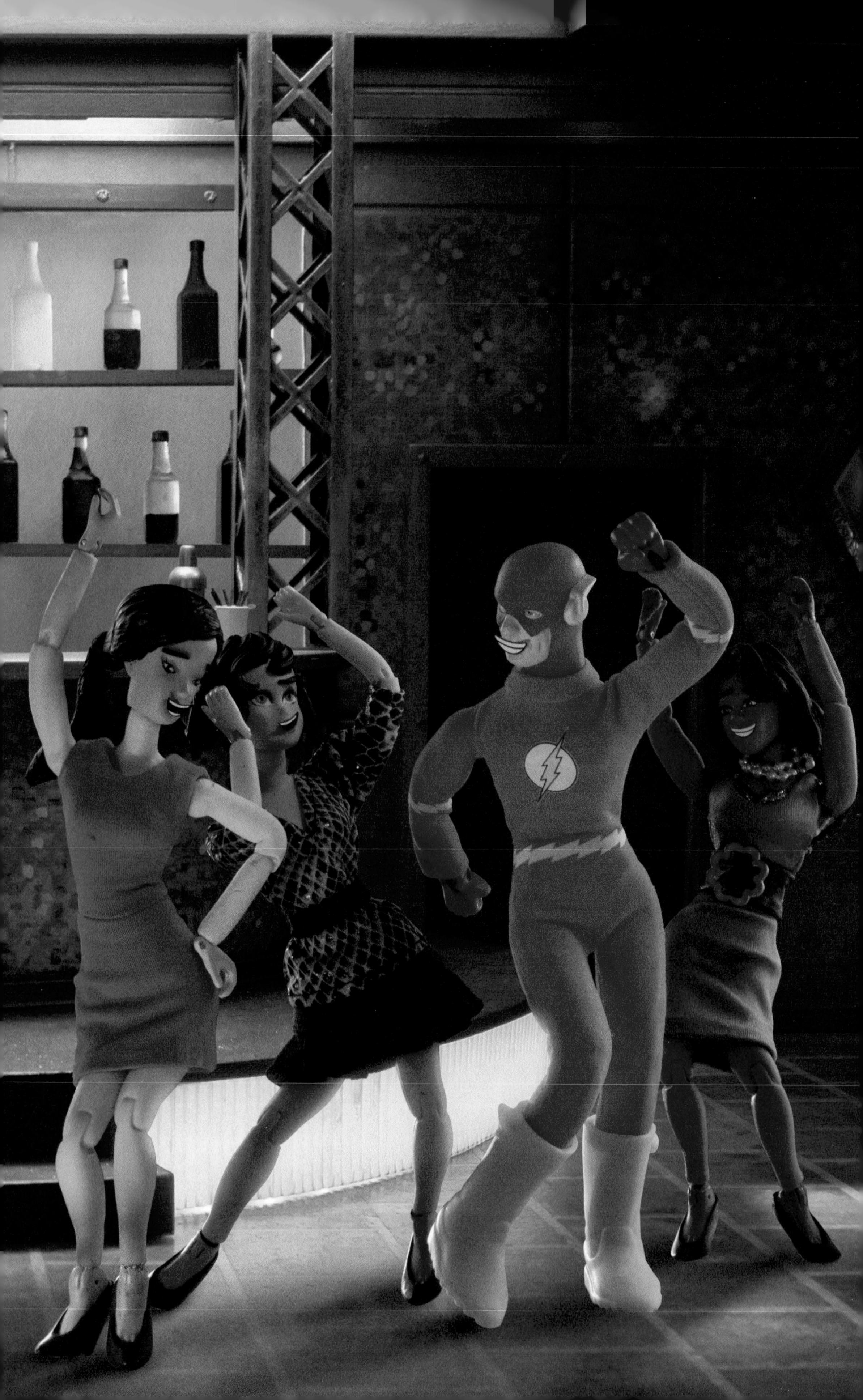

The Flash by Patrick Zircher

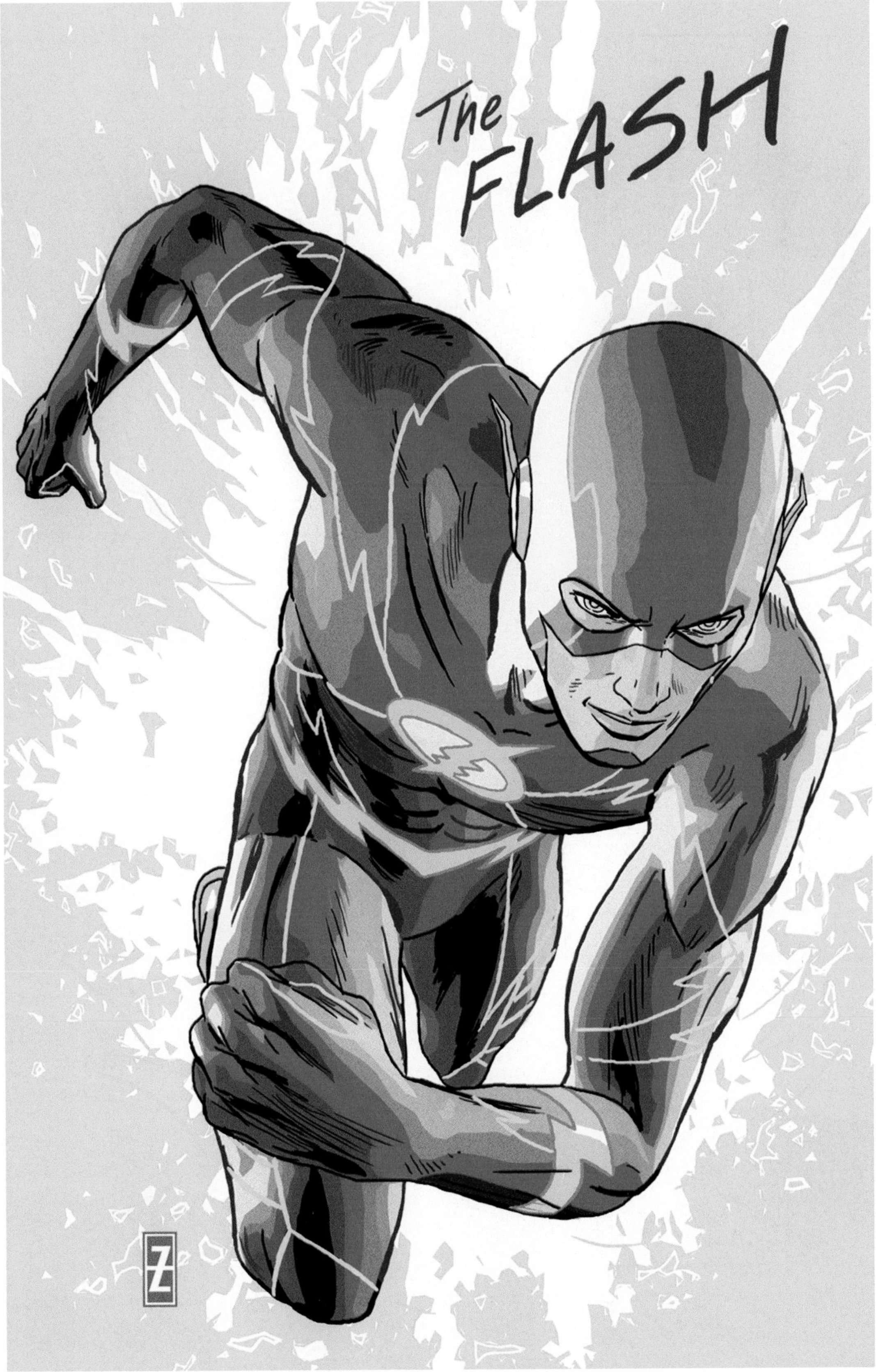
The FLASH

The Flash by Patrick Zircher

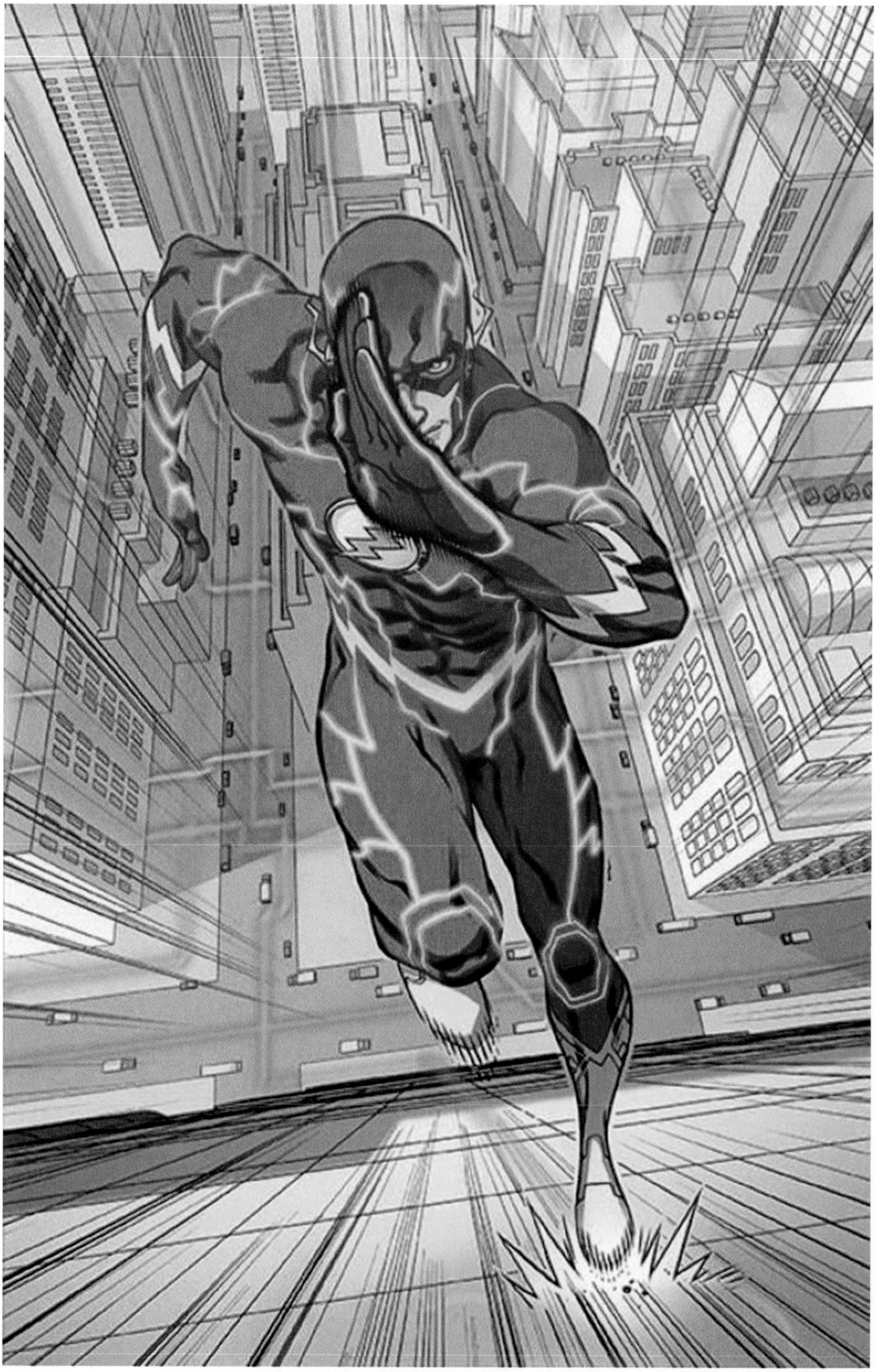

THE FLASH Annual #2 layouts by Sami Basri

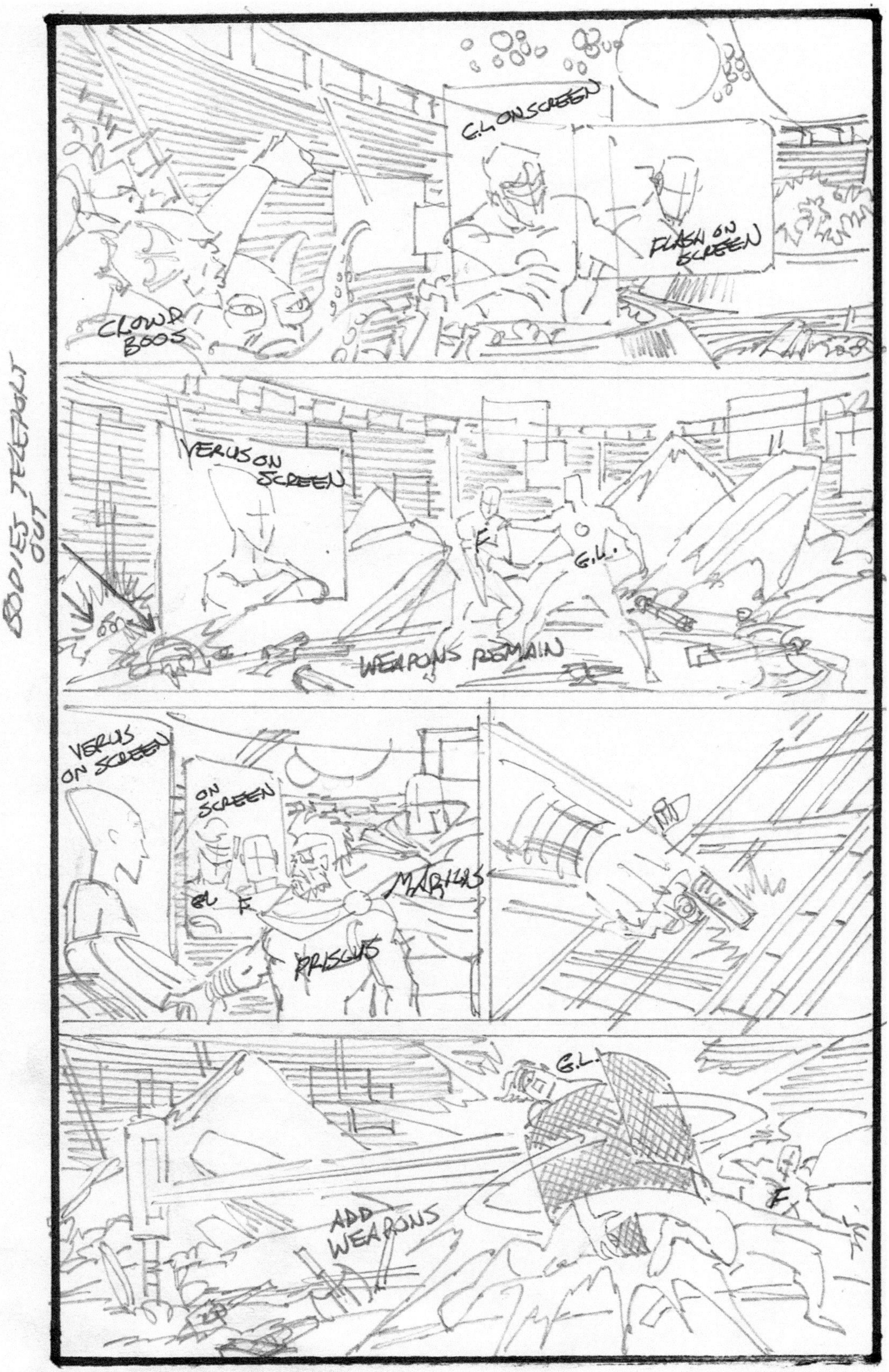
CROWD BOOS
G.L ONSCREEN
FLASH ON SCREEN
BODIES TELEPORT OUT
VERUS ON SCREEN
F
G.L.
WEAPONS REMAIN
VERUS ON SCREEN
ON SCREEN
GL F
MARIUS
PRISCUS
G.L.
ADD WEAPONS
F

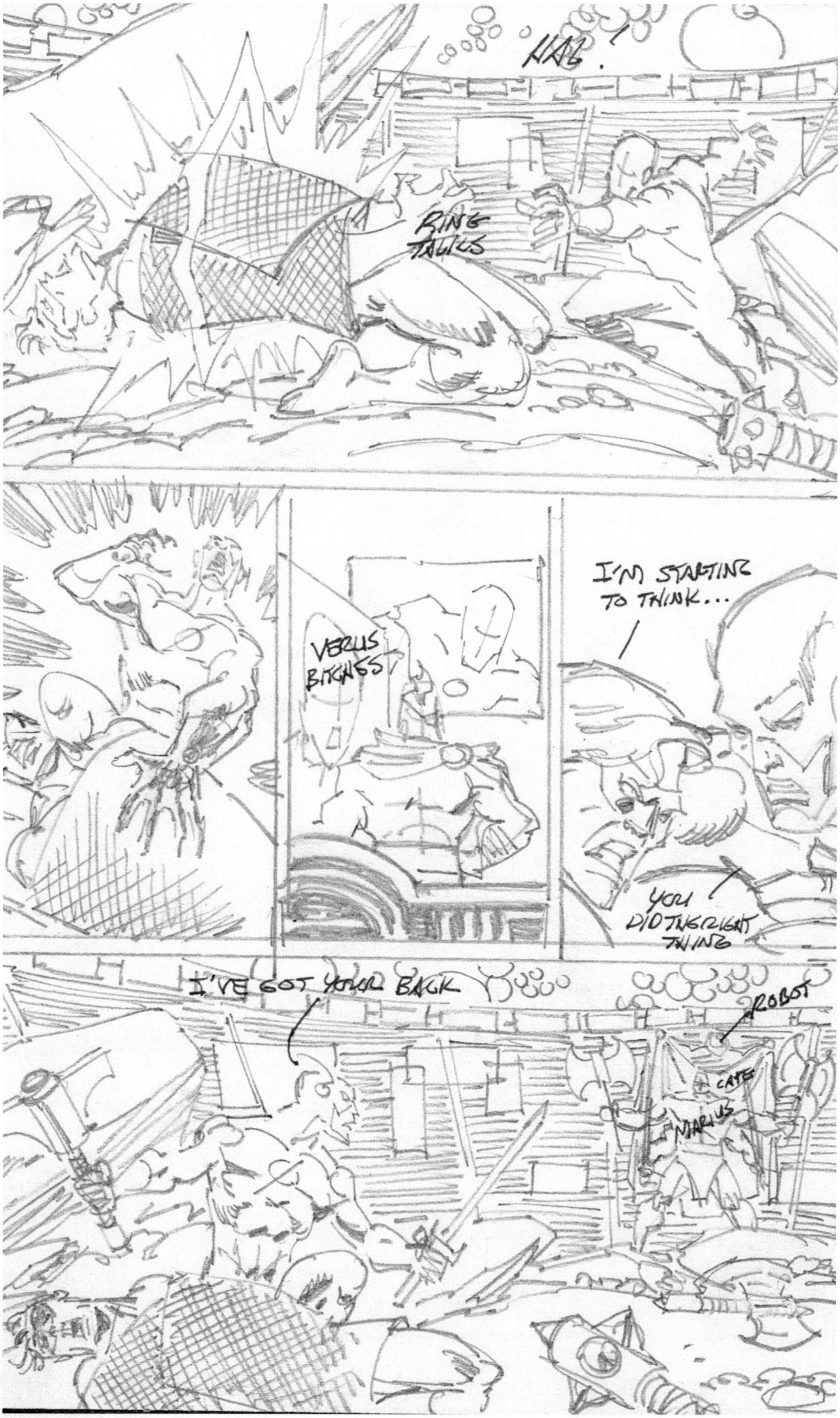
HAG!
RING TALKS
VERUS BITCHES
I'M STARTING TO THINK...
YOU DID THE RIGHT THING
I'VE GOT YOUR BACK
ROBOT
CATE
MARIUS

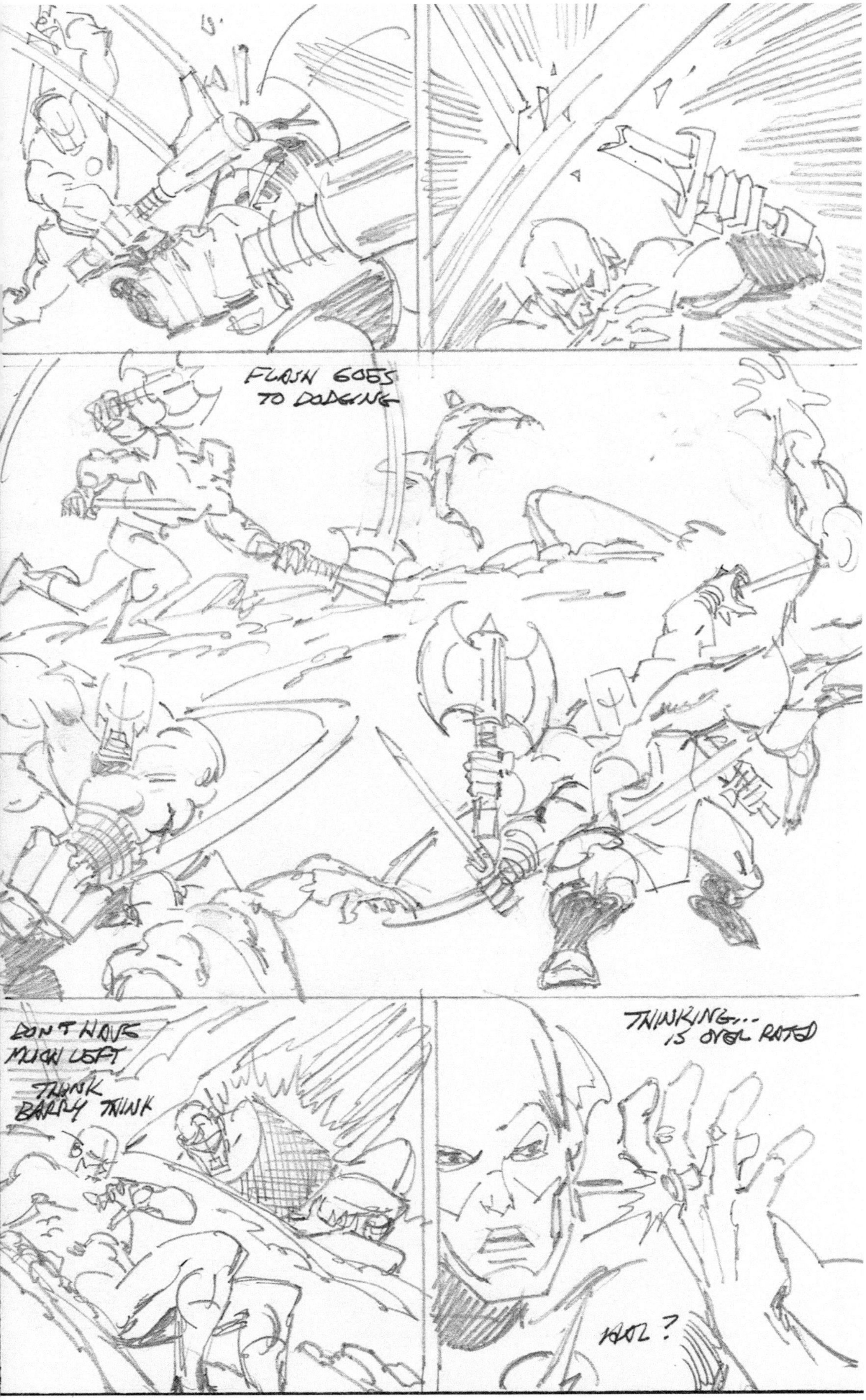
FLASH GOES TO DODGING
DON'T HAVE MUCH LEFT
THINK BARRY THINK
THINKING... IS OVER RATED

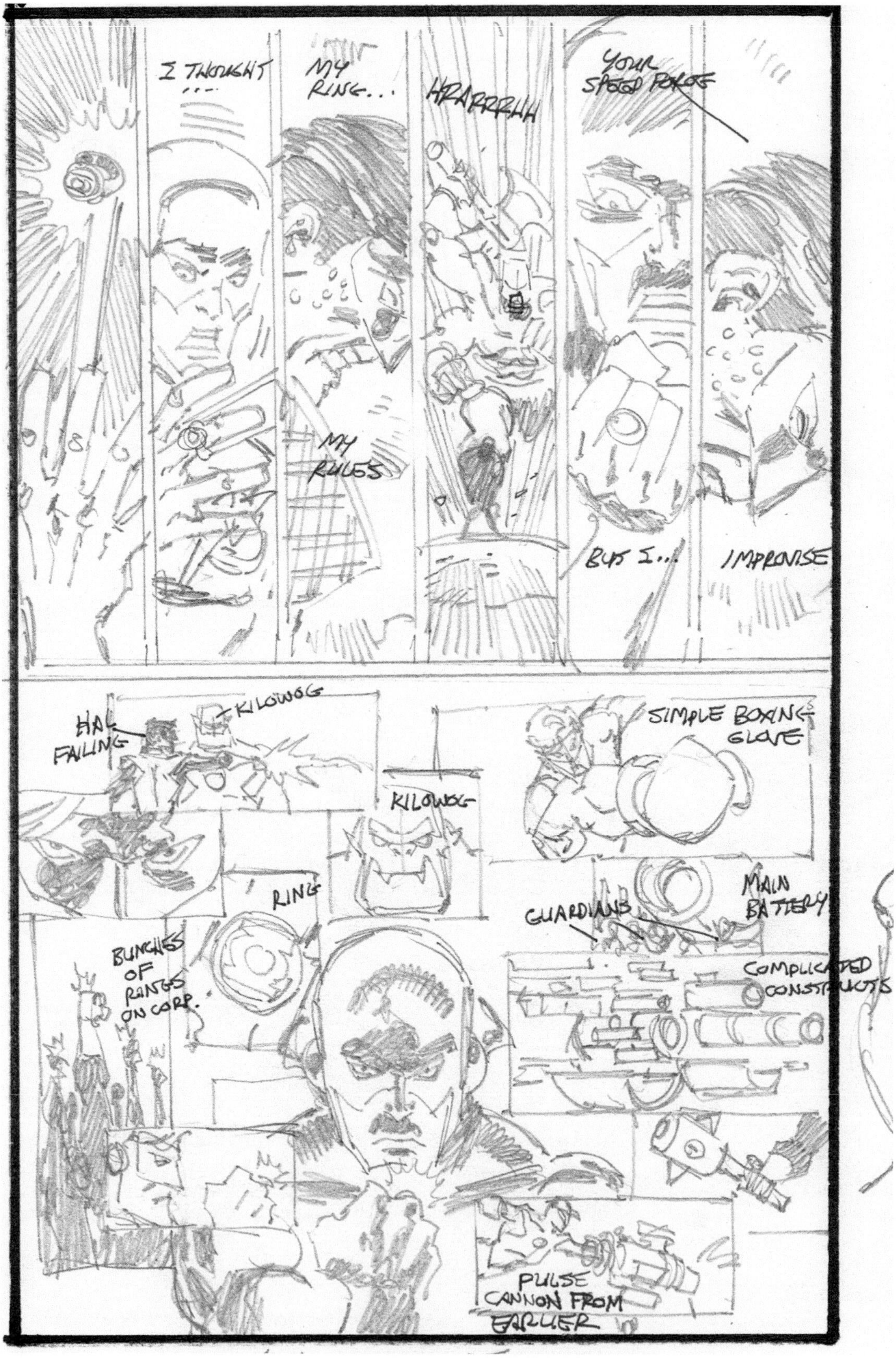

I THOUGHT ...
MY RING...
MY RULES
HRARRRLLH
YOUR SPEED FORCE
BUT I...
IMPROVISE
HAL FAILING
KILOWOG
SIMPLE BOXING GLOVE
KILOWOG
RING
MAIN BATTERY
GUARDIANS
BUNCHES OF RINGS ON CORP.
COMPLICATED CONSTRUCTS
PULSE CANNON FROM EARLIER

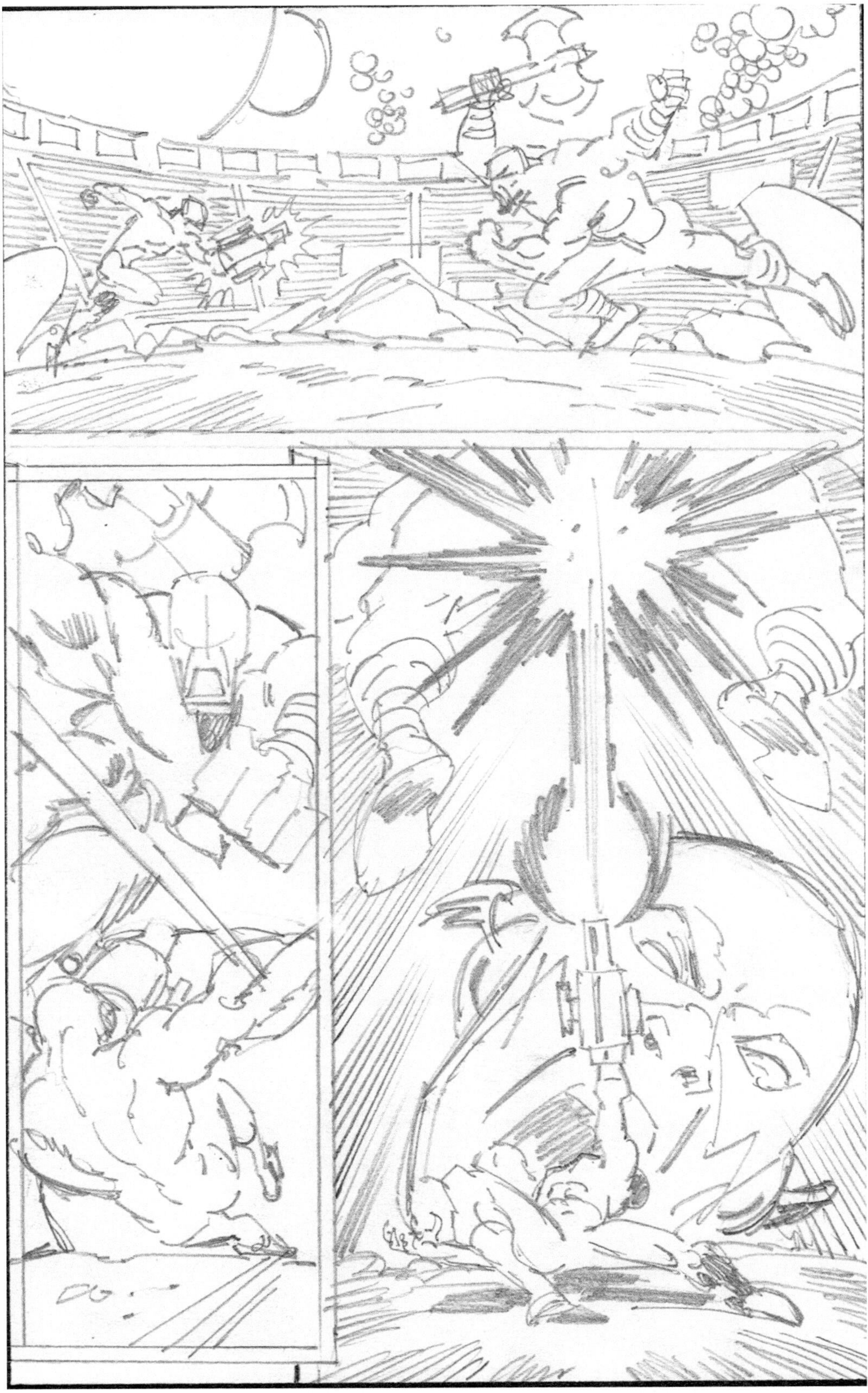

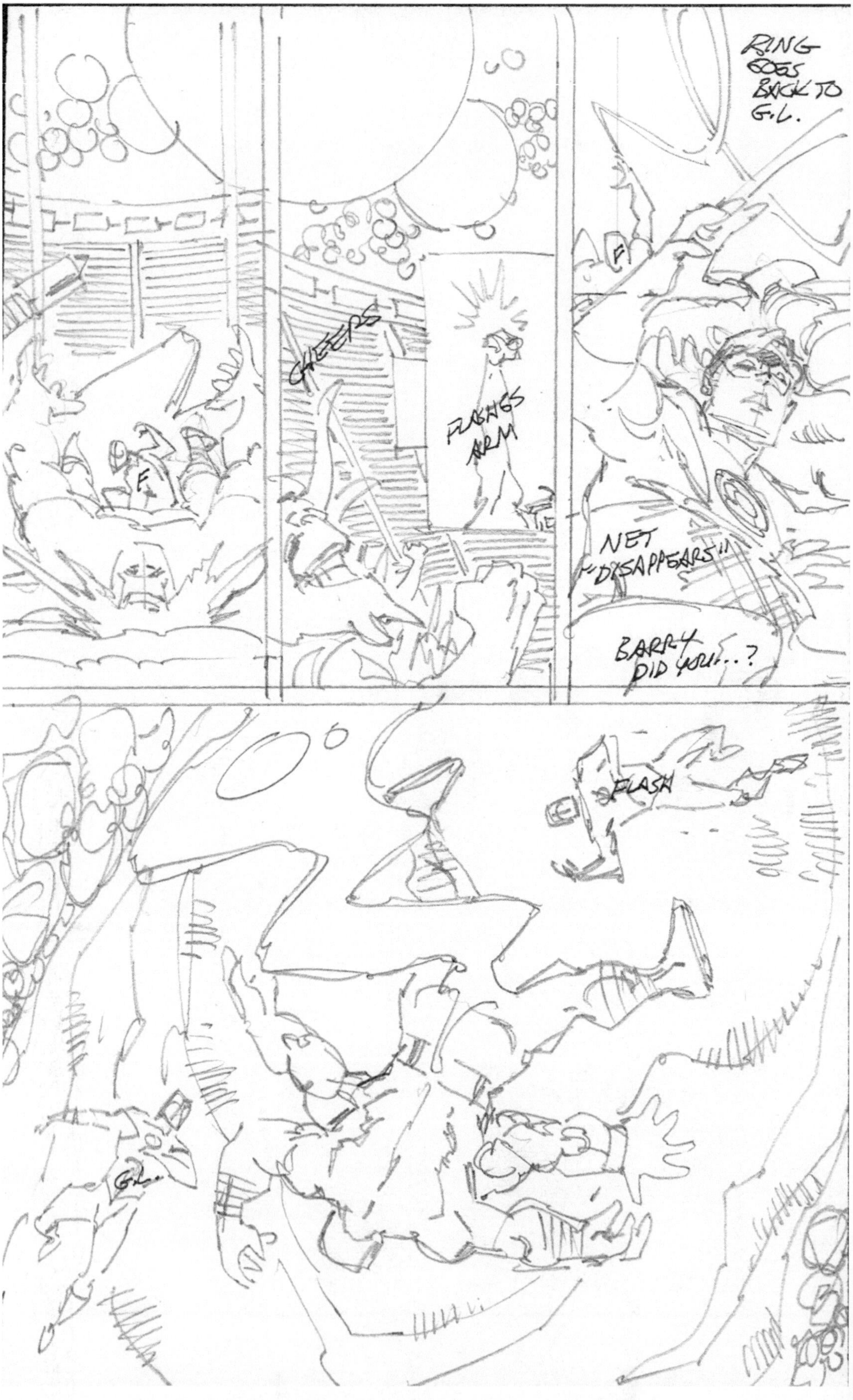
F
CHEERS
FLASH'S ARM
RING GOES BACK TO G.L.
F
NET DISAPPEARS!!
BARRY DID YOU...?
FLASH
G.L.